THE TEAM THAT MANAGED ITSELF

Wodtke, Christina. *The Team That Managed Itself: A Story of Leadership*. Print Edition.

The Team
that
MANAGED ITSELF

A Story of Leadership

CHRISTINA WODTKE

FOREWORD

I STARTED MY CAREER 25 YEARS AGO AND HAVE BEEN BOTH A member and a leader of dozens of teams all over the world which means I feel fairly confident when I say that I've seen almost every management style and team dynamic under the sun, from the functional to the deeply dysfunctional. Because despite how much lip service we pay to the importance of teams and teamwork (especially in today's increasingly complex environments), we spend far too little time actually focused on our teams and how they work together.

After much experimenting with all the wrong ways to lead teams, around 10 years ago my CTO and I realized that the closer we put decision making to the customer, the better the decisions became—so we started exploring how to give our teams more and more autonomy. It sounds so easy—hire people who are smarter than you are and get out of the way. Empowering our teams this way makes an innate sense and I've yet to meet anyone who disagrees with the sentiment, but actually doing it well is surprisingly difficult.

As always the devil is in the details, and in the intervening years I've learned that just hiring smart people isn't enough—we have to make sure they work (and play) well together too. So I've spent the best part of the last 10 years figuring out how to make this happen, by trying (and sometimes failing) to implement autonomous teams in various companies as well as through evangelizing and learning about it through the product community I founded as well as hundreds of interviews with product leaders for my own book on the topic.

When Christina shared her first draft of this book so many of those different threads suddenly clicked together, and in her storytelling, she walked the hero of the story through the same journey I'd been on for so long, in just a few short chapters. In short, this is the book I wish I'd had 10 years ago, and I know it will make your journey to building high performing, autonomous, learning teams *so* much easier.

Martin Eriksson
London
September 30, 2019

THE BOOK THAT DIDN'T WANT TO BE WRITTEN

An Introduction to
The Team That Managed Itself

THIS BOOK. OY, THIS BOOK.

Radical Focus was a tough book to write, but in the way most books are hard to write. This book, *The Team That Managed Itself,* has been borderline cursed.

I started it in the NaNoWriMo of 2016. If you aren't familiar with NaNoWriMo, it's National Novel Writing Month, a goofy but wildly popular event in which you write a 50,000-word novel in one month. I took a class with the founder, Chris Baty, and every week I'd sit in a room with twenty other intrepid writers desperately trying to hit my 1,667 words a day.

Chris wrote the book, *No Plot? No Problem.* Following that approach caused my first problem. "Write whatever comes to mind!" he'd say, and I would. When I was done, I would have 50K words of ... stuff. I wanted to write a story about a young woman who was promoted before she was ready, and suddenly had to figure out how to hire, fire, and give effective feedback so she could have the team she needed to succeed. What I had was a disastrous manuscript based on some of my worst work experiences that was 20 percent potential and 80 percent therapy.

I recall walking around a SoHo alleyway after giving a workshop, talking to my editor, Cathy Yardley, and crying, "Can this book be saved?" She said it could.

And then she got breast cancer. I was devastated. First, I had come to love her. She gives difficult feedback in a way that makes you feel you can fix anything, in a way that makes you believe you can be an author. And when she praises what's working, the insight and truth of it makes you feel like a superhero. She sees the writer you can be, and helps you become it.

I couldn't do this book without her. She went off to heal, and so did I (in a much much, much smaller way). I put the book I had code named *"Continuous Feedback"* away. I started drawing. A lot. I made a cute little workbook based on what I was learning about drawing.

My editor beat her cancer, and I am so grateful, mostly because the world needs her, but selfishly, because *I* need her. But our American health-care system made it necessary she take a full-time job to pay for her care. She left the thing she loved—writing and editing—to pay the bills. So I left *Continuous Feedback* in the drawer, so to speak. (Literally, in the Dropbox folder. But whaddya gonna do?) I couldn't face trying to make sense of the damn thing without Cathy.

Thus *Pencil Me In* was born. I wrote a book that didn't need her kind of editing. I wrote a book about drawing: How to draw and when to draw.

Pencil Me In was a work of pure joy. Every day I spent on it made me happy. It was a love poem to making marks that make you smart. It was the book that I hoped would sell, but didn't really need to, because writing it made me so much smarter. The book had done its job for at least one person.

Continuous Feedback was the opposite. Nothing about it was fun.

It was looking back at one of the hardest times of my life, combined with two other hardest times of my life. But then a miracle occurred: Cathy came back. She had found a way to afford to do the work she loved. And if she was willing to attack this beast, so could I. We ripped into it, bouncing outlines back and forth until we had a book that had hope in the darkness.

Continuous Feedback is a book about trying to make a good team in a toxic workplace, so I wrote a toxic workplace and immediately wanted out of there. In my head, I was screaming at my protagonist Allie to quit already! But I also knew *why* she wouldn't.

I wanted to have protagonists of color. But putting them in a toxic workplace meant dealing with microaggressions and mysterious career blockers. If you are a woman or a person of color in the Valley, you always wonder if you aren't getting promoted because you aren't good enough, or if it's something else. There is an unsettling randomness in who gets ahead. Sometimes it's you, but mostly it's not. I don't know anyone who doesn't wonder, *is it me or is it sexism/racism?* The magazines celebrate those who make it despite prejudice, and you wonder why you aren't that person. You wonder, "What if I was just a bit smarter/tougher/nicer?"

I also chose to make her a rarity in the Silicon Valley: a female general manager. I gave her an all-male engineering team, and the only women she worked with regularly were in design and human resources. I did this to increase the pressure on her. Any woman who has sat, as I have sat, in a room full of men knows how exhausting it can be. You feel like a freak. You wonder if you chose the right profession. You wonder if you might better have gone into marketing or HR. And then you take a big breath and move on.

As well, I wanted to do a lot of things I don't see in fiction enough. I wanted to write about friendships between men and women that didn't have to become romantic. I wanted a husband and wife who loved each other and were willing to put the work in to make the marriage function. Unspoken assumptions kill marriages as well as team health. The tensions between Allie and Derek's conflicting needs were a reflection of Allie's workplace where so much was assumed and so much of that was wrong.

And finally, I have mixed feelings about the business fable. I wanted to write more than a morality play. I wanted to write a real story, full of hopes and dreams, and rooms that felt like real rooms, and people who seemed like complete people.

This. Damn. Book.

Well, it's done. I believe it is the best thing I have ever written about the most important topic in business: How do we work with each other when we are all so different? We are promised diversity will make us great, but how do we stop fighting long enough to reap those benefits?

The answer is not simple. Yes, we have to set good goals and have clear roles. But we also have to learn to understand each other. We have to question the behavior we have never thought twice about. We have to have a lot of honest conversations.

The Team That Managed Itself (or T3MI as I like to type it) is both a follow-up to *Radical Focus* and a departure. It was born out of questions from clients about other aspects of managing strong teams beyond OKRs. It was born from research on how to make good teams and the exercises I developed to make teams great. It was born out of my hard-won experience in managing teams under dysfunctional conditions. It is the book I wish I'd had.

Just like *Radical Focus*, this book starts with a fictional case study based on real experiences and follows up with a nonfiction section that covers the core concepts and how you might implement them in your workplace. Unlike *Radical Focus*, the case study is written as real fiction. It gets dark, it is nuanced, and sometimes you may feel like you are working at one of the toughest companies in Silicon Valley. It's three times as long as *Radical Focus*, three times as complicated, and three times as deep. It's also nine times more powerful. This book may not be for you, but if you want to commit to the work it takes to make a truly high-performing team, this is the book you need to read.

This is a complicated book about a complicated topic. I hope you will go on this journey with me. Since I got out my machete three years ago to try to find a way in the wilderness, I've paved the road for you with models and storytelling. I hope it's less bumpy for you than it was for me.

The reward is working with the kind of team you've only dreamed of. It's worth it.

This book is dedicated to Cathy Yardley,

my editor and best cheerleader.

The Story

WE'RE IN VEGAS, BABY

"BABY NEEDS A NEW PAIR OF SHOES!" ALLIE SCREAMED.

Rob laughed out loud at that. "Really?"

She threw the dice. "When in Vegas, roll like you're in Vegas! You got to live every damn movie cliché!"

Rob nodded. Her best friend might be sober and keeping his money off the table, but he was whooping and cheering with their team. Tonight, they were celebrating.

"Snake eyes!" the croupier announced.

The table groaned, and the dice passed to George.

"Let me show you how it's done, honey," purred the studio general manager.

Allie had a sudden sense of perfection, like a key snapping into a lock. She had her best friend on one side, and her dream boss on the other. Rob was a tall African American, and Allie was a tiny mestizo. George was something and Chinese, and even if they didn't look like the usual bro-co team, they had managed to snare the third quarter of top earnings at SOS. And they had done it all with a game that was basically Minecraft with quilting squares—a girly game. Allie wished the first-person shooter fanboys she went to high school with could see her now.

Allie placed her bet next to Rob and George's. Why not? Her bet on QuiltWorld was winning, as it had been for months now.

Then her phone vibrated against her hip, where she had stuck it in the waistband of her skirt. She didn't dare leave it in her purse in the noisy casino. Weekend or not, she was always on call.

She pulled it out and looked. Midnight stats were in.

"Easy fours!" called the croupier.

Yep, George had gotten her another win. Allie grabbed her chips and stepped back from the table to look at her game's numbers.

As lead product manager on top-earning mobile game QuiltWorld, it was her right to be here in Vegas with the team. They had blown away revenue expectations and her CEO Rick had rewarded the QuiltWorld team with a trip to Vegas. But as lead PM, she still needed to keep an eye on numbers, in case something went sideways. Her boss could chill out and get drunk, because he knew his team had his back.

Plus, she wanted to watch the numbers. She was excited. She had crafted a new bold beat—a special event designed for the game—under the tutelage of the lead game designer. She was dying to see how it performed. She didn't consider herself creative, not like the game designers or the art team, but she had correlated numbers across the various games in the studio and had seen a pattern that inspired a fresh idea.

In late summer, all the games at SOS got the doldrums. Their biggest competitor was a sunny day. Games that spoke to the desire to play in the sun could get a lift midafternoon in the workday. You can't sneak outside, but you can sneak a peek at a pretend outdoors on your computer. Allie had come up with an idea that was all about playing outside on a playground, with swings and slides and a baseball field. They packaged it up as a "sewing kit"—QuiltWorld's name for mini-expansions to the game— and offered it to players so they could make their own playground.

QuiltWorld was a strange beast inside of SOS. SOS had started out as just another game company trying to ride the popularity wave of mobile games. They began with a combination of gambling and pulp-fiction inspired games. Vampires, cops and robbers, gangsters. But then a tiny mythical group—George, Pete, and Christie—had a new idea. They took the popularity of a sandbox game, where you take modular units and build things with them, and rethemed it with quilts. It was Minecraft, but with quilts. The CEO Rick had thought it was the stupidest idea he'd ever seen, but because it was George, and George had a track record at another company of taking stupid ideas and making a lot of money from them, he'd funded it—given them their time, plus an engineer and a game artist to make the images. They launched an alpha and the numbers were beyond any anyone had seen. Players went insane for it. Rick still couldn't understand it, but it didn't stop him from taking credit for it.

QuiltWorld was now the biggest studio in SOS, dwarfing even Baccarat. SOS had cloned the core concept to great success. ClayTown, another sandbox game but themed on claymation, was the second biggest, and

Sketchworld was the up-and-comer. Rick was overjoyed. A serial entrepreneur, he always told them at company meetings that SOS was what his entire life had led up to, and they would be reinventing the very nature of fun. He was so proud he was able to be profitable and respectable at the same time.

The Vegas trip tradition came from the time when all the games at SOS were on the sleazy end of respectability. You made the most money, you got to go to Vegas. No matter how many times at the company meetings Rick talked about "forever games" and "innovation" and "high quality production," what got you to Vegas was revenue. At SOS, a good game was a game that made money.

George lost the dice and peeled back from the table. "Waitress hasn't been by in a while. Want to get a drink?"

The two of them wove through the crowded casino. When they had claimed the craps table, the casino was sparsely populated by a handful of dedicated gamblers. Now every square inch of floor space had a human on it. The bar itself was also lined with humanity—drinking, laughing, flirting. An unrepentantly cheesy piano man swore to play any song for the right tip.

Allie wedged her way in near a tall middle-aged man and leaned in to get the bartender's attention. In her outstretched hand she held a twenty, in case money was a better bartender lure than cleavage. The man next to her caught notice.

"Hey, where you from?" Vegas's standard opening line, from hawkers on the sidewalks to men at bars.

Allie was used to a bit too much attention. Her hard to place ethnic features and hip-length black hair were a magnet for certain kinds of men.

"She's with me," George said, placing an arm on her shoulder. The man turned away with the complacency of the unsober.

"Ew!" Allie laughed, shrugging George's arm off her. "What will your wife say?"

"She'll say I'm watching out for you."

The bartender finally swung by and got their order. Allie ordered two shots of Patron.

"So, we're toasting?" asked George.

"Toasting what?" grinned back Allie. She gestured at the Patron.

"You got the midnight numbers. I can look at them on my phone, or you can tell me."

"SummerQuest is doing quite well. Even in the evening, we're up 8 percent!"

George offered a hand for a high five, and Allie smacked it. They turned to their shots and downed them.

"Good work, half-pint! You've got a knack for this!"

"Ah, the numbers just like me. They tell me their secrets."

"The number whisperer." George ordered a margarita. "Never mix, never worry."

Allie ordered a soda water. She believed drinking was like a game: It was all about pacing. She looked back at the table where her team played on. They screamed as one and went into an impromptu wave.

"We're going to get kicked out," she said.

"No way," George replied. "It's Vegas, baby. To QuiltWorld!"

They clicked glasses merrily.

Allie felt a tap on her shoulder. Where her admirer had stood now was a middle-aged woman. She was perhaps from the south, with very tall hair and a thick layer of makeup. "Excuse me, but did I hear you work on QuiltWorld?"

"Why, yes," Allie replied. George's smile faded from his eyes, though it remained on his lips.

"Oh, I love that game! My quilts are so beautiful. I work on them every day when the kids are at school!"

"Have you tried Original Martha?"

"Oh my God!" she squealed. "Oh, gracious, didn't mean to curse! I love it so much! It was like traveling back in time."

Allie heard George mutter, "Not quite."

"I felt so patriotic, like I was part of history! And so good of you to donate to history education. My sister made her first in-app purchase to help out!"

Allie shot George a look. It was her idea to use a donation element to up in-app purchases. It had bumped revenue, got positive PR, and raised money for history books for public schools.

George returned her look with one that said, "Okay, okay," with a slight eyeroll.

"Would you like to see my quilt?"

"See it?" Allie responded.

"I have my iPad! I took screenshots!"

"I'd love to," Allie said quite sincerely.

George stepped back, then off toward the table. Pete, his CTO, greeted him with a fist bump and a bro-hug. Pete's mass almost knocked George over. Allie was glad to not participate in the ritual. She preferred spending time with her players. The woman showed her screenshots of her quilt structures, including the quilted White House that was part of the Fourth of July bold beat, and then showed off her QuiltWorld towns. She had two—one a miniature New York and one that looked like a small midwestern town. She must have spent a fortune over the years on these.

"I'm trying to make my hometown," she admitted shyly. "I know some people take apart the kits and make their own QTs," she said, pronouncing it "cuties,'" "and I thought I'd try to do it, too."

"It's darling! Is your house here?" Allie asked, fascinated. *Is this common?* She thought rolling-your-own was an advanced player trick, but if it was spreading, then maybe they should consider how to build that in for more players.

"It's right here." The woman smiled widely, yet Allie could see she was anxious about sharing her work.

"Wow, you did that!" Allie knew there was only one right response when a creator was brave enough to share.

Now the woman was beaming. "Sure did! I actually found our house's blueprints, you know, to get ideas for how to make it. You see here, I'm using some of the Valentine's Day kit to get the lattice work on the porch right!"

"That is beautiful." Allie sighed. She meant it. The house was fine, but what was beautiful was this woman finding her way to creativity and the pride of making something new. That's why she loved working on QuiltWorld. When she met the players and found they were unlocking their creativity, she felt proud. And perhaps a little jealous. But mostly proud.

Her phone vibrated. She ignored it for a second, but it vibrated again and again. A call. She smiled at the woman. "I have to take this," she said, and moved toward what she hoped was a quieter corner of the casino as she answered, "Jenova."

It was Noam, one of the engineering pod leaders. He had volunteered to stay behind to mind the shop because "I hate Vegas. It's a pit of despair."

He sounded tense. "The new bold beat is in freefall. We can't tell if it's a reporting problem or a bug in the back end. I just know everything's testing fine here. Can you grab Rob or Pete?"

Allie pivoted and headed toward the table. She tapped Rob, her lead dev, on the shoulder. He looked up as she said into the phone, "Okay, we'll poke around and get back to you."

Rob gave her a look that said, "Of course." He shook his head and walked away. He didn't gamble, but he believed deeply and completely in the importance of spending face time with his team and was sad to have to step away from the celebration. They walked to the elevators.

"I can't really tell much from my phone," Allie said. "But Noam is right, something isn't working. There is no way our numbers can be taking such a severe hit. I really hope it's a reporting error or I'll be having fun explaining this to Rick Monday."

Rob punched the number 32 on the console, and the elevator smoothly ascended. Allie's ears popped.

He sighed deeply. "Something always breaks. If George would give us time to work on code rot, instead of always chasing the next bold beat, we could elevate and maintain all of our numbers instead of this moronic roller coaster ride."

"You've made that argument."

"So I have."

George's counterargument was that a dead game with good code was not as valuable as a spaghetti code that made money.

They walked to Rob's room, and he sat at his laptop on the small desk. Allie eyed the two beds, one made neatly, and one covered with jeans and T-shirts celebrating game releases.

"You're sharing with Pete?"

"Why not? He doesn't sleep at night while he's in Vegas. It's a lot like no roommate at all. Plus, I think it comforts Marie to know I'm rooming with comic book guy."

"Fair. Can I help?"

"Not yet. Hold on."

Rob played his laptop like a jazz pianist. Allie sat on the edge of the clean bed and flipped through her emails on her phone. There were no clues. Her eyes wandered over to the T-shirts. Pete had been at SOS since the beginning and wore nothing but SOS release T-shirts as a badge of honor. She saw one on the bed from six years ago, before she'd joined, once a dark blue but now a faded sky blue. His first big hit. He must've worn it a lot to remind people what he'd accomplished. SOS had no memory, so it was probably a decent strategy. The blue shirt was the size of a small blanket, probably a triple X—as Pete liked to joke he was. He was a walking caricature of an old-school nerd. She sighed and thumbed back through the midnight numbers. Might as well bask in the one thing that was going right.

"Got it. API change. Give me a second …" He typed, then snapped his lid shut. His lips pressed together hard, like he was struggling to hold back a string of obscenities.

"I can announce the fix then?" she asked.

"Yes. But it will break again. This," he waved his hands in frustration over his laptop, as if it held the entire code base of QuiltWorld, "is a frigging house of cards. One strong breeze …" His voice trailed off as he contemplated the various ways it could break next.

Allie was taken aback. Rob never swore. Never showed anger. She knew he was unhappy about the state of QuiltWorld's code and ached to fix it. There was nothing quite so alarming as when a quiet man was angry. She ducked back to her phone to forward his fix and add a few notes.

When she looked up, his anger had passed like a tropical storm.

"Sorry," he said. "I just don't think this is how one should run a technical team."

"No need to apologize," she replied. "Shall we head back?" She noticed Rob was absent-mindedly rubbing his left forearm, his fingers kneading into the muscles afflicted with carpal tunnel. She didn't know if he was in pain just now, or this was an anxiety reflex. She knew that even if his face was calm, his mind wasn't.

"Go ahead. I'd like to take a moment to look over the fix again." He looked at her blandly, but she wasn't fooled.

"Sure. Later!"

As Allie rode down the elevator, she wondered if they really deserved to be celebrating tonight. Her ears popped.

SUNDAY AFTERNOON

ALLIE GOT OUT OF THE SHUTTLE VAN AND WAVED AT HER TEAM-mates as they dispersed, some heading to the parking garage, some calling for rides. None of them had slept much; more than a few were still drunk. It had been an amazing weekend. She had spent the entire night at the craps table and left seventy-five bucks up. She didn't care about the win, but she loved craps. There was camaraderie in screaming at dice together.

She looked up at the SOS building and sighed. It'd feel good to go home, but she really wanted to run a couple of database queries before Derek picked her up after his softball game. She looked at her watch. 3:20. Yeah, she could sneak in an hour of work.

She paused indecisively for a moment and looked again at the concrete building. It was shaped a bit like an early game controller, two rounded towers connected by a lower flat building. It was mostly glass, a giant '80s style post-modernist monument. It had held Sega at one point, and then had been broken into smaller offices when they moved to cheaper property. Shiny Object Syndrome, or SOS as it was known to all, had started in a single office on the third floor, now owned the first through the third floor on the left hand of the controller, and was negotiating to own the entire building. She started to trudge toward the front door when she recognized the man standing outside of it.

"Derek!"

Her husband walked toward her, swift yet unhurried, and swept her up in his arms. "Darling, you smell like an ashtray!"

"Flatterer! You could have waited until I got home and showered." He looked fresh as a daisy. "Shouldn't you be at your game?"

"I didn't dare let you go upstairs. I knew if I didn't collect you, I'd be eating another pizza alone."

"Not after a weekend away!"

"Maybe." He put an arm around her. "Anyhow, here I am."

"Here you are." Her arm fit nicely around his waist, and she squeezed him. He was a solidly built blond, a blend of the British Isles and something that let him tan rather than burn in the sun. He didn't approve of the team trips to Vegas, either personally or professionally. SOS frowned on bringing spouses—said it interfered with team bonding, though Allie suspected it was cheapness. And while he trusted her to stay out of trouble, he found it questionable that they'd go on a business trip to a place committed to a variety of sins. He'd put on his HR hat to complain that it was unfair to addicts or put on his husband hat to complain it was yet more time he didn't get to spend with her.

"You know, I'd like to go lie by the pool with a daiquiri and catch a show." His husband hat was jealous in a variety of ways.

Allie decided to defuse the issue. "Why don't we just go sometime? It's a short flight."

"My birthday is next month." He looked down at her and fluttered his eyelashes.

"Be a good boy until then and we'll see."

"Hmmp."

Thirty minutes into the drive, they'd finished catching up and he started fiddling around with his phone to get music playing.

"Stop that, it's dangerous."

"Not as dangerous as your taste."

"No, dearest, it isn't. Drive." She grabbed the device away from him and put on one of his playlists.

After a few moments, he spoke up again. "I really don't like it, you know."

Allie turned the music down. "I know. You know it's good for team morale."

"Abusive spouses always separate their victims from friends and family."

"It's one weekend a month when we are the top-earning team! Hardly a plot."

"Maybe. But when you have your own company, you won't take them to Vegas, will you?"

"No. I'll take them to Disneyland."

"And you'll take me?"

"Every time." She gave his knee a light squeeze. *When* she had her own company. *If* was more like it. She grew up in East Palo Alto, on the wrong side of this very highway they were driving on. On her left, her family. On the right, Stanford and all the startups it fathered. Instead of attending Stanford, she had taken over her half-brother's Nintendo when he'd grown bored with it, and his computer when he moved to New York, and then used the Internet to teach herself what she needed to get a customer service job at Hurricane, the best game company in the country (in her opinion).

Then she just worked harder than everyone else and look at her now. No degree, but hey, enough stock options to be a millionaire if the IPO went well. She just needed to keep hustling and eventually, she'd get promoted to general manager. Then she'd know enough to finally found her own start-up. She was living the Silicon Valley dream.

ROB LEAVING QUILTWORLD

AT 7 A.M., SOS FELT DESERTED TO ALLIE. THE PARKING LOT HELD a half-dozen cars, so she knew someone was here, which made the office even more eerie. The front door was locked, so she swiped in with her keycard. There was no receptionist at the front desk. The grand staircase could hold more than a hundred people at a time and dids when they took their annual year-end photo. She hopped up the stairs, eschewing the elevator, eking out what exercise she could from the office since who knew when she'd get to the gym. Her mind chattered at her, avoiding the question of how to explain the latest numbers dip to her CEO. The kindest thing one could say about Rick was that he was mercurial. She'd seen him go from delighted to incensed in seconds. He was determined, ambitious, and driven by inner demons without names, and had built up SOS from zero to six hundred people in under three years.

He had an unerring instinct for trends and drove everyone faster and faster trying to stay on top of each opportunity as it appeared, generally succeeding. She had learned more in her two years there than her entire career before and had paid in blood. It was clear that the payments were not stopping anytime soon.

Allie walked into the studio. A glance around the open space showed only one person in the cavernous room. SOS eschewed cubes in favor of tables in rows with computers on each table. It had a sweatshop for nerds quality. Rob called it the panopticon—a prison where you were always watched. And Rob was the room's sole occupant. Most of the engineering crew stayed until 2 a.m. most nights and wandered in around ten. Rob preferred silence to program, so he'd become a lark rather than a night owl. On a launch night, she'd still be there when he came in at 5 a.m. She'd learned that just because he came in that early didn't mean he wanted to talk to people at that hour. She looked at him as she entered, and he gave her a slight nod, suggesting perhaps he'd had enough coffee to be social. That made one of them.

She dropped her coat at her desk and headed to the break room to pour a second cup. She heard Rob come up behind her.

"What's brought you in before ten? I thought you resolved the dB error?" Rob's face showed only the slightest trace of concern.

"Metrics meeting."

Rob winced. "I thought that was on Thursday."

"Rick moved it."

"Again? Typical." Rob looked into his milky coffee. "Heya, so, I wanted to ask you something."

"What's up?"

"There's a slot opening up for CTO in the Bagboy Race studio, and Davis is offering it to me."

"That Diner Dash rip-off?"

"It's not a great game, sure, but it's a break. It's a step up. And I can run things the way it should be."

Of course. Pete wouldn't give him time to deal with code debt. Rob was sick of having to stay late to deal with major crashes caused by malingering bugs.

Allie felt sad, and then knew she wasn't allowed to feel sad. "Congratulations!"

"So, I should go for it?"

"You've already decided, haven't you?" she teased.

"We have lunch today. I was mostly sure I'd take it. Just wondered if it's a decent bet. CTO is the right title, but Bagboy has never found its audience."

"No one cares if you're CTO of a dead game, just that you're CTO. It's not like GM, where you're held responsible for game numbers. Just that you stop it from crashing all the time."

Rob nodded. Being a general manager of a game in free fall could be a career killer, especially if the game never found its feet. Strong technical leaders were more precious than gold. He should have been promoted years ago.

"Congrats!" she repeated and raised her mug for a clink. Rob smiled, and tapped his mug gently against hers.

Allie stared into her coffee. "You make me think. Is QuiltWorld as big is it's going to get?"

"What do you mean?" Rob asked. He probably knew what she meant, but they were wading into tricky waters.

"Well, acquisition has been off for almost the entire quarter, even below seasonal drops. You know Rick's motto, 'If you aren't growing, you're dying.'"

"We aren't seeing any usage drop off. MAU is steady." They lived by usage acronyms at SOS. Monthly Active Users, Daily Active Users … they lived by their numbers, period.

Allie sighed. "Sure, retention is fine. Usual ups and downs, but no increase." She took a small sip of the hot brew. "I just worry. We've never had a game thrive over eighteen months. QuiltWorld should have been moved to exploit mode a year ago. Rick's theory is sandbox games could have longer lifespans than content driven ones." Sandbox games were Allie's favorite kind of games, much more than casino games. They gave players the tools to make whatever they could imagine, and human imagination is endless. "He hopes QuiltWorld will be a forever game, like Baccarat. But what if it isn't? What if it has a lifespan in between?"

"Maybe. I don't know. Minecraft is still going strong. Legos have been around forever."

They both knew how Rick handled games in decline. He started taking your headcount away, reinvesting it in growing games. You had to do more with less, as he pushed you toward higher revenue numbers. It didn't matter how happy your users were, as long as the whales—big spenders—were milked of every possible dollar. You couldn't do daring creative explorations; instead, you had to optimize every single aspect of the game with a numerical analysis. Brainstorms and charettes were replaced with multivariate test planning meetings.

Right now, Allie was proud to say she worked on QuiltWorld. But QuiltWorld's reputation as an innovative game would disappear quickly if it stopped being that and became a money sink for its most valuable players.

"Maybe I should consider shopping around also." She finally broke the silence. "Have lunch with Sketchworld."

"Oh, come on, Allie. QuiltWorld is fine. Probably a bug somewhere. Don't give up on the old girl yet." He gave her a goofy grin.

"I'd feel much better if we had some historical data."

"Not everything can be calculated. Sometimes you have to take a leap of faith."

"Not a fan."

"Not a choice! That's the problem with living on the bleeding edge. Sometimes you have to go with your gut."

By midmorning, Allie was back at her desk, trying to scry the numbers for some kind of hint about the future when she was interrupted.

"I need to talk to you."

Allie looked up from her spreadsheet. Kendra stood in front of her desk, hands on hips. She was planted in the Wonder Woman pose as if ready to catch bullets with her bracelets. Her straight honey blonde hair was pushed behind her ears, which were bright red, as were her cheeks. She was clearly steaming mad. Kendra had been hired straight out of Stanford to do game UI work, mostly to improve the chrome of the game—the dashboard, controls, and leaderboards. She had talent and had started working on special events under the tutelage of the lead game designer. But her idealism sometimes led to clashes with teammates, and Allie found herself playing referee more than once.

"Okay." Allie rolled her chair back and motioned to the second one that was always near her desk. Product management was at least as much about conversations as numbers. Her desk needed two chairs.

"Privately," Kendra said through tight lips.

"You have a room booked?"

"We can find one. Let's check Braid."

As Kendra predicted, it was empty.

Allie shut the door behind her. Kendra didn't even bother sitting down before she began her rant. "I want to talk to you about Mick."

"Alright, go ahead." Mick was one of the three product managers who reported to her. He'd been a growth hacker for hire that she'd managed to convert to full-time. He was a wizard at optimization. He was not a wizard at interpersonal communication.

"He's wrecking Thanksgiving!" Kendra slapped the conference table with the flats of both hands.

"The entire holiday? What, does he hate turkey or something?" Allie replied. She pulled out a chair and sat down. Kendra mirrored her, sitting down but not one bit calmer.

"He is making me crazy."

Obviously, Allie did not say. She gestured to say, *go on*.

"He's pre-optimizing."

This Allie was familiar with.

In SOS, and a lot of other game companies, product managers were mostly in charge of managing metrics. Their job was to make sure that the holy trinity of acquisition, conversion, and revenue was watched over and constantly grown. SOS was even more intensely metric focused than most game companies and had been developing a playbook on how to maximize revenue over time. Games were understood to have a life cycle.

First, they would be fun toys, and be terrific at acquisition—their only job was to get as many people as fast as possible. The clever mechanics, charming art, and inviting themes would create wonderful word of mouth and supercharge virals—growth based on recommendations. People felt perfectly comfortable sending the game to their friends. After all, they were just games—just fun, relaxing time wasters.

Then gently, a product manager would work on conversion to paid, and try to build the habit of spending money on in-app purchases. After all, there were salaries and rent to be paid.... It was an agreement with the player: We give you fun, you give us money.

Eventually, there would be a moment when a game would stop being able to grow. Usually, at the two-year mark, there was no need to focus on fun and getting new players. Your main job was to get increasingly higher amounts of money from the "whales," people so invested in the game they'd buy anything. The game would be tuned to its most invested players ... literally invested, but with no hope of return. NoirTown had one player who gave it $10,000 a month. He was a former rap star who was now a producer, and he'd even visited the game studio a few times to provide his feedback. Really, Allie thought, SOS should just sell him the game so he could make it whatever he wanted.

Pre-optimizing was the act of tuning the game for optimization before it had been creatively thought through. Arguably QuiltWorld was at the cash cow stage, but if it was going to outlive its brethren, new users had to be delighted as well. Allie could see both sides of the argument, but her love of the game led her to side with Kendra.

Kendra ran her hands through her mass of blonde hair. "He's an asshole. He keeps telling me what to do! He won't give me time to work through the *feel* of the event. I won't work with him on the Advent calendar. I won't. I refuse. He keeps coming to my desk! I can't get an hour to think! He keeps coming by and saying, 'I've got another thing for you to put in Thanksgiving.' I tell him, 'Email is your friend.' But does he listen? He tells me to write things down while he talks, like a secretary! He tells me!" She was near incoherent.

Allie felt responsible. She had met Mick working on Baccarat and coaxed him to switch to QuiltWorld. He was her first direct report. "That's not okay. I'll talk to him."

"You'd better! Because we'll be late otherwise! I'm behind!" She stood, shoving her chair backward. "I'm going home for the day." She crossed her arms. "And turning off my phone."

"Good idea. You need to get yourself some thinking time." Allie stood also, trying to placate her.

Kendra nodded. "Yes, I need some quiet. I'll turn off Wi-Fi. In fact, I'll draw! I'll just work on paper for a while."

Allie exhaled. Kendra seemed to be calming down. Allie opened the door. "Go, go home and catch up. Drop me a note end of day and let me know how it's going. I'll chat with Mick today."

"Great. Thank you, Allie. I knew you'd understand. You've got a creative nature." She beamed at Allie.

Allie resisted rolling her eyes. If she had a creative side, she'd better find it, if she was going to change Mick's behavior.

Allie made her way back to her desk. As she passed Mario, George waved to her to come in. She opened the door.

"Hey, I'm going to have to skip our one-on-one this week. Pete and I are in the middle of something," he said.

"Didn't really expect you!" Allie said, before she could stop herself. They hadn't had their weekly one-on-one for a month.

George frowned. "Hey now, you look worried. Do we need to sit down? You can put something on my calendar, you know."

"Nope, I got this." She paused. "If I don't, I'll swing by later, okay?"

"Sure."

Often as not, they chatted late in the evening, after the chaos of the day had passed. And they were in meetings together all the time as well. In fact, they talked so often, what was the point of a one-on-one anyhow?

As soon as she sat down at her desk, she saw a series of messages from Paul, one of the folks on their data team. While she could do most ordinary queries herself, this growth problem was making her crazy, and she'd put in a request for a senior analyst to look at it.

"This is weird. You should come see…. Oh, maybe not…. No, definitely."

Paul was talking to himself more than her, which probably was a bad sign. Allie dashed down the stairs to the second floor, where the data team was located, and a minute later she was sitting with Paul.

He stroked his scrubby goatee as he gazed at his screen. "Yes, this is not right."

"What do you mean, this is not right?"

"Well, look, the players are sending a ton of friend requests, but they aren't converting at the usual rate. It just falls off a cliff. I don't think it's a fail in intent. I think something is broken."

"What?"

"It's a mystery, honestly. Could be a usability issue, could be a weak message, even a bug … dunno. Something is broken."

"I can't do anything with that!"

He shrugged unperturbed, as if product managers freaking out were what he dealt with all day. Which was probably true. "I only tell the stories the data tells. That's what the data says. Talk to your engineers. Test the flow." He turned to her, as if just noticing how worried she looked. "Hey, at least no one hates your game."

"Okay, fair. Thanks."

He nodded, already eyes on his screen.

She started upstairs. She thought, *Nobody hates your game.* That was something.

On her way toward Mick's desk, she swung by the researcher's desk to talk to him about the report he'd done on the new invite flow, looking for clues to the drop. And then stopped by the invite engineer's desk, to ask him to run some tests. And decided maybe she might as well ask the QA engineer to go over the flow one more time ... and before she knew it, the day was gone.

Around 5 p.m., Allie was toast. She'd woken up too early and had had too many emotions for one day. She knew she should run through numbers one more time. After all, the last revenue drop had been a reporting error. Instead, she sat sideways in her chair, looking at the wall behind the design team. It was covered with maps of QuiltWorld, sketches, and screenshots. There were a few posters of archetypal players as well. The designers called them "personas" and they represented an amalgamation of research into someone the team could design for.

Right then, Allie was looking at one persona in particular. A woman in her late twenties with long straight blonde hair, a dark blonde that didn't see enough sun. She had a shy smile. Her quote, which Allie could not read from here, but still knew by heart was, "The kids are screaming, the dog threw up on the kitchen rug, but my quilt ... my quilt is beautiful." She'd heard almost that exact phrase in a play testing session. SOS games couldn't change the world, but games could make someone's life a little richer. Was it enough? She worked so hard and for what?

Noam ran up to her then. He was the most senior programmer in the studio after Rob. He was twenty-four, tall and gangly and indecently brilliant. He had thick horn-rimmed glasses like Buddy Holly and spoke in the thickest Israeli accent she'd ever heard outside of their team in Tel Aviv.

"I found the acquisition problem! Facebook changed the API, but didn't announce."

"Are you sure?"

"Am I sure?" He gave her a look like she had insulted not only his honor, but the honor of every programmer who had ever lived before him.

"Okay, okay. Forward me the code, and I'll call Dave and we'll talk to them. It's happened before...."

Noam nodded and trotted back to his desk.

Allie got up from her desk, stretched, and walked over to where Mick sat. Mick was hunched over his keyboard, his nose nearly touching the monitor screen. He was utterly intent on whatever he was looking at. He wore his noise-canceling headphones, huge black padded circles giving him offset Mickey Mouse ears. He was a generically handsome guy who would fit in nicely in any frat house at an Ivy League college and had a shape that spoke to soccer or baseball or some regular weekend sport. There was a time in which he might have gone into management consulting or ended up on Wall Street, but the rise of tech meant numbers-savvy guys were willing to take on the risk of early-stage startups. She circled around his desk so he could see her and waved gently in his peripheral vision until he emerged from his trance.

He pushed back from the monitor and lowered his headphones, so they hung around his neck. "What's up, boss?"

"Noam may have found the root of our acquisitions dip. Unannounced API update. It may have been breaking the share flows."

"Nuh-uh. Any flows break, we have alerts set to notify me. I watch all my numbers."

Allie shrugged.

"Go talk to him. See if what he found matches the problem."

Mick leaned way back in his seat and crossed his hands across his belly as if bored and considering a nap.

"Look, buddy. Talking to people is the first job of product management. Talking to numbers is after. You wanted out of data analysis. You wanted to affect the game features. That means we talk to people. Suck it up, cowboy." Then she recalled Kendra's complaint. "Just make sure you set up a time with him first. You ever read *Maker's Schedule, Manager's Schedule*?"

A blank look from Mick.

"By Paul Graham."

A hint of interest. Famous VC=worth his attention.

She continued. "Look it up. Basically, it says people who make things need time to get their head around the problem. If you interrupt them every five minutes, they can't concentrate and can't get work done."

"That's why God gave us headphones."

Headphones were a common solution to the panopticon's noise problem, as well as a signal to leave a person alone. Everyone got a pair when they started.

"Not everyone likes them. Take Kendra. She says they give her earaches."

Mick rolled his eyes expressively. It wasn't a reaction; it was commentary.

"Hey, if you want something from her, you need to give her time to make it! Just saying."

"Okay, I'll talk to Noam." Mick spun his chair around, hopped up, and strode to the engineering pods.

In one ear, out the other, Allie thought. She decided to go home before anything else broke.

AT HOME WITH DEREK

NO MATTER HOW CRAZY THE WEEK, SATURDAY ALWAYS CAME eventually. That weekend Allie wasn't on call, and she was taking full advantage of it by being especially unproductive.

The late afternoon sun shone into their condo patio doors. Derek got up to close the shades. In October, Mountain View could be as hot as August some days. Plus, the light was obscuring the TV.

"Maybe we should go for a walk," he said.

"Maybe you should come back here and let me finish kicking your ass," Allie replied.

"That's just my strategy." Derek sat down and patted her leg, then picked up the controller. "I'm lulling you into a false sense of security."

She restarted the game and said in a Spanish accent, "Prepare to die."

Their two tiny characters walked over the rolling dunes. They were in cloaks, so you couldn't tell if they were male or female or human. Just tiny figures eclipsed by the immensity of the desert. The sun was coming up and the stars faded as the horizon turned a rosy orange. Derek sighed with pleasure. It was so beautiful. They scrambled over the next dune and saw a small metal pipe poking out of the sand.

"I saw it first!" shouted Derek. They both raced for it.

"What is it?"

"I'm not sure. It looks like a periscope?"

They zoomed in closer. Derek's little person looked into it, and the screen showed a giant eye looking back. They both fell backward with laughter.

"What is it?" Allie asked.

"Can we dig?"

"Let's try!"

They hit the sand near the base, but it didn't work.

"The old shack?" Derek suggested.

"I don't remember anything there."

"Oh, c'mon, this isn't working."

"You go, I'll keep trying."

Derek's avatar, a squat bear-like person in a bright blue cloak, walked away from Allie's, a hedgehog in a top hat with a red cloak. As they wandered the expanse of the desert, the screen was split into two horizontally, echoing the expanse of the desert. But when they went into the cabin, it faded into a dark space, and as their eyes adjusted to the darkness, the screen split vertically. This emphasized the change in mood and supported the change in behavior from traveling to exploring the space. It was one of the elegant moments in the game's two-player mode, cinematic and evocative. Allie sighed at the transition.

Her games were limited by technology, and by the free-to-play model. SOS had to have constant nag screens to try this or that quest that would make them money. What a pleasure it was to get lost in a gorgeous game like this. And it even was successful, a breakout hit for the little indie studio that made it.

"I got it!" Derek shouted. His avatar held a broomstick.

"Really?" Allie replied.

"No, wait!" He took a jackalope head that was mounted on a wooden plaque down from the wall. He pulled the head away from the plaque … and an entire jackalope came out, like a rabbit from a magician's hat. The jackalope bounded away, and Allie and Derek collapsed with laughter. Then Derek pushed the broomstick into the plaque, and it became a shovel.

"Oh, honey. My baby is the smartest baby."

"You know it, darling love."

His avatar walked across the desert again, and the screens merged into each other like water as the two tiny figures were reunited.

"Shall I order pizza?" Allie asked.

"The finder of the shovel chooses the cuisine." Derek said solemnly. "We are leaving the house!"

After dinner, they decided to grab some gelato. There was always a line at the gelato place, but the hot weather made it twice as long. Still, it was pleasant to wait together and chat.

"I've talked your ear off all dinner," Allie said. "How'd your penultimate week go?"

Derek shrugged. "Fine. Can't start much, obviously. We filled the director role. And next week, as a going away gift, I get to sit in on the firing of everyone's favorite VP."

"Ugh, I'm sorry." The line inched forward.

He shrugged. "I don't enjoy it. But every time we let someone go, the entire team gets better."

"What do you mean? I thought it was depressing." Allie thought of her first job. It was a startup that had run out of money, and they started laying folks off, starting with the worst performers. When she joined, they looked so healthy, but after a year they hadn't had a follow-up to their first big hit, and then they started trimming costs. It was one of the most miserable work experiences of her life, sitting among the empty desks and wondering who was next. She tried not to think about QuiltWorld.

Derek knew what she was thinking of. "Layoffs are different. They are part of larger organizational issues." He paused, thinking. They stepped closer to the counter. "Not firing is also a sign of organizational issues. If you keep a bad hire around, it causes a lot of issues. If they don't work hard, everyone wonders why they should work hard. If they work hard, but are a jerk, people don't want to work with them. If they are incompetent, it undermines trust in management … it goes on and on."

The clerk came over to them. "The usual?"

Allie snapped back to reality. "Oh. Yes. Thanks." Derek ordered while Allie thought about the layoffs. At first, they were a relief in a weird way. There was one guy who just made her job harder. It was easier to do things alone. But later … seeing friends go. That hurt. Giving up the dream of success—that hurt, too. Eventually she had quit, before they got to her.

At SOS, she'd seen something similar with dying games. First the rats left the ship, as they say. Those super-political folks who wanted to be associated with whatever was hot would jump studio to whatever looked like the next big thing. Then Rick would firmly move people out. If you didn't pick a better place to be, you'd get a message you were now working on whatever Rick thought you should work on. It didn't matter if you were loyal to your team, or if you thought you could turn things around. You were moved like a chess piece.

"Hey, come back to me, hon." Derek nudged her softly with his shoulder, his hands busy with gelato cup and spoon.

Allie refocused and realized they were halfway home. "Sorry, what were you saying?"

Derek laughed. "You don't even have to be on that damn phone to be working. I was just telling you all of the fine qualities of our 'special VP.'"

"Mm?" Allie replied, eating her gelato.

Derek sighed. "It's too long. Let me sum up. He's poison for everyone, and when he's gone, everything will get better. More important, management will be seen as willing to take on the hard problems, which will grow trust. It's taken us six months to get the documentation right, but it'll be worth it when he's gone."

"Six months? That's crazy!"

"Well, he's an exec. Half my meetings are with legal, half are with HR."

"So, are you happy or unhappy to do this firing? I can't tell."

"The CEO is doing the actual act. I'm just there to witness and take notes." Derek paused to think about it. "I guess both. Firing is one of the hardest jobs in anyone's life. But it really does make the job better. It's often a wake-up call for an employee. I dunno. I do like hiring better. It's all sunshine and rainbows at the beginning."

"Well, congrats on the new job then."

"Hah! I'm just glad I don't have that stupid commute anymore. More time for us!"

The phone in Allie's back pocket vibrated. Derek's eyes widened. Allie laughed. "Don't tempt the gods!"

She pulled out her phone. Another anomaly in the sign-up numbers. "Oh, I need to deal with this. Five minutes, I swear."

Derek shook his head and walked ahead. Allie tossed her melted gelato into a trash bin, and dialed Mick.

BE CAREFUL WHAT YOU WISH FOR

ALLIE WOKE UP AT SIX, HER PHONE ALARM VIBRATING UNDER her pillow. She turned it off and silently got out of bed, navigating from the phone's light into the hall. She didn't want to wake up Derek. Bad enough she had to join him in bed after he was asleep and leave before he woke up. She'd forget what color his eyes were at this rate. She pulled a robe off the back of the bathroom door and shuffled into the kitchen to flick on the electric kettle. Derek had ground the beans last night before going to bed, and two pour-over cones sat next to the kettle, waiting for water to transform them into the magic elixir of life.

Allie sat down at the kitchen table and popped open her laptop. Maybe she could go in a little later today, get breakfast with Derek first. The last week had been littered with problems, though, and she was far from certain that they were over yet.

Wi-Fi was out, and she rebooted the router, then looked through last night's emails. Today's numbers looked good. Allie loved that a "woman's game" had managed to outperform SOS's previous hit, Angels and Assassins. But more, she loved the players' creations. The community manger had sent her screenshots of the latest, including a quilted reproduction of Wat Pho, Thailand's temple represented in virtual gold and cream fabric squares. No matter how clever the lead designer thought he was being with new fabric kits, the players took them apart and recreated them into more and more fabulous quilt creations.

This week, revenue had taken a freakish tumble out of nowhere. She was in the office from Tuesday until Wednesday morning before she'd managed to track down what turned out to be a reporting error. Sadly, both the acquisition numbers and a gently downward sloping revenue curve were accurate. Sleep would have to take a back seat until she had a plan.

She watched as her email list suddenly doubled then tripled as Wi-Fi connected. Triage time. She scanned for any flagged red, and by some miracle, nothing had burned down overnight. She got up and released the coffee into the mug. She permitted herself a moment to inhale deeply the fragrant liquid, and joyfully scalded her mouth with it. She sat back down and got ready to sort out the noise from the signal. Then another email popped in, flagged and with the subject line "URGENT 8:30 meeting w/Rick." Her stomach dropped. A meeting with SOS's CEO was never a good thing.

She wouldn't be having breakfast with Derek after all.

She got to meeting room Mario at 8:15 and plugged in her computer to make sure the projector worked. She opened both PowerPoint and Excel, making sure she could toggle from the presentation she'd whipped up to the raw numbers if needed. Rick had been known to yell at people for showing him numbers and not showing him numbers, and since she had no idea how deep they'd go, she wanted to be ready for anything. She reviewed the lines of numbers again.

Why were the acquisition numbers dropping? Game growth usually showed one of two curves. Acquisitions either popped out of the gate and then settled, or they started slow and then picked up into a hockey stick if players loved it enough to make sure the viral growth was strong. Allie had been promoted to lead PM because of her work designing for virality. She was extremely talented at figuring out how to get new players to share their progress and invite others to play. QuiltWorld was a game based on the pleasure of creativity; those always had great sharing metrics. Yet out of nowhere, the shares were faltering. Why? If Rick went into numbers, he couldn't fail to notice this. Less worrisome than their trajectory was the fact that she didn't know why they were faltering. The coffee sloshed in her stomach.

"Greensleeves, Greensleeves is my heart's delight and who but my lady Greensleeves," sang an off-key baritone. Allie jerked her head around anxiously. It wasn't Rick. No way on earth.

In walked Felix, one of the board members. He was a former EA executive, at Sega and Atari and everywhere else. He was now a VC, but weirdly omnipresent in the halls of SOS.

He sat down and gave her a grin. "Play anything good lately?" he asked. "I'm liking the mod on Baccarat the team just released."

"I mean outside these halls!" He threw his bulk down into a chair and put his feet up on the table. His pupils were hugely dilated, and she wondered what that meant, and if it was even a safe thing to wonder. "You don't only play our games."

Allie didn't talk much with board members. And by not much, she meant never. What was the right answer? Was there a right answer? Every day was like another test.

"Honestly, I've been playing mostly Korean MMOs. They are doing great things with collaboration mechanics, and the art is surreal beyond belief."

"Write down the names of them for me." He slid his feet on the conference table, leaving a slight smudge of mud.

I wonder if it's raining, she thought. I wonder how high up in the org you have to get before you feel comfortable putting your feet on the conference table.

At that moment Rick walked in, talking to her GM, George. George always spoke slightly too loudly and seemed to take up all the room, except when Rick was there. Then Rick's tiny form and giant personality overwhelmed everyone else, the only star in the system. Right behind George came QuiltWorld's CTO, Pete. George pulled the door shut behind them. Weird. Was this it? What meeting could this possibly be, with this group? She petted her Mac absentmindedly, finding the cool aluminum comforting.

"Okay, then. Allie." Rick's eyes locked on her. The brown was so dark she couldn't tell how much was iris and how much was pupil, like a badger's eyes. She glanced back to Felix. Felix's glassy eyes seemed inward looking, half-dreaming, while Rick was all-noticing.

"We've been talking." Rick glanced over to her GM. "George, you want to take this?"

Allie sat up a little. What was going on here?

George sipped from a bottle of water, then glanced slowly in her direction, almost reluctantly.

"QuiltWorld is where I hoped it would be. But I need new challenges. It's time for me to move."

At SOS, movement was the only constant. Everyone changed studios. If you succeeded, you left. If you failed, you left. If you got bored, you left. If you loved where you were, you'd probably get nudged.

"I'm going to start a new studio for a new game." He began to twinkle with excitement. "I've been looking at the passive games, the way they integrate into lives. I think this could unlock an entire new market for us."

Rick interrupted. "You're funded. You can stop pitching."

George sat back again, almost embarrassed by his show of excitement. "Well, so I'll be moving on."

Allie couldn't help herself. "Who's the new GM?"

Felix broke in. "You are."

Allie's jaw hit the Mac. She snapped her mouth shut, then asked cautiously, "Oh?"

"We think you've got a lot of talent. This is your moment," Felix said.

When did she ever see Felix? Or more important, when did he see her? She couldn't recall even being introduced.

Rick was nodding softly, as if he'd gotten wise insights from his *consigliere*. "Interim GM, for now. I'd like to see what you can do with the game."

Pete smiled at her, still saying nothing, but there was approval in his expression.

"Time to step up, kid." George smiled.

Rick said, "We'll announce at ten, when everyone is in. Do you have any questions?"

There was no asking her if she wanted it. It was understood that she did. Everyone did. At SOS, there was a constant jostling upward. You tried for a better title, a better game, a better market, a better team. All who worked there had a silent stack rank in their head of what was ahead of you and what was behind you. QuiltWorld's numbers were faltering, sure, but it still was the cash cow and darling of the company.

Allie swallowed. She had not seen this coming. She was lead PM, but she thought she'd get a smaller game first, maybe be offered one in "exploit" mode. So, when you were promoted, you'd usually step up and down, as they said. But she'd stepped up and sideways. She allowed a little fire of excitement to light up in her breast. Her baby would become *her* baby? She could take QuiltWorld to its next iteration? It was something she hadn't even considered as a dream. She loved that fucking game. And now she'd be its shepherd? This was the best day of her life.

* * *

This was the worst day of her life.

At ten she was shifting anxiously from foot to foot, thrilled at what was about to be announced. She'd pulled a pair of pumps and a jacket from her file cabinet, feeling she should look a bit more respectable when her promotion was announced. And sometimes she felt better with a couple extra inches of height. Rob sidled up to her, still towering above.

"You look spiffy!"

"Shut up."

"What's up? Do we have VIPs swinging by today?" Rob pronounced VIPs to rhyme with zips, knowing it annoyed her. A little friendly teasing to try to get her to relax. It didn't work, but she appreciated his effort.

"I can't tell you yet. Just hang out a bit."

"Heya, I ran into Davis downstairs in line for breakfast."

"And?"

"I went ahead and told him I'm in."

"Wonderful! I've got good news too, but it has to wait just a ..."

Rick swept into the studio. Immediately every eye was on him. No one knew what to do, but all watched him surreptitiously, as if he were a king in a poor disguise walking the marketplace. Again, George was at his elbow, and Pete a few paces behind. Allie stood a little taller, excited.

"Hey, folks, gather round, got an announcement," George called out.

The panopticon turned its sixty eyes to him, and the room rumbled to life as chairs were pushed back and people stood. People walked around the desks to the front, where George and Pete's desks stood next to each other. Rick was sitting back in George's chair, lending his approval to the scene.

George cleared his throat, then spoke in his theater voice, effortlessly projecting to the back of the large room. "Okay, folks, it's been an amazing couple of years ..."

A frisson of fear seemed to move across the room. If you'd worked at SOS for any length of time, you knew to regard announcements with suspicion.

"We've done incredible things! No studio has gone to Vegas more than we have!" A cautious cheer arose.

"But it's time for the next QuiltWorld to be created!" And again, Allie felt the room move as one, this time leaning slightly forward with interest.

"Pete and I are going to be starting a new studio, to look into the future of passive games." Now a cautious cheer—a polite cheer, if there was such a thing. George was a good GM, but not all the studios had good leaders. Some were neglectful, some were bullies. Change might not be a good thing. But Allie knew better.

"I know what you are all thinking ... who can step into my giant shoes?" He paused, savoring the tension. "Tiny feet make big steps ... your GM has been with you all the time! Allie, please step forward!"

Allie came to stand next to George, Pete, and Rick. This time the team gave an enthusiastic cheer. Whew. And Rick hadn't used the word "interim," so people would take her seriously. She hadn't forgotten that, though.

Rick then stood. "Allie has led this studio along with George," with a nod toward George, "to become the most profitable in the company. I have complete faith she will continue to keep QuiltWorld our shining star." He smiled at her and shook her hand. Allie didn't shake hands often, and missed slightly, hitting the inside of his palm with her fingers, but he recovered as if he hadn't noticed. Then he nodded to George and Pete and glided out to his next appointment.

Later, while she was pouring her fourth cup of coffee, Rob stepped up. "Good news all around! Congrats!"

She gave him an impromptu hug. They didn't usually hug; Rob was not demonstrative, but he gave her a quick tight squeeze of pride and happiness.

"I can't believe this! It's too good to be true!"

Rob looked at her thoughtfully. "Maybe. So, Pete is going with George?"

"Yep, they are a team."

"Who you going to get for CTO?"

Allie froze in place. "Oh. I hadn't thought of. Would you?" She looked up at him.

"Oh, honey."

She blinked.

"I can't break my word. I committed already."

"Oh. I get it," she rushed to say. "Of course, of course. Really, it's cool."

"I'm happy to vet people for you."

"OMG, that would be great! I've hired PMs, but never technical before."

"No prob. So, who else is going?"

"What do you mean?"

"I mean, who else is George taking? Rick gave him twelve heads, I hear. I imagine he'd want to take people he'd know."

Allie put down her coffee cup. Suddenly she felt very sloshy. She looked around the room. SHE KNEW THESE PEOPLE. They were her people. She knew who was good at what, who could be motivated by chocolate and who needed scotch. She knew who was a morning person and who was a night owl. And suddenly she was going to lose that?

They hadn't discussed that at all in the meeting. They'd talked timing, logistics, about having regular one-on-ones with George to discuss handover issues—but nowhere did he mention taking her crew. Her crew. His crew.

She walked over to where George was leaning against his desk, Rick long disappeared. He was deep in conversation with Victor, her second in command on product. She walked into the space between them, making an equilateral triangle.

"Hey, George."

"Hey, kid." He turned to face her.

She smiled guilelessly. "So, have you picked out your crew yet?"

"Working on it. I'll get you a list." He turned back to Victor.

Victor said, "So things were dropping a little in August, but we thought that was seasonal...."

"Okay," she said, and retreated to Rob.

"You're right. He's going to take everyone good."

When Allie walked into the studio Monday morning, George's desk was empty. As were Pete's, Victor's, Janice's, and Steve's. George had basically wiped away senior leadership, leaving her with strong teams led by no one but her. If only Rob hadn't left literally minutes before her promotion.

She stood looking at the studio, about a fourth filled. It was only 9:15; few would come in before they had to for the 10 a.m. stand-ups. She walked over to Jheryn, a senior engineer who was quietly staring at his monitor. He turned to her as she walked up and gave her a shy smile.

"Hey, seen George and his crew?"

"He's up on the third floor. I think by Dark Room." The third-floor conference rooms were named for iOS games.

"Thanks!"

She shot up the stairs, taking two when she could. George was NOT going to worm out of their one-on-one today! If he was near Dark Room, it meant he was near the mobile team. She wondered if that was an accident or meant something. Probably it meant something. George was nothing if not strategic. All choices meant something.

She caught her breath as she topped the staircase and stepped into the community kitchen. She grabbed a bottle of water and took a sip to slow herself down a bit. Then she made her way through the open room toward where she recalled the Joust conference room was. The space was about fifty percent occupied, if desk decor was any hint. Only a quarter ago, they had no mobile dev team. This was some crazy growth. But that was SOS. It doubled every six months.

She found George sitting against a window, his desk already adorned with his collection of Lord of the Rings action figures. "Hey, buddy. Ready?"

"Hmm?" He looked up at her. "Oh, yeah, hi!" Was he really as absent-minded as he came across? He was like a parody of a professor. Brilliant, but only loosely fixed in time and space. He waved at a nearby chair. "Shall we just meet here?"

"I'd prefer to grab a room, if you don't mind."

George stood and walked over to Dark Room. Ironically, it was a terrific room, full of light and space. One wall was all windows, and it had a large table in the center that could hold twelve people easily.

George strode to the head of the table and sat. Allie took the seat to his right, and they pushed out their chairs and swiveled to face each other. Today the dance felt meaning-filled to Allie. First his right-hand man, now his equal.

Allie spread her hands out, as if to receive a physical package of his experience.

George shifted a little, perhaps trying to get comfortable in the office chair. "I'm taking a core team, but nothing crippling."

"It looks like you are taking the CTO, art director, lead game designer, and the most senior PM."

"You're the most senior PM."

"What do you even need a PM for? You don't have anything to optimize!"

"Victor is interested in learning about early stage game development." George was not rising in reaction to her anger. "And he can do analysis on emerging trends and generally keep us focused and on schedule."

"Janice is critical to our next upcoming launch. Couldn't you have taken another staff member? Aaron? He's really good."

"Come on, Allie. The style guide will keep everyone on brand, and you've got enough bodies. Janice is bored with just executing against the guide. She deserves to shape a game to her vision, don't you think?"

'Don't you think.' That always meant you should think, as far as Allie could tell. She sat for a second, trying to put a finger on what she did think. What she felt.

"You've taken all the senior managers from QuiltWorld. I've never run a team this big. Not even close. I would have liked to have had some support."

"I'm just a floor up!"

"You know it's not the same. I could barely find you when we were in the same office. Now I'll have to form an all-new leadership team."

"You can do this, Allie. Rick picked you for a reason. Felix and I both recommended you. Your work on maximizing revenue on special events is unmatched, and the team admires you."

"I don't need a pep talk, George! I need a crew!"

George regarded her calmly, and then said, "Well, I have some good news then."

Allie stared at George. She could see the crinkles of his eyes that said he was smiling. Why was he pleased with himself?

"Yosi will be your interim CTO."

Allie sat back in her chair, semi-stunned. "Yosef Beinart?" She was stunned.

"Yep," George said, looking much like he had eaten a canary.

"He's going to Tel Aviv!" she replied.

"Not until after Q1. His wife wants to have the baby here with her primary care physician. She feels more comfortable with the devil she knows, he says."

Yosi had been the first CTO of SOS. He was not a people person. He was a code person. He spoke to it like a horse whisperer. And he could hire. He could talk to someone for five minutes and know if they could code worth a crap. Pattern recognition, he called it. But no one enjoyed working for him. He was a micromanager. Apparently, he couldn't recognize his own patterns.

They'd placed a VP of engineering under him at first, to deal with management issues. But he had a way of profoundly annoying investors and embarrassing Rick in meetings. He'd been gently nudged over into an R&D role, chief scientist or something. She hadn't heard much for a while. Last she'd heard, he'd been working on a new platform to assemble game components more quickly, and he was moving back to Tel Aviv to work with their engineering team there.

Allie thought through the repercussions. The thing was everyone agreed he was brilliant. There was zero question about that. And there was some prestige in having a founder in your studio.

"He can help you with your searches. Evaluate talent. And of course, keep the lights on. When I found out he was staying, I wrangled him for you." George was smiling broadly now, like he had just given her a kitten. After stealing her new bike, of course. And scooter. And skateboard.

"This breaks all the rules, George. You aren't supposed to just pillage one studio to build a new one."

"Rick approved it. He felt you had enough headcount to handle it. You should get back to your studio. Yosi will be there to listen in on standup."

Allie glanced at the clock. 9:45 already. Fuck. Nothing to do but suck it up. She stood, and George followed suit. "I look forward to our next one-to-one. You can teach me how to hire an art director."

"My pleasure, Allie. You've always been my favorite protégé."

Allie managed to leave the room without punching him in the face.

ARE WE CELEBRATING?

SHE GOT HOME BEFORE DEREK. SHE'D GONE IN SO EARLY, THEY couldn't commute together anyhow, so he probably didn't expect her to be there. She ordered from his favorite Italian place, adding a couple extra dishes just to be decadent. And to not have to cook tomorrow. She then walked downstairs to the corner grocery to grab a bottle of bubbles to stick in the freezer.

She kicked off her shoes and laid back on the couch, considered playing some Call of Duty, but then, exhausted, put on the ballgame. She shut her eyes just for a second.

Then she was wide awake, her phone vibrating madly on the glass coffee table.

"Food's here," Derek said. He sat across from her on the sectional, smiling at her. The Prosecco was sitting on the table, and he poured her a glass. Then he stood and walked to the door to meet the delivery guy.

He put the boxes on the table.

"How long was I out?"

"Ask your phone. I've only been here five minutes."

"And you went right for the Prosecco?"

"How many bottles have exploded in the freezer? I always look there when I get home."

She nodded ruefully and helped open and spread out the boxes. They served themselves plates overflowing and sat back on the couch. The dinner table was too buried by paper and electronics to be eaten at.

"So, what's the announcement you texted me about?" He gestured at the food and bubbles. "Vegas?"

"Silly, the quarter has barely started. No, this is much bigger."

"And scarier?" He looked into her eyes. They had dated for eight years before they'd finally gotten married three years ago. He knew her like no one did. Or would.

She blew air through her lips, a silent whistle. "I dunno." She took a sip of Prosecco. "I dunno. Hon, I'm the general manager. Of QuiltWorld. I got promoted."

Derek gave her a quizzical smile. "This is what you always wanted, right?"

"Yes." She smiled but couldn't smile all the way.

"You said you didn't want to start your own thing until you got a shot at leading. Well, you couldn't have a better shot than this!"

She blinked. Yes, she had said that. Years ago, Derek had asked her when she'd start her own company. He believed in her. And he also thought that if she became a boss, she could build a company with a better culture than the one she was currently experiencing, one that would allow her come home for dinner.

Then when she'd taken a job at notoriously miserable SOS, he'd asked her why she would join that sweatshop. She'd said so she could learn to lead under stress. SOS was big enough you could get promoted and she could get mentorship. And now that it had happened? "I'm terrified."

"Why?"

"It's all wrong. I thought I'd get to take over a little game, or an older one first. I thought it would be a smaller team and a much smaller P&L. This is one of the most important games in the company." Her voice was higher; she spoke faster. She could feel the tension grip her throat. "I'm a great right-hand man."

Derek snorted at that. "You're a terrible feminist, hon."

Allie ignored him, continuing. "Right-hand person. I can make just about anything happen. But I've never had to be the one to decide what should happen."

Derek moved slightly back, as if to take in all of her. He smiled comfortingly.

"Oh, you're putting on your HR face, I see!" she teased. More like his husband face, when he looked at her like that, eyes shining with faith and admiration.

"You are overdue to step up." Derek's lips smiled, but his eyes said he was serious. "When we moved here from Austin, you said you wanted to start your own thing. That was eight years ago."

"Startups are hard. The game business has not gotten any easier."

Derek took her hands in his. "It was hard when we moved here. Don't let the jacked-up culture at SOS keep you from remembering your goals. Today, you made a huge step forward toward them. The general manager is CEO of the game studio. Sure, the stakes are higher than you expected. But at SOS, you've got a support system in place. You've got recruiters, more experienced peers who can mentor you, and a great bench of talent to pull on. This is perfect—it's the role you want with training wheels. You'll be fine. In fact, you'll be better than fine. I know you, babe. You can do this."

Allie gazed past Derek, out the window of their condo. Squirrels frolicked in the leaves, flirting and collecting food. She missed the simplicity of her days waiting tables sometimes. You came in, did your job, and left without looking back. You never took your work home. And when you were at work, everything was understood. You knew how to greet, how to take an order, how to serve, how to close a check. There was enough variety in the people that it was never boring, yet the routine was profoundly relaxing. It had been years since work was like that.

"Yeah, I get training wheels, but my bike is on a narrow bridge over a pool of piranhas swimming around waiting for me to fall off my bike so they can eat me alive. Every GM of a lesser game has been waiting for George to step away. They know he's a starter, not a finisher. They all want my job, so they can enjoy the glory before the numbers collapse. They'll be watching me every second."

"Then they'll see you succeed." Derek was not budging. He took his role as husband seriously, including unwavering support.

He was right; she'd left Blizzard for a reason. She wanted to up her skills and explore this new game platform. She wanted a chance to work with and meet top game designers and engineers and get what she needed to step out on her own. She had chosen this life. She had to remember she was aiming at something better than SOS. She would leave this place with the knowledge she needed, and she would start a company that treated people right and built games players loved. This had been her promise to herself when they moved out here. She would keep that promise.

"So how is the new gig?" she asked, changing the subject.

"Pretty cool. Right now, I'm running a harassment training marathon."

"Welcome to big company life!" Allie laughed. "It's CYA all the way."

"Actually, it's not. I mean, this training is not just so they can check off the 'did I warn people to not make lewd jokes in meetings.' The training has been incredible. They actually bring in professors from Stanford to teach us methods for supporting our employees."

"Well, they print money there. I guess it's nice they spend it on you?" Allie looked at Derek. He had his glowy *I'm learning* face on.

"Agreed." He grinned. "I got the coolest model today. Can I share?"

"Can I stop you?"

"No!" Derek reached for a notebook from a stack of papers he had piled on his end of the couch. The giant sectional was fifty percent sitting room, twenty percent electronics, and the rest piles of printouts and books. Lifetime learning was a survival skill in the Valley.

"Okay, it's called GROW. It's an acronym."

"Of course it is."

"Shush. It's for coaching. So, this tennis coach guy realized his coaching style could be used for coaching anything, because he just got people to coach themselves."

"Very Zen."

Derek leaned back toward his pile of books and papers and pulled out two books. "Here."

Allie took them. One said *The Inner Game of Tennis* and the other said *The Inner Game of Stress*. "I can certainly use this one," she said, waving the second in the air.

Derek gave her a quizzical look. "Yes, actually. Keep that one."

Allie sighed dramatically.

Derek continued. "Okay, so GROW was developed by this guy Whitmore who took the ideas from the tennis guy and codified them."

Allie gestured for him to get on with it.

"It's how you run a coaching session. *G* is for goals. You ask people what their goals for the session are. You want to try it?"

"Sounds like therapy."

"Oh, come on, Allie, if I try it out, I can learn it better."

"Okay. My goal for our session is to get you naked instead of talking about work."

"Allie. First the work, then the reward. You just got promoted, and you look like you ate a lemon! I know there is something you're freaking out about."

Allie shook her head. There were so many things running in circles in her head. So many things that were fucked up about her situation. "I don't even know where to start. I have so much to do. I shouldn't even be sitting here. I should be working."

Derek's face fell. She suspected she'd hurt his feelings, but she wasn't sure how. She could guess, though. He'd been a work widower so long, and now it was about to get worse. She had better give him some quality time.

And if he wanted to play coach, why not? "Okay, hon. I need to figure out how to sort out the studio. It's not just that I don't know how to manage. It's that George took all the good people when he left to start this new game."

Derek nodded. "Okay. *R* is for reality. What are the factors that are making this so difficult?" He took her hands.

She smiled. "Are coaches allowed to hold hands?"

"Husband coaches are." He sat very still, very quietly watching her. Silence was one of Derek's superpowers. His silence was like a warm blanket wrapped around her shoulders.

Allie's stress and fear that she'd been holding at bay came flooding back. She was safe enough with him to be insecure. "I don't even know what to do." She felt her throat close, a sign tears might be on the way.

"Just tell me what is going on."

She recapped her day for him. "And I feel so overwhelmed. I don't even know what to do first. There is so much. I have at least three positions I need to hire for yesterday, I've got people who aren't doing their jobs, I'm not doing my job, I don't know what my job is, George isn't helping, Rick will demote me or worse the moment I mess up, and everyone is just waiting for me to prove I'm not good enough so they can grab my job." She wasn't crying yet, though the tightness in her throat was still there. Maybe she'd learned to hold off tears until she was private.

Derek was watching her still, perhaps trying to decide if he should keep coaching or hug her. His warm hands still held hers firmly. She could see his Adam's apple as he swallowed. "*O* is for options. What do you think you can do in this situation?"

Allie nodded. Problem solving felt better than wallowing in helplessness. She felt her throat loosen. "I have to hire. Period. I need to get job postings out. I might need to pull a George and steal from other studios."

"What are the pluses and minuses of that?"

"Fresh blood can be great. Get folks from other companies to increase our body of knowledge. But it's slow. And it's harder to get honest references. Inside the company, I can buy someone a cup of coffee and get the skinny."

"Okay," Derek said.

"My current team is a mess. Mick makes everyone angry just by walking into the room, Noam is smart but won't make a decision unless he talks to me three times, I swear, Kendra is a sweetie, but she is no game designer, Jheryn is a mute…."

"An actual mute?"

"No, I just mean, he never talks to anyone. You ask him to work on something, he does it, and he never even tells you when it's done, and God forbid he gets stuck because you won't know until you go talk to him. He just stops working and starts playtesting the latest game."

"So, you've got some feedback to give."

"Yeah, no kidding, but I need to get on hiring first. No amount of feedback is going to make an orange into an apple. And I have got to sort out the conversion drop. I have to get the numbers at least stable before the next numbers review with Rick or we're dead in the water. I was looking through the new set of numbers I just pulled...."

Derek looked like he was bursting with something to say, but Allie was on a roll. She went deep into the analytics work she was doing until Derek had to unhook his hands to lay a finger on her lips.

"Hon, can I please make a small suggestion?"

"Oh, I'm sorry. I know the tech stuff is boring."

"No, not that." He smiled. "I think you really need to focus on the people problem. You don't scale. If you can get these roles filled, you can live a sustainable life. You can't just keep working longer hours."

Allie knew he didn't want that. He'd changed jobs to get rid of his commute so they could spend more time together. She hadn't asked him to. And now she was going to work even longer hours, and they both knew it. She felt guilty.

Derek said, "The _W_ is for 'What will you do?' Knowing what you know about the reality of the situation, and your options, what will you do to meet your goal?"

Allie thought he was asking more than that. He was asking when life would become normal. She left the elephant in the corner sleeping, though. "It's triage time. I need to get these roles hired, but until then, I need to make sure I keep our numbers stable. Otherwise we chance getting written off by Rick as a dying game, and then he'll start taking away head count and it's all over. I'm sorry, but before bed I do need to do some work tonight."

She didn't tell him it was going to get worse before it got better. They both knew.

DAY ONE: MEETING YOSI

THE NEXT DAY AT THE QUILTWORLD STUDIO, EVERYONE WAS IN early and the office was buzzing. Allie supposed people were interested in seeing what was going to happen next and meet the infamous Yosi. She eyed the empty seats where George and his band of pirates had decamped. Annoying.

Derek was right; she needed to hire. Which meant she had to write job descriptions. She'd start with the one for art director. What did they really do, anyhow? They ran the art team, they made the game art, and what else? What else?

At least she understood CTO and game designer. Or did she? A CTO hired, fired, and managed the team, but what else? Code reviews? CTOs didn't project manage, but she knew they certainly had opinions. She could ask Yosi later. And the game designer designed the game behavior; this she knew from years of sitting together. Look, behavior, functionality.

She flipped to her email tab and jotted a note to the recruiter, Jayla:

Please send previous job descriptions and/or job descriptions for other studios for

* Art director
* CTO
* Game designer
And any other listings you think relevant.

Thank you,
Al

She sighed. Probably would take a few minutes or so to get a response. She hopped over to a job site, looking for an art director position. Hmmm, nothing but stuff for advertising agencies. Ugh. She went to a competitor's site and found a listing. It was not horrible. She cut and pasted it into a new document. She also found a listing for a junior game designer. She threw it into her document also.

She checked her email. Jayla had already replied.

Here's what we have on file for role currently. Let me know if you'd like me to go into my archives and find more examples.

Have a good day!

Jayla

Unflaggingly pleasant, unflaggingly polite. That was Jayla. Then she realized she'd forgotten to ask for a product manager description. She wrote a quick reply and sent it.

Allie cut and pasted the descriptions into her document and compared them to the ones she'd found online. She decided to start with game designer. It was the role she felt more comfortable with. It was practically what she did, once the game was established.

In the beginning, when the game was being conceived, a game designer was really the only person who could bring balance and fun to a game. They had to decide dozens of things—from how to mix skill and chance, how much narrative to put in, what the players' roles and interactions would be, and more. Allie found it fascinating, especially choosing between collaboration and competition in the social aspects.

QuiltWorld was nominally a collaborative game in which you made worlds apart and together, but in playtesting she'd seen rivalries in which players constantly tried to outdo each other's works. Steve, the previous game designer, always said that games were a series of continuums, and the game designer had to choose which to make explicit and which to allow the player to own. Watching hundreds of players create quilts in her game had shown how right he was.

But once a game was launched and tuned, a product manager could use the mechanic's wiki to create new "beats"—minigames in the master game—often themed around special events such as holidays. Allie loved making them, and hers were always successful, bumping up revenue and engagement.

The studio needed a lead game designer to design more complex expansions and big "bold beats"—special events that tried out new mechanics in hopes of exponential metrics. As well, the game designer reviewed the beats put together by the PMs, to make sure they didn't unbalance the game.

Allie looked over both descriptions. Jayla had sent her a standard game designer listing, not a lead. Oh, it was her own fault, she hadn't specified. Well, it wasn't so different, and she felt a bit embarrassed burying Jayla with emails. She made a few tweaks to the description and borrowed a phrase she liked from the competitor's junior description— "unchecked imagination that frightens your coworkers"—and then turned to the other descriptions.

She felt suddenly tired and overwhelmed. How could something new and complex also be so boring? Writing these made her feel like her energy was being drained. Or maybe she was just hungry.

It was almost time for lunch, and she had a lunch-and-learn session with free food to go to. She decided to just send Jayla the other two descriptions to post, untouched.

Jayla,

These are great, thanks! I made a couple tweaks on the game designer role, but left the others as is. Go ahead and post. Cheers!

Allie glanced at the clock in the conference room through the glass wall. Five minutes to ten. It was time to run stand-up, when all the teams gave short updates on progress. She suddenly realized she wasn't sure who she would be doing stand-up with. Before her promotion, she'd check in with the team that was working on her project, and George would run stand-up with Pete and Janice. She should run a stand-up with her exec team, but she had no exec team. She had a list of people to hire, thanks to George.

Just then Yosi walked in. He was a not a tall man, maybe 5'7", but was solidly built and walked as if he was claiming each bit of earth as he stepped foot upon it. His hair was a dirty blond and was receding like a general from a losing battle. His belly, however, had all the boldness his hair had lost, and had claimed the territory beyond his belt. He strode into the studio, looked around, spotted Allie, and walked straight for her as if they'd met a dozen times before, when in reality they had exchanged maybe a half dozen words at various events over the years. First Felix, then Rick, now Yosi. How long had people been watching her? Or did they watch everyone who didn't flee from the unremitting stress and workload?

"So. You heard?" he said, holding out a hand to be shaken.

Allie shook it awkwardly. At SOS, and for that matter, most companies in California, folks either nodded or hugged, and not much in between.

"Yes. Thank you so much for agreeing to help out."

He shrugged. "Nothing else to do but wait for the baby. And who doesn't love QuiltWorld?"

Allie didn't even know she was holding her breath until he said that, but suddenly a great deal of tension fell off her. She loved her game, and anyone who also loved her game had a foothold toward friendship.

"Shall we listen in?" he asked.

"Absolutely," she replied. "Here, this is my old team." She walked him over to the corner where Noam's desk was. He was standing, of course, along with the rest of the members of his pod, going over what everyone had accomplished last week. When he saw her, he paused. "Hey."

"Hey."

"Should we start over?"

"Nah. Go on."

Each engineer reported on what he had promised to get done yesterday, said what he planned to do today, and brought up dependencies and blockers. Allie listened, nodding. She'd only missed one update. Yosi also listened, his head tilted to one side as if he was listening to the words, not just reading them.

Yosi was staring off into the distance, reading a white board that was sitting in the middle of another pod.

"Would you like to go over? I can introduce you around?"

"Okay," he said. "Do you have lunch plans?"

She was surprised by the sudden change of topic. "Not on Mondays. I usually just grab something downstairs and eat at my desk."

"We'll go out. Meet me out front at 11:45. I hate lines."

He walked over to the pod with the intriguing white board, leaving Allie a bit thrown. Maddening to have so many elements moving all at once. She longed to settle for just an hour into something familiar. But instead she trotted over to Yosi to introduce him to the cross-game marketing team.

Yosi moved from pod to pod, chatting with everyone amiably. His reputation as an antisocial engineer had been greatly undone as he smiled at each member of the studio, asked who they were, what game they were playing, where they'd been before SOS. He was better at small talk than Allie, and she felt like her skills were respectable. Around 10:45, he'd returned to his desk, still by Rick's, in order to catch up on email. He promised he'd be in the studio later that day, and he'd have IT move his things over lunch.

Now she stood outside the SOS doors and glanced down at her watch. 11:44. And right as her watch changed to 11:45, Yosi appeared at her side.

"Shall we?"

Allie nodded in assent.

Yosi led, not asking her where she'd like to go. They walked by the sand-wich place, then the Mexican place, and the odd little Brazilian joint in the World Gym, crossed 16th, and went to a small strip mall, really a mini, only five stores wide that held four restaurants and a bakery.

They had changed. There used to be an English bakery there where she'd get sausage rolls when she was hungover. Now it was a place selling organic and gluten-free foods. The mom-and-pop diner had been replaced by a hip brewery. And she couldn't recall what had been in the spot now sporting the sign "Oren's Hummus." Allie realized she hadn't been beyond a one-block radius of SOS for over a year.

"Hey! It's up here now!"

"You know it?"

"I live in Mountain View. I get takeout from it all the time. It's great."

"I know Oren. Angel investor, from Tel Aviv. He missed good hummus, and had a machine brought over from Israel."

They went into the bustling space and found a small table. It was an odd place; it had table service but was incredibly unfussy. The servers were fast and pleasant. On the wall was a big blackboard exhorting customers to call and share any complaint they had or just give feedback.

"He runs this place like a startup. Prototyped it, iterates, constant cus-tomer feedback."

"That's cool." She meant it, but at the same time felt too off-balance to really appreciate anything.

"Shall I order for us?"

"As long as you get the chicken skewers."

Yosi smiled. "Not vegetarian?"

"Not even a little."

"Good to know."

He ordered a variety of food, the chicken the only meat.

"Are you vegetarian? I hope you don't mind?" Allie didn't mean to insult her new ally.

"No, not at all. I'm just reducing my meat intake. Health reasons. And with falafel this good, I don't miss it!"

Allie bit her tongue. Oren's chicken was the best she'd ever eaten. *She'd* miss it. But why torture him? "So, you wanted to talk?"

"Yes! We need to talk plans. The baby is due in January, and babies keep their own schedule. I could be out early or late."

"I thought you were heading back to Tel Aviv?"

"Yes, but my wife is American, and our first was … difficult. It was good to have her family so close, and she decided she didn't want to make the move until after. The American health system is crap, but better the devil you know."

The devil you know was something Allie understood, though not why anyone would want to have a second kid after the first one was such a hassle. She hadn't decided if she wanted kids. Derek said he'd like to, someday. Allie wasn't so sure. They had good jobs; they enjoyed each other's company … why mess with perfection?

"So, you're still moving, but just a bit later? How long can I keep you?" She flashed one of her most winning smiles.

"Nothing in life is certain, and less so at SOS. But we think we'll move in April. Still. Have you hired a CTO before?"

"No," she replied.

"It's slow. You need to be careful. It's like finding the right person to marry. You need someone who is not only good at his job. Or her job. But also, one you can trust. Lean into. It's hard work, bringing a game into the world. It takes a strong partnership."

Jeez, this guy has babies on the brain, she thought. "Okay, I get it. Good teams make good games. So can you help me figure it out?"

"That's what I'm here for!"

"Where do I start?"

"You need to change how you think about hiring. Hiring is just one piece of the puzzle. A role, a job, it has three parts. Set, check, and correct. You set the role and hire someone into it."

"What?"

"You design a job."

"Jobs are pretty much the same, here."

"Are they? Are you sure you want the same kind of game designer that NoirTown has? Or Baccarat?"

"Hmm."

"So you've hired someone. Now you want to have regular check-ins to give feedback to make sure you get what you need from the role."

"One-on-ones."

"Yes, or even just having lunch and saying, 'There is something I've been meaning to mention....'"

"Ugh. Sounds like an ambush." She eyed him suspiciously.

Yosi shrugged. "You do what you need to. Anyhow, all those little check-ins are all right, but eventually you need to step back and ask yourself if the person is right for the job."

"Performance reviews."

"You got it. You can promote, you can fire, or you can do something in between."

"Sure, bonuses, raises, whatever ... this is pretty straightforward. It's what everyone does."

"No! What everyone does is grab a job description off the Internet, hire whomever the team likes, then live with the results."

Great, thought Allie, *I'm halfway to mediocrity.* "Okay, so what should you do instead?"

"You have to define the role and then interview the person so you can make sure they can fulfill it. Then you use that same role description for one-on-ones and performance reviews."

That made decent sense, Allie thought as she grabbed some pita bread that had magically appeared in front of her. "Oh, this bread is magic."

The conversation drifted to the proper way to make pita bread, then hummus, then the virtues of dark meat for chicken skewers. Allie knew she was going to enjoy working with Yosi. Anyone who loved well-made games and well-made food was her kind of person.

ROB AND ALLIE DISCUSS BAGBOY DYSFUNCTION

ALLIE WAS JUST FINISHING UP HER CTO JOB DESCRIPTION WHEN she got a text from Rob.

"Free? I haz sleepies."

"Y"

She met Rob at the lobby.

"Coffee or walk?"

"Can't I have both?" replied Rob.

They stepped outside. It was drizzling a little bit.

"Winter is coming," Rob pronounced direly.

"Ha. Not around here. This is just an aggressive fog."

They crossed the roundabout and went into the design center building across the way. On the ground floor was a very good coffee shop. They walked over and Rob ordered a latte. Allie ordered a double espresso.

They took the drinks from the barista and Rob grabbed three sugars. He placed them next to each other, then ripped them all open in one go, pouring them into his cup.

"Don't you like coffee?" Allie inquired for the hundred and first time, as straight-faced as she could manage.

Rob declined to answer, merely rolled his eyes and headed upstairs. When the weather was bad, they'd walk the halls of the design center, looking at the little shops of the interior designers.

"What's up in QuiltWorld-land?" asked Rob.

"I posted the job descriptions for all the people George stole."

Rob guffawed. "They were *his* people. He had them first."

"Thanks, Dad." She slugged him lightly on the arm.

"Can you hit me somewhere else? I'm starting to bruise up there!"

"Baby."

They walked down the hall.

"So. I'm thinking … I hate hiring. Too much risk. Can I promote? What do you think about Noam as CTO after Yosi goes?"

"Noam?"

"He's a great programmer. He's been killing it since he got here."

"He's pretty young."

"Who isn't?"

"Hmmm." Rob sipped his latte. "Maybe. Have you talked to his team?"

"No. Should I? Will they be jealous? Is that weird?"

"Well, maybe, but mostly to find out if he can people manage."

"Argh! I don't know how to do any of this!"

Rob stopped in front of a slightly bigger shop, full of couches, chairs, and tables that all looked like they came from the set of Star Trek. "Mind?"

"No, go ahead." Allie followed Rob into the store.

Rob sat on each piece of furniture. "I hate our couch," he said by way of explanation.

"And all your chairs?" She grinned as he struggled to emerge from a deep armchair.

"I like things to match," he replied. He sat on a long modernist couch and patted the spot next to him. Allie knew he was going into professor mode.

"Programming is not managing. It's an orthogonal skill." He got up from the couch, and sat on the one across from her, the same model in red.

"How does color change the comfort?"

"Red is much warmer." He wiggled his eyebrows at her. "Lots of individual contributors can't get the handle on managing. The skills are different. For example, if you are in meetings all day as a programmer, you aren't doing your job. If you are in meetings all day as a manager, you're doing your job perfectly. You have to be able to talk to people. Give them feedback. Broker deals with other teams. You go from typing code to speaking it."

Allie thought about that. She'd spent this week in a spreadsheet. Was she spending her time wisely?

"Talk to Noam's team, see how he manages their time. He's the lead of his pod, so he manages the work."

Rob looked over the room. "Nope, nope, nope, nope, nope," he said, as he pointed at each piece of furniture. He waved at the salesperson as they walked out.

"Also, talk to Barak over in Backgammon. I hear he's unhappy."

"Thanks!"

They walked back downstairs and past the coffee counter. The barista waved at Rob and he waved back. He made friends everywhere he went.

Allie thought about that and wondered if it was part of his management-fu. "Always be networking," he'd told her more than once before. Speaking of, "So how is Bagboy Race?"

"Complete shitshow." He sighed. "I've been there one week, and I can't tell you how I'm going to get anything fixed."

"Why is it so bad? I thought you scoped it out before you went in?"

Rob flopped down on one of the coffee shop couches. He gestured at the couch across the glass coffee table from it. "Got time?"

She nodded and sat down. "Is this one for sale?"

Rob grinned. "I wish! It's actually comfortable!"

"So. Spill."

"Young is the most unscrupulous GM I have ever worked for. And I worked on 21town."

"Ew."

"He's all about the hack. He took over the studio and he's optimizing the holy hell out of the game, misleading dialogs, spamming people's network and breaking TOS. He's going to have the lawyers on us."

"And the codebase?"

"It is an epic mess. Luckily, he knows he can boost numbers by reducing speed, or else I wouldn't be allowed to attempt a cleanup. But I'm not sure I can. The programming team is a bunch of kids who graduated San Jose State a year ago. As far as I can tell, my predecessor just hired them all, and has been firing as they turn out useless. They are adequate, but they don't know what to do, and I desperately need a lead who can level them up. But no one is going to want to touch our codebase. It's worse than a ball of Christmas tree lights. Tangles within tangles."

"So what are you going to do?"

"We've got no headcount. It was slashed when our numbers went into freefall. I'm going to PIP out at least two of the worst and try to place a couple of more senior folks in."

"PIP? That will take forever." A PIP, or a performance improvement plan, was the type of cover-your-ass strategy HR preferred. First, you let the employee know every way in which they had failed the company, then gave them ninety days to turn it around. You had to document every infraction to create an airtight case against the employee suing the company for wrongful termination.

"I know. I'm going to talk to Patricia, see if she has any more ideas."

Patricia was the head of HR. Allie had had maybe two encounters with her, once when she was being recruited, and once at a company party. "What do you think of Patricia?"

"I'll be honest. I don't have an opinion. I've mostly worked with her recruiters, and they seem fine. They source good folks for me. And the person who helped me set up benefits was super nice." He shrugged. "You don't know anything about HR until there is a crisis."

"I've heard mixed reports." Allie wasn't really sure if she should spread gossip, but it could affect Rob. "Christie told me when she was pregnant, she was told she could take two weeks off or quit, and come back when she was ready to work again. I couldn't believe it. Christie designed our best game."

"And that's illegal." Rob sighed, sinking more deeply into the couch. "And yet they get away with it. It's just like Ephemeral Arts here. Except you don't know whom to trust."

QUILTWORLD IS BREAKING; ALLIE IS DROWNING

MONDAYS WERE FOR THE QUILTWORLD NUMBERS MEETING. IT felt strange to be receiving reports rather than giving them. She sat at her desk, giving the team a moment to set up. She knew from experience letting them have a couple minutes to settle was a good thing. She wasn't exactly raring to go herself. Yosi, Kendra, and Mick had sent their updates to her to collate into a deck, and it wasn't looking good. She was about to hear why and how bad, and wasn't excited for that adventure.

When George set the studio's objective only a few weeks ago she'd been thrilled to launch a groundbreaking expansion. The objective was a crazy stretch goal, but crazy stretch goals were what her team had been doing since day one. The key results involved press attention, reactivating lapsed users, and revenue. Always revenue. George and Pete's departure changed the studio's ability to accomplish anything, but Rick had a hard-and-fast rule about never changing an OKR set once it was finalized. Which he had reiterated when she had asked him about them. The key results now looked ridiculous rather than challenging. She shut down her desktop, then walked into the conference room where Mick had the same damn slide with the same damn OKRs already up on the wall. No hiding.

The big table was sparsely populated. It could hold ten people, yet it was just her, Mick, Kendra, and Yosi. She sat down at the empty chair at the foot of the table. "Okay. Let's go."

The team leaned forward, except Yosi who leaned back to such a degree that she wondered if his chair would tip over.

"Let's start with the OKRs. Confidence has dropped on all our key results. Other than the obvious staffing issue, what's up here?"

There was a moment of silence, as the team hesitated before opening the Pandora's box of speculation.

Yosi broke the silence. "My confidence has dropped because I can't tell what I'm dealing with. I've got code that keeps breaking and essentially no documentation. Hardly any commenting, even, except some idiot who left *Hitchhiker's Guide to the Galaxy* quotes throughout. I'm low confidence because I'm still trying to figure out what's going on, although poor documentation is an early sign of poor coding."

"Fair. So this might not be permanent?" Allie asked.

Yosi shrugged.

Kendra spoke up next. "For me it *is* mostly staffing. I'm not a manager. I have to drop my work to cover Janice's work while trying to replace her. Plus, Atsuko left for Cat Detectives, so I'm down an illustrator *and* we've got no lead game designer. You should try to borrow someone or steal or *something*. It's ridiculous!"

Allie interrupted, "Yes, we all know we're short-staffed now. I'm on it. Are those the only issues?"

There was silence. Mick yawned.

"Okay, so same deal here in the health metrics. Team health is bad. Yes, we are missing people. How are the rest doing?"

Again, Yosi was the first to speak. "The engineering pods are fine. Pete was not particularly hands-on, so Noam and Jheryn stepped up long ago to make sure everyone was communicating. They've got a host of bad habits, but morale is fine. Also, I do have a little good news. I've talked Simon into joining."

Simon was a tall pale Goth with a bad attitude and unearthly coding skills. He was legendary at SOS both for skills and his ability to say no to Rick. He refused to be relocated from NoirTown. He said he liked the game's feel (he dressed like one of the game's vampire detectives) and had told Rick if he wanted him to leave the game, there were lots of other interesting companies to work at. Allie had to know how Yosi had convinced him to join. But not now.

"Thank you, that is good news."

"Well, design is very worried," Kendra burst in.

Mick finally spoke. "Yes, Kendra, design is always very worried."

"You should be worried! There is no one to make your little experiments!"

"If you'd work as much as everyone else …"

"Who says I don't, just because I have to go somewhere quiet to get away from you."

Yosi slammed his hand on the table, flat, making a loud sound. Mick and Kendra stopped bickering. Then Yosi gestured to Allie.

Allie swallowed. "So that's the sound of one hand clapping," she joked nervously. "Okay, so let's talk about what's coming up next week …"

Mick shot out of the room as soon as the meeting was over. Kendra waited a moment, but Allie moved to speak to Yosi in a preemptive move to avoid listening to complaints about something she couldn't fix any faster. Kendra vacillated, then stepped out.

"It's only the first week," Yosi said softly, sensing her dismay.

"Yes, I know." She was so frustrated. "I just hate working in the dark. I feel like all the things I took for granted are proving false, and I don't know where to start."

"Start by getting your head clear." Yosi walked over to the board. "Let's get all the problems where we can look at them."

"Okay. Just a sec." She looked at her watch. She was supposed to meet with Mick. She texted him to say she'd reschedule for afternoon. "Well, there are all the hires, of course."

"Let's put them up on the wall." He drew an org chart with Allie at the top. Then CTO, and he drew an empty box next to it, "Since I'm a temp." He drew a box for Lead Game Designer, Art Director, Lead PM, and wrote Lawrence's name in the QA spot. "Let's get the next levels in, in case we can move anyone around." And he filled in the chart with the pod leads and engineers in each pod, Kendra under Lead Game Designer, and only one name, Emma, under Art Director. She was a recent CCA graduate and not ready to do much beyond what she was hired to do: make gorgeous illustrations. Allie would have traded places with her in a second, though. Lawrence's team was complete and tight. He commanded fierce loyalty.

"Why wasn't he here today?" asked Yosi.

"George never had him come."

"Does that make sense to you?"

"No." Not at all. She'd fix that. "What about Simon?"

Yosi had put him on a line by himself, rather than in a pod. "Doesn't play nice with others. I promised him he could do what he wanted, as long as he commented extensively."

"Is that a good idea?"

"It's an experiment. We'll see. Right now, though, I can't make head nor tail of the code, and he likes 'unhorking' things." He shrugged. "He did have one request."

"Oh?"

"He'd like to see a few vampires put in QuiltWorld by Halloween."

"Hah." It'd be well worth it if he was as good as rumored.

Allie looked at the wall of empty positions and sighed. At least she could see the size of the problem now. QA was fine. Engineering was fine for now. But the creative team had a hole she could drive a truck through. "Better the devil you know," she muttered, and went back to work.

The next Monday, Allie arrived at eight a.m. but didn't go straight into the studio. Instead she headed to the cafeteria. Her stomach still clenched when she considered the ever-increasing list of issues George had left her with. She decided it'd be best to grab a coffee downstairs first, then sit a moment and gather her thoughts.

The cafeteria was a tribute to Rick's ego. Hungry for success, he'd clearly modeled it after many of the successful software companies' "work hard play hard" decor style. It sported old arcade games throughout, as well as pinball games, foosball, and Ping-Pong tables. Mixed in amidst the games were tables for eating at (or playing board games), and along the wall were the highly coveted booths in which you could get a modicum of privacy.

The windows were shaded to allow for maximum atmosphere, which helped the arcade game players and hurt the Ping-Pong ones. A fireman's pole led down from her studio to the cafeteria, though it was roped off. Apparently, HR had decided it was too big a liability to be actually used, though PR removed the ropes every time there was a photo shoot of their incredibly cool HQ.

She gave her order to the barista and glanced around to see who was in at this hour. A few folks sat with coffee and laptops. The balding VP of new games was in the corner with several gray-haired business development cronies, talking about who knows what over bacon and eggs. Tucked away in one of the furthest booths was Brenda Madsen. Allie wouldn't have noticed her, except for her platinum blonde hair lit by the screen of her laptop, illuminating her and making her look positively elfin. Brenda looked up from her laptop and at Allie, as if she felt Allie's eyes on her. She smiled and waved her over. Allie held up a forefinger and mouthed, "Just a sec." The barista passed Allie her double latte, and she walked over to Brenda's booth.

"And then there were two," Brenda said softly.

"Oh?" Allie replied, puzzled.

"Sit!" said Brenda with a sly smile.

Allie sat.

"We now have two female GM's. Congratulations!"

"What about Virginia?"

"Busted down to producer. Her game numbers sank, and they gave NoirTown to Mike."

"Huh." Allie wondered if that helped Yosi's acquisition of Simon.

"Rick's in a mood. He pulled Jim off HoldemFoldem as well."

"What's Jim doing?"

"Floating."

"Huh." Allie sipped the caffeine, not feeling quite verbal. Rick did what Rick did. She never could figure out why some GMs got to float around until they had a funded game or a new position, and why some others were demoted to producer. Producers at SOS were a blend of art director and project managers. Cat herders at best, schedule keepers at worst, and almost always female.

Brenda hadn't been pulled off a game ever. She was a "starter"—a GM who could take a tiny creative team through the initial good idea into a new franchise. Her current game was a niche game so far. It was a multiplayer game in which you had to defend your cookie farms against marauding but super-cute monsters. It had a small but passionate following of players. Allie was pretty sure it wasn't going to get any bigger than it'd been for the past year. SOS had several games like that. Base hits, Felix called them. QuiltWorld was a home run. Base hits were safe, the middle of the pack where you could hang out for a while as a GM. It was what she thought she'd start with when she was promoted to GM, or maybe even taking over one of Brenda's games when she got bored.

"How's it lookin'? Have you taken stock yet?" Brenda asked. She had an empty mug next to her. A spoon sat next to it, with a tea bag tightly bound to the spoon by its own string.

"Today is all one-on-ones. I'll be honest. I lost key people to George's new effort. He built his development team solely from QuiltWorld."

"That's against rules of engagement!"

"It seems QuiltWorld is considered big enough to be able to take it. I'm not so sure."

"George is Rick's golden boy."

"George managed to take Pete, Victor, Carlos, *and* Janice. I need to find a new CTO, game designer, art director, and lead PM."

"He's a bit manager heavy, isn't he? Who's going to do actual work?"

"I *know*. I guess he thinks he can make the same magic he did when he started QuiltWorld, since it's pretty much the same crew, minus Christie."

"How many of them have been in the trenches recently, though?" Brenda looked into her empty cup.

Allie shook her head and rolled her eyes. "I can't explain anything. I have no idea how I'm going to recover from this."

Now Brenda looked up and at her sharply. "Don't admit that. Ever. Darling, you think product management is vicious. You are swimming in the deep waters now. Jim is floating. He'd love to step in if he heard you weren't feeling ready. And any of the other GMs of the base hits. They are all looking to step up, and QuiltWorld still has the numbers they could take credit for. You can't show indecision."

"Would you want to ... ?" Allie wondered if she had made a mistake, as soon as she started the sentence.

"No. I like to roll my own games. And I don't like the big hits, too much attention from above. No danger from me. In fact, if you need advice, feel free to visit. I'm here most mornings. But be careful whom you talk with. Including Patricia."

Patricia was head of HR. Allie had a meeting with her this afternoon.

"Patricia? But why?"

"She's Rick's creature. Her loyalty is completely to him. You show any sign you aren't up to the task, and he'll know it before you set foot back in your office."

"Ah, come on. Isn't HR's job to help us grow, to succeed?" That's what Derek always said.

"Human resources. Humans are resources. For the company. Their job is to make sure the company succeeds. Patricia has made a lot of things go away for Rick over the years. That one ..." She pointed at the VP of new games, now laughing uproariously with his tablemates " ... gets handsy with his assistant, suddenly *she's* pipped out. Not him. A dev on Baccarat get sick, turns out it's chronic fatigue, but he's suddenly let go for underperforming. Why he didn't sue, I have no idea." She tried to sip at her empty cup, then slammed it down annoyed. "Use HR, but don't lean on HR. And be careful. And best not sit with me at estaff, I'm not popular. Sit with Baccarat, Rick loves them. Keep your head down, listen, and don't contribute until you're certain how it'll be received."

"Really?" Allie was appalled.

"My advice is worth every penny you paid for it." Brenda leaned back.

Allie had always thought Brenda pretty easygoing, but now she saw the anger in her eyes.

"Thank you." Allie gulped. "No really. Thank you."

Brenda seemed to relax a little bit. "You'll figure it out. Just go slow and be careful what you say. Be careful whom you say it to."

She got up to refill her mug. Allie took a sip from hers. It was cold.

REFUSAL TO CHANGE

ALLIE CUT ACROSS THE ROUNDABOUT ON HER WAY TO THE restaurant to meet Christie. She didn't know why Christie had reached out to her to grab lunch, but she figured, why not accept? She could use all the advice she could get. Christie had been the first game designer on QuiltWorld. She'd come up with the initial idea, worked with George and Pete on the pitch prototype, and crafted the largest debut launch in SOS history. And had gone off on maternity leave almost two years ago. The rumor mill said Christie had extended it without pay, but with the right to return and start vesting again at the same amount.

Christie was a bit of a legend. She'd given a talk to 1,200 people at GDC about shaping a game for fulfilling the fantasy of order in an increasingly crazy world and had done it eight months pregnant. She was known as The Iron Woman in some circles, having continually designed successful new modules and expansions to QuiltWorld as her girth increased. Her ever-lengthening leave had given some pause. Julie Bee, head of marketing, had come back two weeks after giving birth, and that was the new standard for parenthood at SOS.

Allie entered the atrium of Design Center South. The brick building housed interior design companies full of beautiful things that Allie couldn't afford. Space-age couches and ancient Pakistan rugs, up-and-coming painters who could make work to match your color theme, and lighting that was a centerpiece or invisible. And in the center of all this was an echo chamber housing an outpost of one of San Francisco's oldest restaurants, Perry's. The menu told the story: Caesar salad, Sole Meunier, steak and frites. Bistro food, done as if the last fifty years of food revolutions had not happened, as if the fashion that surrounded the restaurant had only proven that classics were best.

Christie sat at a table at the far end of the rotunda and stood briefly as Allie wove past waiters and tables to join her. They shook hands and sat.

"Thanks for meeting me. I'm not quite ready to return to the compound."

"Ha! Can't blame you," Allie replied. "The crazy has a way of pulling you in. In fact, thanks for giving me an excuse to step out. I've got a lot on my mind. In fact, if you're willing, I'd love to bounce some things off you."

Christie smiled. "Of course. But let's order first."

Allie didn't really need to peruse the menu. Though she never came here—no one at SOS did—it was as familiar as the place in Dallas her grandparents used to take her on birthdays and other celebrations. The waiter came by.

"Caesar salad with grilled chicken. Iced tea," she ordered.

"Make that two iced teas. And trout almandine," Christie added. The waiter made a note and scooted away.

Christie looked into Allie's eyes. "So, you have things to ask. As do I. Who goes first?"

"Please." Allie spread her hands out.

"You're QuiltWorld's GM now."

"Yup."

Christie sat back. She was soft and round and dressed in loose, flowing clothes that wouldn't inform her when she overate. Allie could feel her jeans pressing against her stomach even before lunch started. But more than that, Christie looked relaxed and comfortable, more than any SOS exec she worked with. She looked like she knew a secret that kept her from making bad decisions. Or maybe that kept bad decisions from bothering her.

"I'm considering coming back to work."

Allie should have seen that coming. A lunch offsite. Christie was interviewing her. What did she think of this? Good thing? Bad thing? Did she want Christie?

"I've had lunch with George as well."

Ah, George! Did he have to steal everyone good?

"George is a great guy, and we had an amazing partnership with QuiltWorld. But do you know what his new game concept is?"

"No?"

"Gun running. Seriously."

Allie made a face, though honestly, she wasn't sure it was a dreadful idea. A gross one, but possibly a profitable one.

Christie leaned forward. "Let me be honest. I'm worried about QuiltWorld. I knew when I made it, the day would come when it'd be time to move from explore to exploit. Then the PMs would be unleashed to optimize the game to death, and you …"

Yep, Allie had been a product manager until recently.

Christie continued, "I've heard good things about you. The designers you've worked with say you are respectful of their ideas, and you don't set an unreasonable pace. So what do you think the future of QuiltWorld is?"

The waiter showed up with their iced tea. Allie took a long sip. What was the future of QuiltWorld? Was it time to start squeezing the whales for every penny they had? Or could she spend more time growing it? She didn't know what the answer was, but she knew what she wanted it to be.

"I refuse to believe it's time to start optimizing for revenue alone. The last couple bold beats underperformed, but I think they were uninspired as well."

"Bold beats?"

"We didn't use that term when you were in the studio?"

She shook her head.

"Oh, okay. Well, Rick recommended we adopt something that NoirTown had used successfully. We have a special event about once a month that players can participate in. It's usually holiday themed, or at least seasonal. It has great virals, and we usually see a revenue spike as well. We did a fun Fourth of July quilt with Martha Washington."

"What's her speaking fee like?"

"Lols," Allie said, rolling her eyes but smiling.

"So then …"

"I get it. I'm—I was a product manager; product managers run the numbers and optimize games for maximum revenue. Therefore, I must have been put in place to grind QuiltWorld down." Allie inhaled deeply. "Nope. Not going to be the one who does that. It's too good a game. There's too much potential still."

Christie nodded. "I'm glad. Because while I was out with the baby, I got an idea for something new and special for QuiltWorld. And I'd like to make it happen."

Allie held her breath. This could solve so much. She exhaled.

"Would you consider returning to QuiltWorld as lead game designer?"

"Yes. I'd like that."

BAD INTERVIEW

A WEEK LATER, VERY LITTLE HAD CHANGED. CHRISTIE WOULDN'T start for another week yet. Mick and Kendra fought. A trail of candidates for the other roles had passed through the door, but nobody was right. Allie wondered if SOS's reputation as a toxic workplace was part of the problem. She rubbed her neck. She was getting a headache.

Noam tapped her shoulder. "You're up." She had an interview with a potential new CTO they hoped to lure away from Epic Arts. Noam held a printed résumé covered with doodles.

"What do you think?" Allie asked. The doodles suggested boredom.

"I would hate to bias your experience."

"Since when? You love to tell me what to think."

"True, but it will be more entertaining if you find out for yourself."

Allie gave him a glare, then stood and walked to the conference room. She could see the candidate through the glass wall, his back to her. He was tall. It was hard to tell as he was sitting down, but he looked over six feet tall. He had a soft layer of fat over a layer of muscle, a baseball player's body, or maybe a golfer. He was sprawled in his chair, legs spread wide, basically taking up as much space as any one human could.

She glanced down at his résumé. It was impressive. He'd run teams in a couple of major game companies and at Microsoft's Xbox. He likely understood both game development and platform. That could prove a serious competitive advantage.

Allie opened the door to the room. He turned his head, and seeing her, pulled himself out of the chair to shake her hand.

"You must be Allie. I've heard good things."

"I pay good money for that. Can I get you something to drink?"

"Noam got me some water." He gestured to a bottle sitting next to him, half full with the label peeled off. He was a fidgeter, then.

Allie sat in front of him, clasped her hands together on the table, and smiled. Then her smile froze. She'd forgotten the questions she'd written down. They were on Post-It notes. At home. On the kitchen table. Her mind raced to recall them, but in the sudden panic, she pulled up a blank. Idiot!

Then she recalled an interview she had had, many years ago. A surreal, weird interview. And she decided to try the same approach the Twitter CTO had used on her so long ago. "You've been asked questions for hours. Do you have any questions for me?"

The candidate looked at her and paused as if to size her up.

"I am wondering how many meetings you have in this company."

Allie was surprised by this question. "Well, we're mostly an Agile shop, so the usual. Standup, planning, retrospective. And there are meetings with the leadership in the studio as well as across SOS, and one-on-ones, of course. There are a fair number of optional meetings to keep in touch with new learnings, and whatever you set with your staff. Nothing out of the ordinary. Why do you ask?"

His face was sour, like he'd bit into underripe fruit. "Meetings break up your day, keep you from real work."

"What is the real work of the CTO?" A question she never imagined she'd ask, but Rob's coaching had taken.

"Programmers like to work with the best programmers. I lead with excellent code."

This was a problem. Programmers did like to work with someone who could outcode them, in her experience. But meetings had to happen, or she'd hire an MIA boss, like George.

"Do you have other questions?"

"What is the relationship of CTO of the studio to CTO of SOS?"

"SOS is probably not very different from other companies. We have a few centralized functions, like HR and data, but each game studio is completely independent. The general manager is essentially the CEO of the game, and has a CTO, lead game designer and art director, and head of QA. Most data analysis is done by product managers here. Some studios have producers, some don't. We don't ... so far."

Allie paused, suddenly realizing she had a chance to change that, if she chose. It might give her more support. If Virginia was free ... she stopped herself. Be here now. "SOS has a CTO at the company level as well, and you'd report to him, matrixed to me. I have input into raises and bonuses."

AKA complete control. The GM was held responsible for the outcomes of the studio, and thus had control of the money that could influence those outcomes. Allie had a budget and a headcount, and it was her call how that was used.

"Other questions?"

The candidate looked at her quizzically. Apparently, he wasn't allowed free rein on questioning very often. Allie smiled at him. She remembered how she felt when she'd been invited to ask all the questions she wanted. Now that she was on the other side of that, she could see how powerful it was. What you ask about is what you value.

He continued on to ask about promotions, bonus structures, hiring practices ... he didn't ask about code health. Which if he had, Allie would have had to tell him was dubious at best. She'd heard Rob rant about it enough times. And he didn't ask about the games, which bothered her even more. She heard a soft knock at the door, and then it cracked open.

"Oh, hi, Yosi. Just a second." She finished up her latest answer, about transfers from one studio to another, then shook his hand. He had a perfect handshake, strong, but not crushing. She thanked him and headed out.

Yosi touched her arm quizzically. She shrugged. "You tell me."

"I will," said Yosi, and headed into the interview.

Allie walked over to Noam.

"Okay, tell me," she demanded.

"What? You were in there," Noam teased.

"Noam!"

"Didn't you just love him? So handsome. So charming."

"Cut it out." Allie was getting impatient.

"But you'll never love him as much as he loves him!"

"Okay, so you don't like him. What else? Can he do the job? Does he know his code?"

"In my opinion, he's a bullshitter. He spews out whatever he reads on a blog, but I don't think he's sat serious at a keyboard in a long time."

"Hmmm. Anything else?"

"Yes. He'll be here as long as it takes him to figure out where is more powerful, then he'll go there."

"Yeah, that, I got."

Allie walked around, gathered feedback. One engineer raved about him, saying he was exactly what the studio needed to update their practices, another dinged him for not being rigorous enough around Agile, another said he was "fine."

"What do you mean, 'fine'?"

"Don't need much for a CTO, so I suppose it might as well be him."

"What?"

"We get tech specs from Uri, so not sure what the CTO does except call meetings. This guy, whatever he is, Shane? Shaun? He doesn't like meetings. So he's fine."

Allie returned to her desk to wait for Yosi to come out. Did she really know what a CTO of the studio did? She hoped Yosi did. She hadn't really thought about it. Pete sat typing at his keyboard, but was it email or actual code? She hadn't noticed. He hired, fired, and gave feedback in between. He went to meetings.

Hell, what was her job? How would she define it, if she had to hire to replace herself? A million tiny things that add up to a healthy studio. So frustrating. She chewed a pencil, which she hadn't done in a long time. What was taking them so long?

Finally, Yosi came out with the candidate. Now Allie couldn't remember his name either. Yosi walked him to the door to the studio, seeing him to the other side of the keycard lock. On the other side was the atrium, and he could easily find his way out, and not into anything else, beyond maybe some free soda.

Yosi walked back toward his desk. "Nope," he said, as he passed.

"Hey, what, wait." Allie hopped up and followed him. "Don't you want to debrief everyone?"

He stopped and turned around to face her. He let out a long sigh. "Not really. He doesn't understand the real work of a CTO. He's in love with the title, but not the work. He'll hurt the team."

"But he's the most qualified candidate we've seen!"

"A bad employee will bring down two good ones. How much worse is it at the exec level? He doesn't understand that the CTO is a people manager. People write code. People need to be inspired, to be coached, to be focused."

Allie knew he was right, but she could feel too keenly that Yosi was also leaving in a couple months. She ground her teeth in frustration.

Yosi saw her face, and replied to the silent thought, "No, Allie. He'll make you do three times the work, just undoing his bad interactions. I was that guy. Trust me."

"You?"

"I'll tell you at lunch Monday."

Great, another long lunch offsite. Well, if it got her a good story about Yosi....

WHAT DOES IT TAKE?

THURSDAY NIGHT ALLIE WENT HOME EARLY AND WAS NOW lying on the couch with her head in Derek's lap. They were watching a cupcake baking contest. Or a baking contest that had a cupcake section. She wasn't really paying full attention, just trying to distract herself as she watched people frost things.

"They all suck," she said.

"Hmm?" he replied, glancing down from the TV.

"The candidates."

"For governor?"

"For the jobs at QuiltWorld! Though that, too. And these bakers are idiots as well." She waved at the TV. "The job candidates I'm interviewing all suck. I don't get why they are applying at all. I don't even want to do a phone screen, but I guess I have to. I've got to get some bodies in place."

"Do you want a body, or the right person?"

"What do you think, Sherlock?"

"What's wrong with them?"

"Some are way too senior, others … not unqualified, but mis-qualified?"

"How did you write your job descriptions?"

"I got previous job descriptions and modded them."

"Hmmm."

"Hey now, with that hmmm. Modding is a great way to get somewhere. We do it in game design all the time. You take rock, paper, scissors, add a new theme, a little story, and boom. Best seller." She nuzzled the warmth of his leg. He smelled pleasantly of fresh laundry and himself.

"It works if you know you've started in the right place. What are you hiring for?"

"Oh, God."

"Okay, what's *one* of the roles you are hiring for?"

"Art director."

"What makes a good art director?"

"They are …"

She stared at the TV. People were running around frantically, building towers of cupcakes.

"They are artistic. I don't know, they make the game pretty."

"Really?" He raised an eyebrow.

"I'm tired."

"Who is the best art director at SOS?"

"Jamie Fittich."

"Why?"

"Everyone says so."

"Interview her … him … they?"

"They."

"Interview them tomorrow."

"For … ?"

"Ask them what makes a good art director. What makes a bad one? What hard skills an art director should have. What soft skills. What kind of experience. Then ask them who else to talk to."

"Because?"

"Now you are messing with me."

"No, you know I love it when you share your secrets of the dark arts of HR with me."

"Promise to only use this knowledge for good?"

"Scout's honor."

"You need to understand what you need in an art director. Not just what the industry wants. Each company is different. Each company has its own ideas of good. Jamie has shown they get it. Talking to them will give you the information you need to write a good job description and hire more accurately."

"Okay."

"You keep telling me SOS is different from most of the game industry, right? It's built on a more Internet approach, focused on metrics and iteration and being goal driven. So not everyone will be able to thrive in that environment."

"I don't want to scare anyone off."

"You *do* want to scare people off—people who will fail in the job. Don't throw a wide net. Throw a tight one and catch the person you really want."

Friday evening everyone had disappeared after happy hour, but Allie grabbed the small conference room and shut the door behind her.

She had held three interviews with good art directors in SOS to understand what the job entailed. She'd collected five job descriptions she'd found on the Internet from companies she respected. But she'd been so busy that week, she hadn't had time to make sense of what she'd gathered. She sat there and went through her notes. She highlighted anything she thought was relevant to her search. It was all over the place, though. Everything from software to "understands creative people." What was she going to do with that?

She sighed, went back to the main room to grab a bottle of wine and some cheese from the Friday happy-hour leftovers. The elves had not appeared yet to clean up, so she made herself a stash and took it back to the conference room.

She had just gone back to her staring contest with the printouts when the door opened a crack.

"Oh, hi!" It was Kendra.

Allie jumped. "I thought everyone was gone!"

"I live in Marin. No need to face *that* traffic on a Friday night. I'm working on a couple of ideas, and then I'm grabbing dinner with some pals. So. Whatcha doing?"

Kendra was cheerfully and unapologetically nosy.

"I'm trying to figure out how to write a description that will get the right next art director to apply."

Kendra zoomed in and sat down on the couch next to Allie. "Let me see."

"Well, there are the notes from interviews with our art directors, previous job descriptions we've posted, and a couple from competitors."

"You've highlighted them."

"Yes." *Duh.*

"Well, let's start making stickies!"

"What?"

"It's just like playtesting! You've done the research, now it's time for synthesis."

"I don't want to keep you from your work."

"Oh, I'm brain-dead anyway. This is much more fun."

Kendra grabbed a pad of Post-Its. "You have to make the information *modular* so you can find the hidden patterns. Copy the stuff you highlighted onto the Post-Its. ONE idea per Post-It. Just one! Modular!"

Why not, Allie thought. *I wasn't getting anywhere with my staring.* She started copying the highlights onto Post-Its. It was mindless, but she was also eating cheese and drinking wine, and it wasn't unpleasant.

"K, you done?" Kendra looked over. Yes, her glass was empty. She filled it back up. And the highlights from the pages were all in a pile of Post-Its.

"Let's get it on the wall!" Kendra erased the whiteboard where it said, "Do not erase," with a date from three weeks ago. "If they haven't documented by now, it's too darn late!" she chirped.

She turned to Allie. "Now we put up the Post-Its, putting like with like. Oh, thank heavens your handwriting is legible. I forgot to say."

She started sticking the notes to the board.

"How are we doing this? I mean, is there a methodology?" Allie asked.

"We don't know what the data has to say, so we just follow our gut. Get it up here where we can see it, put like with like, find the patterns."

"Very game-like," Allie commented.

"Yep! Fun!"

Allie easily found "Photoshop" and added a couple other software programs that had been mentioned. She placed "Works well with product team" with "Understands creative process."

"What the hell is 'Gestalt'?"

"Design philosophy," Kendra replied.

"Thanks for sticking around. That would have driven me crazy."

"Oh, you'd have Googled it, I'm sure." Kendra was swiftly combining Post-Its with the calm efficiency of a master at jigsaw puzzles.

"What am I going to do with 'Nice'?"

"Put it with 'Ass-kicker.'"

"Really?"

"Personality traits?"

"K."

They slowed down and Kendra stepped back. Allie followed, curious.

"Okay, what do we see?"

"That grouping is pretty big."

"Yeah, too big. It's the messy stuff. Personality and knowledge. And miscellanies. And that group is pretty small." She pointed to a list of companies.

"Relevant experience."

"Hmm ..." Kendra paused. "Any missing?"

"It's pretty Bay Area centric. I'd like to see more companies outside the area. Throw Hurricane in the mix. They know community and social dynamics. And Carms, and Super8."

"When you see big groups and small groups, look closely," Kendra lectured. "Big groups often need to be broken up, small groups expanded."

"Where is this coming from?"

"This is just like making personas. We're creating an art director persona!"

Allie looked out the glass wall of the conference room at the wall that held QuiltWorld's personas. "You're right. We're collecting and selecting the characteristics we think matter to decision making."

"So, any of these worth tossing out? Any less relevant?"

"Oh, yes. I'm not buying most of the personality pile. 'Nice'? I don't even know what to do with that."

"But what about ass-kicker? You have to hold people to deadlines."

"That's covered over here, delivery focused."

"Okay." Kendra pulled out the pile of "personality" Post-Its and they flipped through them until they were certain they had the actionable insights. Allie's favorite was "Unflappable."

They looked at the board again.

"Is everything equally important?" Kendra asked.

Allie picked up a whiteboard marker.

"These soft skills: Leads, prioritizes. Respect. Communication." She circled the soft skills cluster. "Art director is a player-coach position. Whoever takes this role, they have to be able to deliver work as well as manage. Not only because we need good work, but because the art team needs to respect the role." Allie stopped to chew the marker cap, another habit she thought she had broken. "I think this is the most important one. It's things they know. Experience. Knowledge. I want someone who has dealt with these issues before. Bad enough I'm new to half of them."

Kendra stared at the wall. "Huh. It looks like a canvas."

"What do you mean?" asked Allie.

"You know, like the business-model canvas. Or an empathy map."

Allie had worked with both, the empathy map more recently in a game creation session. Canvases, as far as she could figure out, were visual worksheets to help you fill in your ideas about something, like a business or a player. The empathy map always helped her to remember to consider sound design, which she had a tendency to forget, because it had a "hear" section.

"Okay, so we have a hiring canvas?"

"Or maybe a role canvas?" Kendra waved the whiteboard marker around the Post-Its, drawing in the air. Then she turned to the other wall, where a whiteboard was covered with utterly mysterious scribbles. She started to erase.

"Are you sure that's okay?"

"No date, no keep." Studio policy was to date all whiteboard drawings and write "Do not erase" if you wanted to keep working with it. This drawing didn't have either.

"Okay, how about this?" She put a person in the middle of her drawing. She always did—she said if she was designing for people, people should be in the picture.

"There!" Kendra said. "You can now use that to brainstorm the other roles you're hiring."

Allie looked at it. It looked like an empathy map, with a person in the middle, and the head, heart, hands model instead of see, think, do ... knowledge, hard skills, soft skills. "What about results?"

Kendra looked at her. "What about them?"

"You know, revenue, hitting your objectives."

"I thought we weren't supposed to use OKRs for performance reviews." Kendra looked at her suspiciously.

"Hmm. If a performance review was based on whether or not people achieved their goals, people tended to set lower goals. On the other hand ... we need to know if they can hit the goals we're hiring them to achieve. What is the point of OKRs if you don't make them at least sometimes?"

Kendra contemplated that for a moment. "It does seem important to determine if a candidate is capable of achieving a goal." She placed a slice of cheese on a cracker and ate, staring at the whiteboard. "Christie always said that when we interview, we shouldn't ask what *would* you do *if* faced with a dilemma, but in the past, did you experience that problem and what did you do?"

Allie looked at her, confused. Maybe it was the wine.

Kendra drew two boxes under her diagram and labeled one "Past" and one "Future."

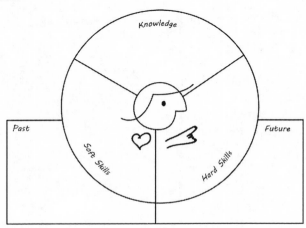

"Okay, so let's say you want the person to do something, right? Like ...?"

"Create a safe workplace for creative work."

Kendra smiled at that. "Okay. So how would you find out if they could do that, using the phrase 'Tell me about a time when ...?'"

Allie grinned mischievously. "Tell me about a time when you had to shelter your team from demanding product managers so they could get work done."

Kendra nodded, and poured herself a glass of wine. "Exactly."

"So, we'll fill in the right with what we want them to be able to do, then put questions in the left."

"Okay. You're still missing goals. And it looks kinda weird, the circle and the box and all. It looks like soft skills has something to do with the past?"

Kendra rolled her eyes. "Everyone's a critic!"

"Can we make it simpler? How about ..." Allie drew a simple four square on the white board, like the one she used every week in the OKR meeting. She began to write in what she wanted, as a test. It worked.

"So boring."

"But easy to draw, so I use it in conversation. I can write the questions here, on the left."

GOAL

MAKE UNIQUE, MEMORABLE AND CHARMING ART FOR QUILTWORLD.

RESPONSIBILITIES

MANAGE TEAM

SKILLS

ILLUSTRATOR

KNOWLEDGE

GAME ART

WORKING IN MULTI-DISCIPLINARY TEAMS

"Actually…it's like a pyramid. You need someone to make a goal and fulfill responsibilities, right, which means they have to have skills and knowledge, therefore you want to ask these questions…."

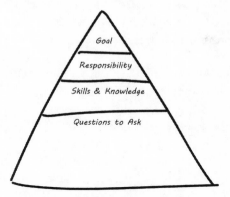

"Except there is no room to write anything at the top."

"Okay. I can see that." Kendra replied. "How about …" She erased part of Allie's drawing and added a new section.

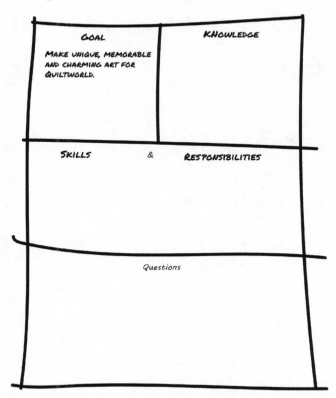

"I can work with that." Allie liked it.

"It's kind of boring." Kendra sighed.

"Let's test it." Allie wrote down the goal and responsibilities of the art director. Then she grabbed the stickie notes with the job qualities that matched and stuck them in "Skills and Knowledge." She tapped her lips with an index finger thoughtfully. "Tell me about a time when … you dealt with timelines being cut in half."

"That's a good question," Kendra replied. "Tragically, it's a key skillset."

"I think we've got something!" Allie liked it. It all made sense.

"I'll cut you in when my bestselling business book is out."

"Ha! If only!" She'd settle for a decent hire.

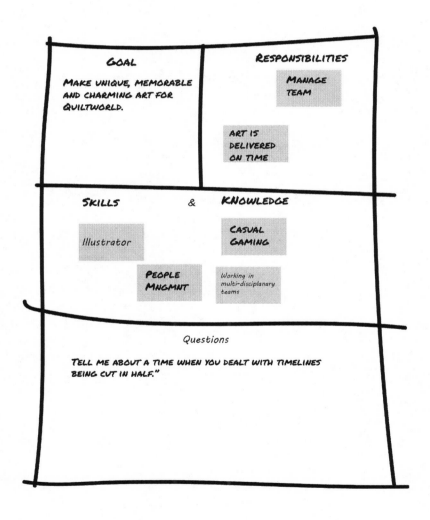

INTERNAL PROSPECTS

THE PRODUCT MANAGERS' LUNCH AND LEARN WAS EVERY Wednesday. Each week a product manager would talk about an insight they had had from the various experiments they ran within their games. It was a time to learn from each other, so SOS could continuously improve. It was attended by far more than just PMs. GMs often came, looking for new ideas, as well as game designers and engineers, and anyone curious about what SOS was doing. It was held in the training room on the first floor and was always packed. Lunch was catered, and usually pretty tasty.

Allie got in the line for the taco buffet. It felt good to be at a product lunch and learn. It felt relaxingly familiar. For an hour, she could just listen and glean insights she could take back to her studio.

"Congrats!" a voice boomed out. She turned around, and Charlie Davis was right behind her, shoveling beans onto his warping paper plate.

"Hey, Davis," Allie replied. "Thank you."

"What a coup!" he continued, not looking at her, just glopping meat onto his strained plate. "Any one of us would have happily stepped into George's shoes! But you nailed it! Rick must like you!" Davis's voice was so loud. It was like he was speaking to the room rather than to her.

"I hope to live up to the faith he's placed in me." She rushed to change the subject. "How's Rob settling in?" As if she didn't know.

"Oh, fine, fine! Miss him, do you?"

This guy! Did he have no social skills, or was he good at psychological warfare?

"Of course. Rob's a great dev. But we can hardly begrudge him a chance to step up, or Bagboy an opportunity to right itself."

Now he looked her in the eye. He replied cautiously, "Rob's good. True."

"We all want to see Bagboy continue. Such a charming concept. Such a fun loop!" she continued. You can't make an enemy of someone who has already decided they are yours, right?

"We should sit down. Looks like they are about to start." He lumbered over to the far corner, near the door, not looking to see if she followed. She didn't. She moved to the middle left and sat with a few PMs she'd worked with before.

"Hey, guys!"

"Hey!" "Hi!" "Congrats!" "Don't forget the little people!" "Yo, good work!" Her old team was sprinkled across the company now.

The first year of SOS's existence, when they were a feisty and rapidly growing online gambling company, Rick had really angered one of his VPs. No one knew what Rick had done, but the VP left and extracted a wicked revenge. SOS had a playbook of everything they'd learned from their year of running multivariate tests. It was on the intranet, and each week after the lunch and learn, the playbook would be updated with that knowledge.

When the VP left, he downloaded the playbook. But he didn't just take it to his next company. He published it publicly. He shared it privately to TechTalk, the news and gossip blog. They had published it from an unknown insider. No one was able to trace it back to the VP, though everyone was sure it was him. The lawyers had tried to sue, but there wasn't any proof. The VP had managed to cover his tracks. And Rick went full paranoid.

SOS had a lot of rules now. Nothing complete was ever put into electronic format and shared widely. At the lunch and learn, the presenter would go through every single number, what it meant, and how you could use it back at your game studio. But when the slides went out, they'd be redacted. No number would be listed in the deck. It would be a hollowed-out shell that was useful only as a reminder of the talk you attended. The wiki documenting each game was the same: a list of mechanics you could use but no indicator of which was good or bad. You either knew, or you knew who could tell you.

This paranoia about information sharing had the interesting effect of everyone attending the lunch and learns, and actually learning. Before the leak, people would skip the presentation, figuring they'd get the deck later. Then the deck would moulder in their inboxes. The most enterprising would read it through, of course, but the rest didn't.

Now everyone who should be in the room was in the room, learning and socializing.

As well—to make sure everyone was learning from each other and not from anything that could be transported out of the company—every single employee started out in a different studio than the one that hired them. They spent a full month there, learning the ropes and the institutional knowledge of that place. Then they returned and taught each other. Rick's paranoia had created an accelerated learning environment.

Allie had downloaded the playbook from TechTalk when she first started. A few things were still true, but mostly it was outdated. She sat with friends she'd made that first month. They still went out for drinks and compared notes. *Social systems are the best way to distribute knowledge*, Allie thought. Rick had that right. He'd been an exec at the first social network, before he left to start his first company. He never forgot the power of weak ties.

This talk was not the most exciting, but it was insightful. One of the PMs on a rugby fantasy league game had run tests on aligning special events to retail calendars. The uptick was about two percent, which didn't do much for their numbers, but probably could net a few extra thousand a week for QuiltWorld. Not a waste of time for her. In fact, the work was well thought through, even if the presenter wasn't able to make a big impact on his studio's numbers. She thought about approaching him, seeing if he was looking for a change.

Then she felt a tap on her shoulder. "Hey, Allie. Your old job is up for grabs, right?"

"Arash! Really? Come on, Allie, if you're taking résumés already, we need to talk." Jason shoved Arash lightly to the side.

"No way! QuiltWorld needs a more feminine touch," Katelyn chimed in.

"Stop!" Allie laughed. What an idiot she was. Of course people would want to join the hottest game at SOS. "Guys, you don't want this getting back to your GMs! If you're serious, just ping me and we'll find a time to talk."

"It's already in your inbox," smiled Arash.

Sure enough, when she got back to her desk, all three of them had sent résumés. Allie wondered if there was a PM other than her that didn't have an up-to-date résumé. She read through them, and they all looked fine.

"Fine." The engineer's words reverberated with her. Everyone looks just fine if you don't have a hiring standard. She reached for her notebook. After Kendra had left Friday night, Allie had stayed working. She managed to create role canvases for each of her hires. Derek had been really pissed when she got home so late, but honestly, it'd be worth it to both of them if she could make these hires and stop running around like a chicken with her head cut off. She flipped to the page with the PM profile. No, that layout was not working for her. It was too hard to decode. It was on the left page, so on the right, she turned the attributes into a stack-ranked checklist. Then she weighted them: five points for must have, three for should have, one for nice to have. Then she graded the résumés.

Arash was an easy win. Jason looked okay. Katelyn was behind Arash, but better than Jason. That made Allie a bit sad. With four women working on QuiltWorld, she had the most women in a top game studio. SOS was a total boys' show. Allie grabbed a pen to chew on.

While looking at the future/past area, she had an idea. She could ask questions for the items she couldn't find in the résumé. Hmm, and verify those she thought she saw. Just to make sure.

She wrote back all three and asked them to coffee.

GOOD INTERVIEW

ALLIE BARRELED UP THE STAIRS TO THE FOURTH FLOOR. SHE had tried to wait for the elevator, but it took forever and it was only two floors up. But now she was out of breath. She stopped at the floor kitchen to grab a water, to try to slow her breathing down. Better to walk in a couple minutes late than to come in out of breath and wild eyed. Oh, and wild haired. Damn it. She'd been running late this morning and had brushed it out quickly, and folded it into the half-bun, half-ponytail she favored for ease and manageability. But it never looked very professional. And she was in jeans and a sweatshirt again. She already looked five years younger than she was, and dressing like a teenager didn't help her look her role. It was comfortable, but it didn't help.

She let her hair down, shoved the hair elastic in her pocket, and took off the sweatshirt. She had a plain, pale blue, long-sleeved T-shirt on today, so she figured it'd pass for very casual business casual. She smoothed her hair out, took another sip of water, and walked over to the conference room where the art director candidate sat. The recruiter spotted her, and smiled and rose. Then Allie realized she'd forgotten to print out the résumé. Oh, well, at least she'd studied it. And she had her notebook in her back pocket where she'd written some questions.

Kendra met her coming out of the conference room, and handed her a printout of his résumé.

"Bless," said Allie.

"No problem. Check out the drawing." Kendra had made a little role canvas on the back with some attributes circled. "Those are the ones I didn't get to!" she said.

"Oh, thanks! That's great."

She walked in and gave the candidate's hand a firm shake. "Allie Jenova," she said.

"Carlton Baronski," he replied. He was average height, and was built like a tree trunk with a gym membership. He had sandy blond hair gelled into good behavior and the same pale blue eyes as seen in huskies.

She sat down across from him and pulled her notebook out of her back pocket. "Okay, so you worked at Hurricane. Tell me about what you did there."

He covered a list of impressive games he'd either done the art for, or led a team on.

She thought about Kendra's advice—well, Christie's advice—about asking about things the candidate had done, and looked down at the role canvas. "Navigating shifting goalposts," Kendra had circled. "Tell me about a time when you"—magic words unleashed—"had to deal with a timeline that suddenly got shorter." Ha!

Carlton paused and ran a hand through his thin blond hair. "Hmm, I feel like our timelines end up weirdly longer than predicted. We're sort of notorious for not launching on time." He smiled. "But I can tell you about this one time, when the timeline didn't move, but the creative direction did?"

Allie nodded. That would do.

As he spoke, she realized how dead-on Christie's advice had been.

"People can't predict what they will do!" Kendra had repeated what Christie had taught her. "But they can talk about things that have happened. And they know you'll check references, so they will stick to the truth. More or less. But then you have something to ask references about."

She made a few notes of things she wanted to double check, and then asked him, "Tell me about a time …"

They chatted amiably for thirty minutes, then suddenly Mick was tapping at the window.

"Oh, I'm sorry! Our time is up. But I'll swing by at the end of the interviews and see if you have any questions."

He rose and shook her hand.

Allie felt better walking out the door. Finally, someone decent.

ROB AND ALLIE COMPARE NOTES

ROB'S QUEST FOR THE PERFECT COUCH WAS NEVER-ENDING. Today it led them to the huge Restoration Hardware store. Allie loved it. It was like being in a dotty old uncle's mansion, full of a mix of styles that somehow belonged together. And she could actually afford some of the pieces. She cheerfully sat on couches with Rob as she talked about the role canvas.

"It worked great!" she said. "I feel like I completely get what I want in the role, and I know who has it."

"Who's got your old job, then?" Rob asked.

"Not Jason!" She chortled. Everyone thought he was a hotshot, but she decided he was also a case of the art of self-promotion. "Arash is a great bet, and so is Katelyn. I wish I could hire them both."

"Why can't you?" Rob thumbed through an upholstery book, pausing to stroke a fabric.

"Well, I only have one headcount."

"That's because you have not dealt with your real problem."

Allie got up. "Thanks, Debbie Downer."

"Okay, let me tell you what I've been doing." Rob sat heavily in the big chair, and Allie sat back down. He looked profoundly tired. There were noticeable purple bags under his eyes and he moved more slowly than usual.

"I'm listening," she said, leaning forward.

"I've been firing. We don't have headcount at all at Bagboy. We're skeleton staff."

"So why get rid of who you have?"

"Because sometimes who we have is worse than not having anyone. I know you've heard me talk about technical debt. But I think there should be such a thing as hiring debt. You went too fast, you hired badly, and now you don't want to take the time to fix it."

"Also, firing sucks."

"Also, firing sucks. And hiring is work."

"Firing takes so looong," Allie whined. "You have to do a warning, then a PIP, and it's all meetings with HR to cover your ass."

"Look, Allie, I love you to death, right? But if someone has been doing a crappy job and you have not been giving them warnings, you are also doing a crappy job. Letting bad behavior continue is sanctioning bad behavior."

Allie put her head in her hands. She knew he was talking about Mick. Her first report at QuiltWorld. He needed to go. Long ago. He'd been easy to ignore before, but now she couldn't.

Rob got up and sat back down next to her. He put a hand on her shoulder. "Hey, you never know. If he realizes his work is not good, he might straighten up. I have seen a PIP actually turn someone around before."

Allie looked up. "No way. Everyone knows when you are on a PIP, it's a countdown between them firing you or you finding a new job before they can."

"No, really," Rob said. "When I started my last job, everyone told me I'd have to fire this one database engineer. Everyone told me what a jerk he was, and how he never got anything done on time. I did a 360 and put together paperwork to put him on a PIP. When we went over the feedback, he started to cry."

"Now I know you're making this up."

"Not sobbing, but he was wiping his eyes. He told me no one had ever told him what he was doing wrong. He thought everyone hated him. He was so relieved he could actually fix his issues."

"And did he?"

"Actually, yes. He got his work done on time and stopped having an attitude about it. I'll admit he was never my star guy, but he became a solid team player."

Allie leaned back and looked at the ceiling. "Fair enough. And worst case, I get another headcount."

"Yep."

They sat silently for a second. Rob broke it. "So can I see this fabulous diagram you've been nattering on about?"

Allie grabbed her backpack off the floor and dug out her notebook.

"Love to!" Her phone buzzed. "Oh. Yosi's wife might be in labor."

"It could be a false alarm. My sister thought she was in labor three times before she really went into labor."

"I need to hire a CTO."

"Honey, you need to hire everyone. You don't scale. You can't be everywhere."

"I'm trying."

"Well, stop. Let things break while you attack your top priority. Which, by the way, is to get a team in place."

"I know, but our numbers …"

"Talk to Mick, ask him to step up and chase the damn numbers, which is his job, by the way. You have to stop being a PM and start being a GM. Otherwise the studio is going to suffer, and Rick will happily give you your old job back."

Allie looked down at her notebook where she had sketched her role canvases. She had this at least. She did know what to do about hiring. But firing. Yuck. "Debbie Downer," she muttered.

YOSI EXPLAINS FEEDBACK

SHE MET YOSI DOWNSTAIRS AT 11:45, AND HE WAS THERE AS always, perfectly on time. He led the way, as ever not asking where she wanted to eat.

She peeled off lunch suspects as they walked the blocks, until she was sure where they were going. Flock. A hip, tiny bistro hidden in the middle of warehouses, run by a husband-and-wife team.

They passed the stone lions that stood on each side of the gate, and walked through the dining patio. There were heat lamps, though not turned on, and blankets folded neatly on the seats. The patio was empty. Even though it was September, this day was foggy and bitterly cold. Only if Flock was completely packed would anyone willingly crawl under a blanket outside.

Allie stepped into the restaurant and into the warmth and smell of onions caramelizing and polenta simmering. The owner came up and gave Yosi a huge hug.

"How are you?"

"Good, good! And how is the baby?"

"Walking! It's terrifying," she replied.

"Yep! I remember well!" They chatted conspiratorially as they wound between glass and wooden tables.

Their table was up against a floor-to-ceiling window. The window radiated cold, but the heat of the room made up for it.

Yosi took his napkin and gave it a dramatic flap to open it, then placed it on his lap. The server was at his side immediately. He ordered the fish special, and Allie got a salad.

"Omega Threes!" he announced. "I do feel like being a little bad today. I'll have a beer."

Allie was surprised, but happily ordered the same.

"One beer is pleasant, two makes for napping." He smiled at her. "But no one to judge us here!"

Allie looked around. She didn't see a single coworker. There were some businessmen, mostly over fifty, and a few people who looked like they worked at the design center, very chic and well dressed. Suddenly she saw the appeal of the place—it was an SOS-free zone. She felt oddly light then, as if the weight of eyes had been removed from her. Sometimes she missed cubes with walls high enough you didn't have to feel like someone was always watching over your shoulder. But of course, she worked at a game company, so when a game was on her screen, she could hardly be judged for spending her time poorly.

Allie slid back into her chair, reveling in the moment of peace. "Okay, lay it on me."

"I promised I would." The beer arrived. Yosi took a long sip, acquiring a foam mustache. He wiped it away and sighed.

"This is Rick's third company, but my first as CTO. We'd worked together at his first, DexTalk, but I left after the first year. I got a terrific offer from IBM and honestly, my wife was not into the startup life of all work and no money. And I can't complain! Sure, there was some money when DexTalk sold, but I had a great salary and was able to save up. When Rick approached me about SOS, we were in a much better place financially, and Rick now had a track record of solid exits. This time his dream is to go IPO."

Everyone knew that.

"It was great when we started. I got to build amazing things, play with different frameworks, and I only hired people who could outcode me. But that didn't last. When Baccarat took off, suddenly we had to scale. Rick and I didn't see eye-to-eye on that. He brought in Chuck then."

Chuck was CTO now, but had started as Yosi's VP of engineering.

"Honestly, I was relieved. I loved to code, I hated to hire, and I hated talking to my team about anything other than the code even more. I believed my job was to create world-class architecture and the code to run on it. So I was delighted to hand over the people stuff to Chuck. I just worked on the code. QuiltWorld runs on my original architecture designs." He beamed with pride. "And look how it's scaled! And Baccarat is still rock solid."

All true.

"But Chuck didn't have my vision. He even hired people I had given a thumbs-down to. But he'd place them in new studios, like NoirWorld."

NoirWorld was notoriously buggy. People bet on which would crash first, their numbers or their game. But it still had enough high spending whales to warrant keeping it running.

"And then I made a deadly error. The sin of pride, maybe. I disparaged Chuck in front of the board."

Allie hadn't even touched her beer. This was the apocryphal story, of how Yosi embarrassed Rick.

Yosi started picking away at the beer label where it had begun to peel off from moisture. "I never got NoirWorld. Not the concept and certainly not how it was built, thrown together overnight with duct tape and string. But it grew like a weed. It had promise beyond the casino games. Rick believed it was the beginning of exponential growth. And I undermined it in front of investors." He shook his head at his own hubris. "And then I wasn't CTO. Rick told me himself. He does his own dirty work. He moved me into R&D, and told me to build platforms for new games, so we could scale faster. And I kept my stock, so," he shrugged. "But it was a new department. I had to learn how to build a team. I knew how to hire, but I also knew I was missing something. I didn't know how to pull people into a unit to work together." He pulled the label off the beer and smoothed it on the table.

Allie reached for her forgotten beer. She had never been at the receiving end of a Rick tongue lashing, but they were legendary.

"I was lucky. My wife was finding me increasingly unpleasant. She talked me into taking Com-19 at Stanford, the T-group. Have you heard of it?"

Allie shook her head slowly, no.

"It's a spinoff from the GSP interpersonal dynamics course." He grinned. "Touchy-feely. We spend four days sitting in a circle and talking. We learn to give feedback, to see ourselves as others see ourselves." Now he shook his head ruefully. "I found out I was an asshole. Yes, probably not news to you, but news to me. It's part of my culture. Israelis are much more straightforward than Californians."

Allie snorted. "That's an understatement!"

Yosi guffawed. "You are passive aggressive nice-niks."

"You think arguing is a sport! You do it even when you agree with me!"

"Ha! True. But *you* aren't too bad. You say what you think sometimes." He tipped his bottle toward her, and they clinked.

The lunch came. They took a moment to settle into the food. Yosi's fish looked amazing—picked yesterday, cooked to perfection. Allie, feeling a bit more relaxed from the beer and regretting her wholesome salad, ordered some fried mushrooms as well.

"Anyhow, T-groups changed me. But they also drove me crazy. All I could remember was sitting around talking to people. And I didn't remember the facilitators doing anything special in particular. Or anything! They seemed to just sit there, or gently remind people 'Feedback is about behavior.' There were a few frameworks they taught us, such as a sort of useful one on relationship types," he waved his fork in the air as if to dismiss it, "and a better one for giving feedback."

Allie silently noted she wanted these frameworks.

"But I couldn't figure out how I'd had so many meaningful conversations. I'd walked in seeing twelve strangers as assholes...."

Allie raised an eyebrow, and Yosi shrugged.

"... You know, the guy who is too old to be a hipster but still tries, the kiss-up guy who agrees with anything someone says, the soccer mom ..."

Allie stiffened.

"No, no, I'm saying that's how I saw them when I first walked in, a bunch of stereotypes I was trapped with for a weekend. But by the end of the weekend, they were all *people*." He emphasized the last word, as if it were a special title, like king or queen. "And I couldn't see how it was done. It was like a magic trick. So I contacted one of the facilitators and he referred me to a coach." Yosi spread his hands wide, as if to say, *there you go!*

Allie took a bit of salad, waiting to see if he'd continue. But he began eating his fish.

"And your coach ... ?" she finally prompted.

"Ed helped me see that my job was not to be first among equals. My job was to be a coach to the best people I could find. To help them reach their potential, so the company can thrive. I had to become a servant leader."

He took another bite and then chewed furiously and swallowed hard, as if gripped by an idea he couldn't wait to get out. He waved his fork at her. "You know what's messed up about companies?"

"That's a long list."

"No, I mean yes, but this is also what's messed up about people! No one likes conflict!"

Another bite, more chewing. Allie waited. She contemplated another beer.

"So we don't give anyone feedback on what they're doing wrong. And then once a year we do annual performance reviews, and all the stuff we have been sitting on, all that resentment, we bundle it up and dump it on some poor schlub's head! And then he's gobsmacked, has a nervous breakdown for a week, and the manager feels guilty and is extra-nice, or worse, avoids him, and there we are!"

"What's the alternative?" Everyone did annuals. Every place she'd worked at, anyhow.

"Continuous feedback." Yosi paused dramatically. "When an employee acts in a way that will make him less successful, we must give that feedback instantly. You see, two things are going wrong with the annual review. One," he held up a thumb, in the European manner, "no one remembers what happened six or nine months ago. An 'annual' review,'" and here he did scare quotes around "annual," "is really only a quarter of a review, unless something dreadful enough to be memorable happened. And if it was that dreadful, the manager probably addressed it then, and it's just opening up old wounds."

Allie nodded. "But that's why we do quarterly reviews here, I thought."

"Yes, that was my idea," Yosi said. "Rick still listens to me. He just won't let me near anyone important I might insult." He smiled. "We do quarterly reviews, and that helps a bit. But not enough. That's the second thing wrong with formal reviews. It's too much feedback. It's overwhelming." Now he opened his hands wide, in a gesture of a reveal. "If you hear one thing when it happens, you can really hear it and change. If you hear twenty things you get overwhelmed. You'll probably just work on one or two. In fact, three!" Now he held up three fingers. "You are so worried about your raise, you probably are hardly listening at all, anyway. We get flooded emotionally, and then listening is too hard."

Allie nodded again. She remembered a horrible review she'd had at one of her first jobs. Her boss droned on and on about everything she'd done wrong, and she had to force herself to nod while he talked, unable to hear anything, just drowning in her misery. In the end, he'd given her a raise anyhow. The standard annual amount, but why he had spent thirty minutes telling her everything that was wrong with her, she would never know.

When she reviewed her guys, she tried to give feedback the way she'd heard to do, say a nice thing, then a thing they did wrong, then another nice thing. She couldn't imagine ever cutting someone down for thirty minutes. "So why are we still doing quarterly reviews?"

"Quarterly reviews are like retrospective, or grading OKRs. They are a formal closing, a chance to reflect. When matched with regular feedback, they can increase organizational learning." Yosi looked at his watch. "We're good for a bit longer."

Allie saw her moment. "I'd like to ask your advice."

"Shoot."

"I need to put Mick on a PIP."

Yosi nodded. "I wondered."

"He's an okay data analyst, but he's a terrible PM. And the team hates working with him. I just wish it didn't take so long to fire someone."

Now Yosi shook his head sorrowfully. "First, you have to change your thinking. There are no bad employees. There are employees who don't know things yet. And there are employees who resist change, but don't know that they are losing power and influence because of their behavior. They conflate behavior with identity. And there are employees who are a bad fit. This last one is very difficult."

"Please continue, Yoda. Wise, you are."

At this Yosi chortled. "I'm starting to look like him! New wrinkles every day!" He took a sip of his drink. "It's not about firing, it's about giving clear feedback. And then making sure that there are consequences to a person's behavior if they choose to ignore the feedback."

Allie shrugged. It was all a bit melodramatic, but not out of keeping with Rob and Derek's advice.

"Let's start by asking why would we ever want feedback? When someone tells you, 'I've got some feedback for you,' how do you feel?"

Allie rolled her eyes. "Here comes trouble."

"Exactly. Most people use feedback as a way to tell you what they don't like about you. But you know what? It's still information. It's a single data point, but it's a data point."

"Not statistically significant."

"Yes, but it's more like a playtest. Playtests are not statistically significant most of the time, as we only test with eight or ten folks at a time. But we start to see the game through their eyes, and gain insights that we can use to make the game better."

Allie nodded.

"So feedback is like that. You can get some information on how you are seen, and you can decide what to do with it. It's a clue to what might be holding you back."

The mushrooms arrived, hot and fragrant fried morsels of delight, with an aioli dipping sauce. Yosi stopped talking to pop one in his mouth. "Ow, hot, hot, hot." He blew past the mushroom, trying to cool it in his mouth.

"I think I'll wait a sec." Allie grinned. "Okay, so I should seek feedback, got it, but most employees don't want it still. Should I try to convince them they should like it?"

"Depends what kind of feedback it is. The simplest format for feedback is behavior, reaction, consequence. 'You did this thing'—something that is observable, that is not a matter of opinion. 'You're an asshole' is an opinion. 'You're trying to mess with me' is also an opinion, because it speaks to intent.

You can't know what someone is thinking. You can only know what you can observe. But keeping to what you can observe, people will feel less judged, less misunderstood. And they can't argue. They may have done something in order to mess with you, but they can deny it and there is no winning that argument. But if they did something that did mess you up, well, there it is. Observable facts."

"Ugh, hypotheticals. I'm already lost."

"Okay, well, in the last estaff, you were suggesting a success metric for the new game, and Brent interrupted you. Talked on top of you."

Allie's lips tightened. That had really pissed her off. She was still mad.

"So did you talk to him about it?"

"No. I didn't know what to say."

"What did you think of saying?"

"You mean after I thought, 'Asshat'?'"

"You didn't say that, and that's good because that is judging, and no one enjoys being judged."

Allie thought, *It's not judging, it's observing the obvious.* She snarked, "Figured that out on my own."

Yosi waved his hands in the air, *So sue me.*

"Okay," Allie put a mushroom on her plate to cool off. "I figured he wouldn't like it if I told him he was mansplaining me. Which he was. How long have I been doing game metrics? But what could I say? 'Please don't interrupt me?' He probably didn't even realize he did it. Half the time the GMs just talk on top of each other."

"That's where the other two parts of feedback come in handy. You might say, 'Brent, when you interrupted me in the meeting, I felt hurt. I'm worried you don't respect my thinking, and that would make it hard for me to work with you effectively.'"

"So many things wrong with saying that," Allie replied. She poked the mushroom with a finger. It was warm, but not too hot. She dipped it in the aoili and bit in. OMG, such deliciousness! Her hackles went down a bit.

Yosi looked puzzled. "Like?"

"I'm not going to say I feel hurt to Brent. He's one of the wolves. He'll classify me down as a weak female. Which means he'll either dismiss me or attack."

"Okay, fair enough. But some other feeling? You look angry?"

"Sure, I'll just say, 'Brent, when you interrupted me, I was really pissed off.'" She tilted her head to the side. "Actually that might work. It's his language."

"And the rest?" Yosi asked.

"Maybe it's the same, it's that touchy-feely language that is not going to fly at SOS. How about, 'Brent, when you interrupted me, I was pissed off. I felt disrespected, and that makes it hard for me to want to work with you.' That should scare him. He needs QuiltWorld traffic."

"In interpersonal dynamics training, we try not to use phrases like 'I felt disrespected' and reserve the word 'feel' for actual feelings."

"Yosi, this is useful, but don't be so dogmatic. I haven't gotten this far without speaking the language of this place."

"I havebeen very effective with this 'touchy-feely' language."

"I'm not you." Allie was growing angry again.

"All right," he replied, his eyes scanning her face. "I respect your experience is not mine. Let's talk about consequences. If people don't see how refusing to change hurts them, they're not going to go through the hassle of changing."

Allie appreciated he was listening to her, not dismissing her feelings, like George always had. George never got that she had to be tougher, work harder just to be seen as equal. But Yosi acknowledged her history. She felt safer, and nodded to him to go on. "Makes sense. Okay, so you were talking about types of problem employees?"

The busser cleared their plates, and Yosi ordered an espresso. Allie gleefully followed his lead. Great, more time to learn.

"Oh, yes. Don't know, don't want, can't. Okay, so if you never give feedback, people don't realize what they are doing that could be holding them back. Have you ever told Kendra it drives you crazy that she never gets her work in on time?"

It was true, Kendra was always late. But why weren't they talking about Mick? Allie replied, "I just add twenty-four hours to her estimates now."

"When you do that, she doesn't learn that her procrastinating is hurting her career. You don't think of her as reliable, right?"

"Not even a little. A few times she's gotten the team her designs two or three days late. But her work is always excellent."

"*You* like her and you like her work, but her next boss may not put up with that, and fire her. You are keeping information from her that could hurt her career. Do you think she'd like to get promoted, lead a game?"

"Yes."

"So. She is a 'don't know.' She thinks being late is acceptable because you have made it so. It would have been easy when she was late the first time to tell her it wasn't okay. Now you'll have to have a longer discussion with her about why it's no longer okay. Or you can pass the problem off to her next boss. Who may not give her feedback either, until he fires her."

"I'm not passing off problems. That's not who I want to be."

"Good. So when you get back to the office, you'll talk to Kendra."

Allie took a very big breath, and blew it out. So many conversations.

"What's the worst that could happen?"

"She could get upset. But she won't. When she knows she's fucking up, she apologizes every time. She just doesn't change."

"Can you think of the last three times it's happened?"

"Yes."

"And were there consequences because of her actions?"

"Oh, yes. Not only that I can't trust her to get critical work done, but she did cause us to miss a launch window. I can probably put a number to that." A week of revenue.

"Okay, now let's go through my guys. I know what I think of them. What do you think? Can you give me a keep and change for each one?"

"Keep and change?"

"Sorry, that's my shorthand. Something that's beneficial, that they should keep doing. And something that is hurting their ability to be effective and have influence. Something that they should change, or stop doing."

Allie went through her pods easily. Then she slowed down as she started considering the engineers in other pods. When it came to the ops crew, she realized there was a guy whose name she didn't even know. He was new, but not that new. She was chagrined.

Yosi shook his head. "You're not a PM anymore. You're responsible for everyone. You need to constantly collect feedback. And constantly give it."

She had to agree. "Okay, you said awareness is the first step. But Kendra knows she's always late."

"She doesn't know it matters. Or she doesn't know how much it matters. That's the second part. We all have quirks. Some are innocuous, but some get in the way of your ability to be effective. Like my accent. When I first got here, people struggled to understand me. But now it's just part of my charm." He winked. "Because you keep letting Kendra get away with being late, you've given her a message it's okay. That's why I suggested you make it clear to her what the consequences are, both in your perception of her and in the world's perception. An observation without consequences is just a fun fact."

"Okay, let's say she doesn't change. She refuses, or maybe she just can't?"

"Do *you* need to know when work will be done? Are you able to estimate how long it takes her to do things?"

"Oh, yes. For so many reasons, yes." Allie had to know how long it took to get work done. After they missed a launch, she padded her timelines with Kendra, and even lied to her about due dates.

"If she doesn't change, you escalate the consequences. You put her on a PIP."

"What do you mean?" Allie was a bit shocked by this escalation.

"Say, 'Unfortunately, Kendra, your lateness problem hasn't changed, and it's causing the studio a lot of problems. While I appreciate the quality of your work, this can't continue. I'd like you to consider if you are willing to commit to change, if you believe that you can. If you can, I can commit to you. But we need to document it via a PIP. If you think you can't commit to this change, I don't think this is the right place for you.'"

The "not the right place for you" line was such HR talk. But Allie liked the idea that if someone committed to her, she could commit to helping them change.

"Okay. I'm going to give it a shot."

"Great! And SOS can pick up this bill. We've done nothing but work!"

When do we do anything else? thought Allie. *This is who we are.*

STRAIGHT TALK

ALLIE LISTENED TO NOAM'S RANT. HIS WAS THE LAST BIT OF feedback she wanted to prepare to speak with Mick.

"And he changes priorities mid-sprint." Noam shook his head ruefully. "He's all over the place and treats us like his minions."

"Thank you, Noam, this is useful feedback for Mick." Allie tried to put on a leadership aura, but wondered if she just came across like a lawyer. It was hard to balance neutral professionalism and showing she cared about the situation. Allie stood to indicate the meeting was over. Noam looked slightly disappointed, as if complaining was the best part of his day.

"Well, thanks for dealing with this, Allie," Noam shrugged. "Can't be fun."

"No, but that's why they pay me the big bucks."

Noam let out a short barking laugh. No one below the C level got paid big bucks. They just waited for the IPO and hoped for bonuses.

Allie had an hour to correlate the feedback before her scheduled time with Mick. It went by too quickly, but at least she was very clear. She reviewed the framework Yosi had given her for formal feedback:

Information—what were observable issues? She had plenty of those now.

Importance—why did they matter? Again, Mick's end-of-quarter status told a story of missed opportunities and delayed results.

Invitation to change—that was what the performance review plan was all about.

Implications—he'd have to leave the studio, perhaps the company.

She had a few notes jotted down for each line, and she was ready to have a productive conversation. She hoped.

* * *

Allie had booked a conference room with clear glass walls facing the main workroom. While she had made her entire career in rooms full of men who towered over her, she didn't relish having what could be an unpleasant confrontation somewhere too private. She didn't think Mick would burst into tears, but she realized her subconscious wasn't sure what else he was capable of. When she hired him, she hadn't seen the signs of a bully, but the 360 certainly painted a clear picture. She went to the conference room, and Mick showed up ten minutes later.

"Hello, Mick. How is your day going?"

He sat down across from her. "Fine. Annual review time?"

That was what the meeting name was, so he was just making small talk as best he could. "Yes. I've read over your quarterly summaries and collected insights from your peers."

At the end of each quarter at SOS, employees wrote up a short summary of their accomplishments. This way what they did could be judged beyond simply if they made their goals or not. It was a strangely pleasant activity, looking back over the last three months and seeing what one had accomplished. Mick had not made any of his OKRs, which was not surprising. She had warned him they were way more than stretch goals.

He'd replied they were shoot-for-the-moon goals, like Google had recommended. Allie believed that the best way to find out what you were capable of is to try to achieve it. Her entire life was like that. If people didn't want to learn from her life experience, they were welcome to make their own.

"Let's go over your progress this quarter. First, it looks like you accomplished none of your OKRs, and made about fifty percent progress toward them."

Mick interrupted her, "I've had a hard time with …"

Allie stopped him. "If you don't mind holding your questions, I'd prefer to go over the summary first. We can then dig into details."

Mick sat back with a *humph*. She noticed he didn't have a notepad with him. He was going to rely on his memory to track what was said. While he had an excellent memory, that was something that got him in trouble. There were just too many moving parts in the QuiltWorld studio to rely on memory. She pushed some Post-Its from the center of the table toward him. "In case you want to take some notes."

He ignored her offer and gestured for her to continue.

"I know you've had a hard time with your teammates. I want you to realize your job as a product manager is very different from being an analyst. It's not enough to watch the numbers; it's not enough to come up with ideas to move the numbers. You have to build up consensus to get work done. Being a product manager means being a people person. We can't get work done without a team. From what I'm hearing, your team is having a hard time working with you. They say you give orders, you don't ask for opinions, you change directions frequently without communicating justification ..." She went down the list.

"Who is saying that about me?"

"Mick, it's not about you and one person. Everyone mentioned the order giving and four people mentioned the direction changes. The team says it feels random."

"That's what Rick does. He follows his gut, and moves fast when he has an idea."

"Well, maybe when you are as successful as Rick, you can emulate his style. But right now, we have pretty convincing data your current approach is not working."

"They need to get on board if they want success."

Allie sighed. "Mick, an old boss of mine used to have a saying. If, during your day, you meet a ..." She paused, decided not to curse. Part of her stepping up. " ... jerk, he might be a jerk. But if all day long all you meet is jerks, *you* might be the jerk."

Mick paused to untangle the story. He didn't laugh. She usually got a laugh.

"I'm sorry, Mick, but too many people are pointing out flaws that are creating issues. And your numbers show you aren't getting the progress you seek. Are you willing to change your behavior? Try to move slower, explain things more clearly, incorporate the team's feedback?"

Mick stared at her like she was speaking Etruscan. She felt nervous.

"I'm sorry, Mick; it's my fault. When I moved you over from data analytics, I should have helped coach you more. You know what upheaval we've been going through. But you still have the potential I saw when I asked you to step into this role. I just need you to try on some new approaches in order to get the kind of results you're seeking. Consider it a very sloppy AB test."

Mick's face was still and Allie noticed his ears were red. It was the only sign of any emotion, though what emotion it represented she couldn't say. She swallowed.

"If you feel like these changes aren't ones you can make, we'll have to talk about if QuiltWorld and SOS are a good fit for you." HR language for *we'll fire you.* Everyone knew what it meant.

Mick finally moved, looking down at the printout she had placed in front of him outlining the changes she wanted him to make.

"Can I take this home? Digest it a bit?"

Allie sighed with relief. Mick had looked like he'd explode for a moment there. Now he was back to his usual reserved self. Perhaps with less arrogance.

"Absolutely. Let me know when you're ready to talk again. But I do need to resolve this by the end of the week."

By the end of the week, Mick had joined another studio.

ROB AND ALLIE BUILD A MODEL FOR SUCCESS

ALLIE LEFT THE Q3 REVIEW SHAKEN BUT RELIEVED. RICK WAS not in a bad mood during the meeting. Then again, he wasn't really in a good mood, either. He hadn't ripped her apart, as she had heard he'd done to Brenda, but rather eyed the roller coaster charts she showed with a reasonable suspicion and congratulated her on her hires with a slight suggestion that they had better pay for themselves. As good a meeting as she could expect for running the studio just over a month.

Next quarter would not be as easy. The two hours of examining every stat in the game, Rick questioning every trend she pointed to, left her longing for good news. Some sign things would head up and to the right. She hoped to find it in the testing lab.

The sign on the door said, "Testing in progress, enter quietly."

Allie turned the handle as softly as she could. She slid into the dark room, lit mostly by the lights on the other side of the two-way mirror. She had timed things perfectly. Inside the room were three rows of chairs, with counters in front of them for taking notes, with candy in small bowls set at regular intervals.

At the table a researcher sat in the front row, a couple members of her team in the middle, and a programmer in the back. From the speed of his typing, Allie suspected he was taking advantage of the dark silence to code rather than to observe, but whatever. He was here; he might pick something up. She sat down in front, next to the researcher, trying to recall his name. She could look it up in his email later.

"What's up?" she asked.

"Almost done building the Quilt Circus ... wait ..."

On the other side of the two-way mirror, a player was silently staring into the world in the monitor, mousing deliberately. She was somewhere in her forties, her hair a dark brown, her eyes the same color. She was slightly over-weight, which lent her a doughy, unformed quality. Next to her sat another researcher, a young Asian woman Allie hadn't met before. The researcher took notes occasionally, and watched the player intently.

Next to the two-way mirror on Allie's side was a sound board and a monitor showing what the player saw. On that monitor Allie saw the rolling green fields of QuiltWorld. The player's quilted city showed in the distance, patchwork buildings inhabited by strolling ragdoll figures. But the player had scrolled to an empty field, her cursor carrying a sewing box icon. She drew a square onto the field, and the box dropped into it. The sewing box sat for a few seconds, shuddering and shaking as if a world of demons were contained inside. Then the lid popped open, and needles and tiny squares of bright color flew out. They spun about in a multi-hued tornado, then started to assemble themselves into ordered space. And thena quilted circus tent appeared.

Allie heard a soft "Oooh" from the player, and looked away from the mirror desktop to the player's face. The player was beaming with delight, her formerly dull eyes twinkling with joy. She looked suddenly younger now, her face alive with pride in her creation, like a little girl having arranged a dollhouse to her satisfaction.

"Look at my circus!"

She then leaned forward to add the other modules, the Ferris wheel and the sideshow.

Allie grinned. This is why she did it. The numbers made it possible to pay the team, but every time a player felt creative and empowered, Allie knew she was in the right job. She hated to leave the testing rooms, but she had to meet Yosi.

As soon as Yosi got the news of Mick's departure, he scheduled her for another of his lunches.

"At least he's gone."

"You need to warn his new GM."

"He should have interviewed Mick! It's not like his attitude is something he hides."

"Don't make your problem someone else's problem."

"Fine, you're right. Is this job ever pleasant?"

"When you launch."

"Yeah," she said softly. They both knew nothing was as deeply satisfying as putting something new and wonderful in the world.

When they left the restaurant, Allie parted from Yosi. She wanted to think a bit. She didn't have a meeting until three, and even though she had a million things waiting for her back at the office, she felt walking was the best use of her time. All her problems would be waiting for her when she returned, so why not spend a little time chasing the solutions that had started to pop into her head. She walked toward the art school first. She passed various interior design shops and closed warehouses that probably held more of the same. So many people playing the game of perfect home. That would make a good game, she thought. *Interior design world?*

The day was sunny now, and she enjoyed the warmth as she walked, shrugging off her jacket. She decided to walk toward the little ballpark near the old SOS offices and turned south. She could feel ideas in her head like puzzle pieces, and she moved them around to see how they fit. It was like working on a new bold beat where you had to find a way to match the joy of creativity with the need to hit the bottom line.

Some aspects of her studio problem she could see easily in front of her. The need to fire, a better way to hire. Other aspects were like shapes walking toward her in a fog. She couldn't hurry them; she had to wait until they became clear. So she walked and thought. For some reason she didn't understand, but she trusted, her mind turned to OKRs.

A company she worked at before SOS had tried to use the goal setting system that Google had made famous. They set their OKRs and had a meeting about them once or twice, then dropped them. Here at SOS they were a religion. You set them, and you measured them at every turn. You looked at them at the start of the Monday numbers meeting. You talked about them when doing demos on Fridays. Your team's OKRs started every status email, before you listed next week's priorities and last week's accomplishments. Goals were integrated into the rhythm of life. They couldn't be forgotten.

She turned a corner and almost ran into two burly guys exiting the local gym. From the open door wafted a strange combination of steamy sweat and Brazilian food from the restaurant that shared the space. Next, a flock of women with yoga mats engulfed her as they rushed in. One class ended, another started, and in between we sweat and eat. Life has a rhythm.

Allie thought, that's what's wrong with hiring and firing. It starts and stops. Like setting OKRs at the beginning of the quarter, then measuring at the end, and hoping a miracle occurred somewhere in between. So what goes between could be feedback. George never did the weekly one-on-ones. He was the king of the drive-by, though. "Managing by walking around," he called it. He had an MBA. Maybe she needed an MBA. Maybe she could go back to school. If she went to Haas or Stanford, people might take her seriously. She'd still be five feet nothing, but she'd have all the good jargon. Maybe then she'd know what she was doing.

"Oh, come on, brain," she said out loud. "Focus." She had reached the park and was tempted to sit on the bleachers, but decided to circle the park first. Kids were playing baseball while their coach shouted out encouragement. She thought about Derek's GROW explanation. Coaching was feedback.

She texted Rob. "Free? Can meet usual?"

His reply came immediately "Sure. 5."

She started walking back toward the design center coffee shop.

* * *

Their coffees acquired, Rob and Allie sat upstairs in the mezzanine. Other than lunchtime, it was empty and quiet. Allie had a notebook out, and was drawing for Rob.

"Okay, so you know OKRs have their rhythm."

"Sure, set, approve, set tasks and confidence Monday, celebrate Friday, finish and grade …"

Allie waved him silent. "Yes, yes. But let's simplify. We make OKRS because they have a regular beginning, middle and end, like a story. We set them, we check in weekly and we do a retrospective to learn. Three stages, really." She drew this on her page.

Rob shrugged. Obviously.

"So I'm thinking, why don't we treat our team members like this? It's a mess. We hire when we need someone, check-ins are all over the place, and we fire when we just can't stand it anymore. It's ridiculous. We could use the same rhythm, to keep it all aligned." She drew a second set of boxes.

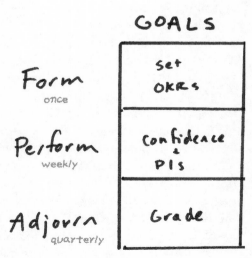

	GOALS	ROLES
Form *once*	set OKRs	set responsibility
Perform *weekly*	confidence & PIs	FEEDBACK
Adjourn *quarterly*	Grade	Promote / Fire

"See this top box? It's when we hire. We write up a role canvas for the job." She remembered her lunch with Yosi, when he said she was thinking about hiring wrong. "But we don't throw it away. We could use it and OKRs in the weekly one-on-one, as a kind of script for the conversation. I was thinking I'd go through the role canvas and see if there was anything I thought people should be doing better, and then ask them about progress toward OKRs."

Rob was nodding. "And we already have quarterly reviews, so we can use that time to go over the job description ..."

"Role canvas," inserted Allie.

"Sure, role canvas, and see if it needs to be updated or changed. Or if the person needs more serious consequence feedback."

"Like a PIP."

Rob nodded thoughtfully and stroked his chin. He had an even layer of stubble Allie hadn't noticed before. That wasn't like him; his wife Marie said she hated how beards felt. Allie wondered if he was keeping the same kind of crazy hours she was. Another SOS widow. Rob interrupted her reverie.

"This keeps it nice and simple. A PIP is ninety days anyhow. You can track feedback from the one-on-ones, have a formal status conversation at the close of quarter. That's the perfect time to discuss consequences. But I think something is missing."

"Okay." Allie gestured to him to continue.

He drew a third column and titled it "Norms."

	GOALS	ROLES	NORMS
Form *once*	Set OKRs	Set responsibility	Set norms
Perform *weekly*	Confidence & PIs	FEEDBACK	Adjust Norms
Adjourn *quarterly*	Grade	Promote / Fire	Question Evolve codify

"What are norms?"

"They are rules of behavior, either emergent or agreed upon. Every group has norms. I had this experience when I was out campaigning for Obama. The guy who trained us how to go door-to-door, Andre something, anyhow, he first had us create norms for our learning experience. We talked about what we liked and didn't like about classrooms. Then we wrote up some rules for our classroom. I really loved it. I've been trying to figure out where else to use it."

Allie hopped in, "Yes, like a team charter! We did that back at Hurricane!" She paused, and frowned. "But it was set and forget, too. Maybe norms need the same rhythm."

"Yeah, but I'm not sure what it is."

"We can certainly make a rule set and update it end of quarter."

"Give Kendra an excuse to make a poster."

Allie burst out at laughing at that. Kendra loved her posters. Then she paused. "No, no posters. It needs to be casual, so we can write on it. Update it when needed. Weekly."

"Flipcharts then, and review during weekly retrospective. Makes sense, tie together all the ceremonies."

"Ceremonies?"

"Agile talk. It's what we call our ritual meetings, like stand-up or retrospective."

"Agile is a cult."

"Do not mock my religion, and I will not mock your worship of the database god."

Allie waved a dismissive hand at him. All service groups worshiped process, and business teams worshiped results. Everyone fixated on the thing that affected their compensation. It was the way of the world. "Okay, so, we set the goals, roles, and norms at the beginning of each quarter. We check them weekly. And we do a formal review end of quarter. Do a norm report card along with performance reviews and grading OKRs."

"Sounds right to me."

"We going to try this Q4?"

"Why not? Davis doesn't care what I do, as long as the code doesn't crash."

Why not? It was really different from how George ran the studio. But maybe that was what she needed. She knew she couldn't just keep going as is and wait for a miracle to occur.

ROLLER COASTER

AT THE BEGINNING OF THE FOURTH QUARTER ALLIE FOUND HER-self standing outside of Rick's office, chatting with Sheila, his assistant. Sheila was sunny natured and happy to discuss her husband, her kids, or her many dogs.

The door opened and George stepped out.

"He's all yours," he said grimly.

She wondered what that was about.

She stepped in and sat down. Rick was on the phone. He gestured toward her, but that was uninterpretable. She hoped it was a "just wait" gesture. When he went back to his call, she figured it was close enough.

His office was huge. She could have put a three-person starter studio in there and they'd have plenty of room for a few more engineers. But it wasn't ostentatious. It was the opposite, in fact; it looked like it was a startup's first office. His desk, while massive, was a door on two sawhorses. He had three big whiteboards on the walls, two on one wall, and another above a large leather couch that looked like it did nap duty. It had a couple of Ikea throws on it. The whiteboard above the couch, despite being blocked by the couch, was covered with diagrams and notes. "Do not erase" was written in at least three different places.

Another wall was covered with a bookshelf, and it was packed solid with books, many sitting on top of other books in the full shelves. He had every book on game design she knew, with a few shelves dedicated to O'Reilly books. He had a couple of windows that looked out at the freeway and the hills beyond. The fog was already licking around them, Allie noted. Rick stood looking at it, asking about negotiations with somebody whom he hadn't named. Even though the sun was low in the sky and the windows faced east, he was in silhouette.

The table in front of the couch was covered with printouts, both spreadsheets and mock-ups. The entire room told the story of a CEO who was very hands-on.

Rick put away his phone and sat down behind his huge desk. He was still backlit, his face in shadows. He clasped his hands together and leaned forward. She could see his expression then, serious but otherwise unreadable.

"Settling in okay?"

"Fine," she said, unready for this question. Past interactions had been in product reviews and had been all about numbers. She wasn't ready for any interest in her as a person.

Now he sat back, disappearing again. "Of course, you've been in QuiltWorld for a while. You know the players. You know the score."

She briefly considered bringing up George's excessive raid of her team, but couldn't find the right words before Rick had moved on.

"Have you tracked down the dip?"

This she was ready for.

"Yes, we found it. Undocumented API change. We'll see real numbers by next release."

"Real numbers? Was it reporting, or were the requests not going through?"

He leaned forward again and his eyes locked on her. Her stomach clenched.

"I just mean real as in normal. The requests were not going through. I have talked to Steve B in Bizdev about this. He promised he'd have stern words about not informing us about API changes."

Rick sat back, a bit more relaxed now. "So what's next?"

"Well, I've got quite a bit more hiring to do …"

"Yes, yes, I know, Patricia says she's on top of it. What else?"

"We're ready for a company-wide playtest of the Christmas Event."

"Excellent! Send me the URL. What else?"

"We're also doing a collectible quest for Hanukkah."

He nodded, "Good, good. Kwanzaa?"

"We don't have anything in the hopper. It was deemed not a high-impact project."

"I know the demographics aren't there, but it makes good press. See if you can put something together."

"Okay, I'll see what we can do," she answered. George had squashed her bid to do something for Kwanzaa when she pitched it, saying he'd handle

Rick, but now she had nothing, no concept, no art, no code, and it was only weeks away.

"Sounds like you are on top of it! Great! Keep up the good work." He turned away from her and started punching a number into his phone.

Allie stood, puzzled, and waited a moment. Rick began chatting into his phone, and she decided to leave.

Outside she saw Davis waiting, shifting from foot to foot like a kid called to the principal's office. Which he well might be.

She headed down to the studio to see if there was anything she could put together for Kwanzaa. If history were any predictor of the future, Rick would want to see concepts in a week. She remembered the apocryphal story of a GM who had told Rick, "There is cheap, good, and fast. Pick two."

To which Rick had apparently said, "I don't like the word 'or.' I like the word 'and.'"

That GM was no longer with SOS, it was also said. Rick asked for miracles, and he got more than most. Allie was out of magic beans and fairy godmothers.

She dialed Derek to tell him she'd be missing dinner again.

ADVENT CALENDAR

ALLIE WALKED INTO THE STUDIO THE NEXT MONDAY, A SPRING in her step. Arash was starting today, and Carlton had accepted their offer. Finally, she'd have a team! Or close. Yosi was doing a great job, and he was a great mentor. She felt less alone, less abandoned. Not that she felt that way. Stupid George.

Allie opened the QuiltWorld Staging Server to playtest the next release. Mick's sudden departure had been a weird relief. She felt like she'd gotten away with something. She was able to send out an offer to Karelyn, as well as Arash. At the same time, she couldn't shake the sense she was being watched. Probably because she was. The time she spent learning about her people was time she was not working on making sure the Advent calendar was the best it could be.

They had just finished the build earlier today, and she knew it'd be buggy from the merge, but she had a few minutes and it'd be nice to help QA. And she was excited. This was the last beat she'd worked on as a PM. It was also, in her opinion, one of the finest beats they'd ever launched. Would launch.

It loaded, and the announcement of the Advent calendar flickered briefly, then it was doubled over the background, semitransparent. That couldn't be right. She hit reload. This time it loaded properly, showing the announcement until she dismissed it.

She smiled at the artwork. It was a cute mouse stuffing an old-fashioned Advent calendar. Then she felt the pang of losing Janice. Janice had just the right touch. Cute, but not cloying. She used currency to buy the mouse some cheese. Now bribed, the mouse scurried across the world and off the screen, then returned with a folded-up cloth. The mouse turned into a pretty girl in a gray dress, and shook out the cloth. The animations were a bit jerky, and she made a note to ask Noam what was up with that. The cloth was now a rolling countryside divided into twenty-four gray squares. Each square held one gray box with gray ribbon. The one closest to her shook a little, and under the lid so tightly tied on was a faint golden glow.

Allie had resisted the gray scale opening state, feeling it was a bit depressing. But Janice had been right. It made the tiny bits of color pop. Allie clicked on the ribbon, and it untied. She clicked on the box, and the lid flew off, allowing an explosion of color to erupt. It appeared as if dozens of colorful scarves were dancing out of the box at once. They then neatly piled themselves to the side of the box. In the box was a piece of paper. She clicked on it and it opened up into a scroll saying,

"On the first day of Christmas,
 my true love gave to me
 A house of silk from the Far East.
 INVENT or GET INSTRUCTIONS"

This was what she was most excited by. There had always been people who took advantage of the ability to create whatever you wanted from the quilt tiles. But she had a strong hunch, backed by data, that most users didn't realize they could make their own designs. And QuiltWorld had such heavy handholding, she believed players had learned to just follow prompts. She hoped the Advent calendar would make more users aware of the sandbox nature of the game, and reengage players who were tired of assembling kits.

If everyone who wanted to create from scratch was already doing it, there would be an uptake of only four percent—the percent of players who currently did free crafting. But if it were higher, she would have tapped into a whole new engagement technique.

She assembled the silk into a little cottage, and when she placed the last square, a note appeared urging her to check back tomorrow (or keep crafting the December 1 square). She hugged herself. If bugs were low enough, she could run a company-wide playtest Friday. She couldn't wait.

"We're going to Vegas," whispered Allie.

Finally she started to look for Yosi around eleven. She was excited to have lunch with him and discuss her ideas around norms. And he always wanted to have a long lunch offsite. She had the time, nothing at one o'clock. But he wasn't there. She texted him.

"Lunch?"

Nothing. She set the phone down on her desk and began to work through the weekly status reports. Then her phone vibrated.

"Sorry, OOO. Ask Patricia."

Out of office? This was oddly brief for the loquacious Yosi. She decided to call Patricia. She answered immediately.

"Hello, Allie. How can I help you?"

"Yosi says he's out?"

"Oh, I thought he had emailed everyone. Oh, I see. It's addressed only to me. So sorry. I suppose he's used to my organizing things, sorting things. His wife's water broke last night."

"But she's only seven months!"

"Exactly. She's in the hospital. He's with her. I suspect he'll be out for a few days at least."

"Well. Thanks."

"My pleasure."

Allie held the phone, warm in her hand. She wasn't sure exactly what had happened. No wonder Yosi had been so short. She sent a short text:

"So sorry, please take care of you both."

And then she wondered if that was the right thing to send. She had no idea if seven months was too soon for a preemie. She didn't know what he was going through. It was amazing Yosi had gone from a notorious asshole to her hero in under three months. That was SOS. Never think you are on top of anything. Okay, no, water breaking early wasn't SOS's fault, no matter how much she suspected the craziness here. As if craziness were a disease that spread through contact. No, it was just life being life. That was crazy enough. Allie reloaded the Advent calendar. Here, in QuiltWorld, it was all order and beauty.

NORMS

IT WAS THE SECOND WEEK OF Q4, AND ALLIE FIGURED THIS WAS the sweet spot to try something new. She felt anxious. She knew Rob was holding the same meeting with his engineering team over in Bagboy. She wondered if it would be more successful, doing it only with engineering, or if it was going to work better with an entire studio. Or if it would work at all. It would be so easy just to have a normal OKR check-in instead, skip this touchy-feely stuff. But no, because if she was right, and she was pretty sure she was, this could make a huge difference in the studio's ability to execute.

She looked around the table. Christie, Kendra, and Carlton represented design. Yosi was at the hospital with his wife, but he sent his lead engineers, Jheryn, Noam, and Nadav. And not to be forgotten, Lawrence and her new PM, Arash. She had a team, all right. Or rather, she had a bunch of resources. Time to make a team.

Allie was secretly shaking. She hoped it didn't show. She was going from her preferred working approach of collecting data and then figuring it out alone to running a touchy-feely session to create team bonding. Argh. But time to test Rob and her theories real time.

"Okay, folks. We're going to start off our team a little differently. You know how most of the time your boss just throws you in a room and says, 'Go solve this impossible problem?'" She got smiles for this, and one of Yosi's engineers chortled. "We're going to take a moment to figure out what kind of team we want to be first. A great team has clear goals, roles, and norms. We're going to set these together, starting with norms."

Jheryn raised his hand. "Norms?" he asked.

"Norms are unspoken rules of behavior. But we … are going to speak them. For example, why did you raise your hand?"

Jheryn shrugged. "Dunno. Made sense to me."

Allie made eye contact with the group, one by one. "Do we want to raise our hands, or do we want to just talk?"

Arash spoke up, "Raising our hand is sort of juvenile. It's like being in school."

Kendra spoke up next. "But you guys are always talking over each other. Mostly talking over us." She nodded to Christie. "This way we know who has the floor."

Allie took back the conversation before it became an argument. "See? Even with something as simple as talking to each other, we all have different expectations of how we should behave. Not talking about it can lead to misunderstandings and hurt. And that will slow us down as a team."

Arash spoke up now. "So raise hands or not?"

Kendra chimed in, "See? One can't even finish a thought around here!"

Allie raised a hand to stop them. "We're going to decide this and more. For now, let's try raising our hands, and see how that works. I want to make sure I hear from the extroverts and the introverts."

Jheryn nodded and his long black bangs fell to obscure his eyes.

She continued, "We're going to create a team charter. But first, I want you to think of the best team you've ever been in. Take a moment and figure out what made it so great. Then raise your hand to share what made it great."

Arash rolled his eyes, but raised his hand. "My team at PayPal trusted each other's good intent. Like, if someone said something stupid," he stopped to point at his own chest, "instead of thinking they were stupid, you'd ask what they meant. And listen to understand what a person meant."

There were a couple nods and Allie wrote on the white board, "Assume good intent."

Jheryn raised his hand. "Everyone trusted that the other person knew what they were doing." He brushed his bangs back from his hazel eyes. "I mean, you didn't doubt the other person was the expert in his field."

Allie nodded, and added, "Trust person to be good at their job."

Another of Yosi's engineers raised his hand and spoke. "Humble enough to ask for help."

Kendra chimed in, "That's a good one, Nadav!" Allie added it to the list on the board.

The team continued, and she wrote:

- Clear common goal
- Knew each other as people
- Could give honest feedback

and several more. Then she turned to the team and asked, "Okay, now think of the worst team you were ever on. The one that made you not want to get out of bed in the morning. This time I want you to just say what you think. Don't bother to raise your hand. We'll try it …"

Noam spoke up, "No leadership."

Allie blinked. "What do you mean by that?"

"No one to make sure we stick to our OKRs. No one takes responsibility. No vision."

Allie wrote up the three definitions. Before she could turn around, she heard Kendra.

"No communication!"

Allie turned around.

"You know, when people are upset about something and they don't say anything, they just pout and snip at you."

Allie wrote on the board *Conflict avoidance*. "Is that okay?" she asked.

Kendra thought about it for a second. "Yes. But can you add, not giving feedback?"

Allie did, then added at the team's urging:

- Chronic lateness
- Over-promising
- Putting your ego before the project
- Shifting goals

Arash then said, "Sabotage."

"That's not a thing here?" Nadav said, uncertainly.

"No, but I've seen it … elsewhere at SOS. The GM believed in competition to promote excellence."

Allie nodded, and added *Internal competition* to the list.

"Is that always a bad thing?" Noam asked. "Rick seems to encourage it between GMs."

"It doesn't matter," Allie answered. "If we think it is bad for us, we don't want it." She looked at the team. "Do we want internal competition between team members?"

The group was all shaking their heads. She didn't see a sign of disagreement beyond Noam's mild curiosity. She took a moment to revel. It was working!

"Okay, this might be a good moment for us to change to creating our rules of engagement. We're going to take these feelings, and turn them into rules we agree to abide by. For example, the last one. How about, *We compete with the competition, not with each other?*"

She saw only smiles and nods to that. She wrote *Rules* on the board, and then: *We compete with the competition, not with each other.*

"So we've tried raising hands and just shouting out ideas. Is there a preference?

Kendra and Arash spoke at once, "Yes … raised hands," "Just say it." Then they laughed.

Arash jumped in. "I feel silly raising my hand."

Kendra replied, "But look at the second list. It's all you, me, and Noam. Jheryn actually talked when we raised our hands."

Allie had to admit Jheryn had talked more in this meeting than a month of meetings before this.

"It's true," Kendra laughed. "No one can suppress me! But Jheryn, why didn't you chime in on bad teams?"

Jheryn sighed. "I dunno, you guys all talk so fast, and on top of each other. It feels like a competition."

There was a moment of silence, then Noam spoke up. "What if we … I dunno … try listening more? And ask each other what we think? Pay attention to who is saying what? Advocate for each other?"

Allie tried wordsmithing it. "How about *Advocate for all voices?* And we try that for a week and see how it works?"

The team looked to Jheryn who shrugged, and Noam who nodded. "Worth a try."

Allie wrote on the whiteboard: *Advocate for all voices.* "We're going to make some more rules now. But just like we experimented with hands and no hands, we'll try another way to brainstorm our rules. Often introverts and marginalized groups feel uncomfortable just calling out ideas. We're going to try a silent technique.

"You all have Post-It notes in front of you. Look at the list on the wall, and think of rules you'd like to propose to the group. Write them down on the Post-Its. We can wordsmith them after."

Allie set a timer for eight minutes and stood silently while people wrote. She twitched with the desire to participate, but also knew she'd have plenty of chances to shape things as a facilitator. She had been a brainstorm facilitator dozens of times, but it felt strange to play this role for something … so important.

Allie noticed that people had slowed down a bit in their writing. She resisted the urge to cut time short, though. Her team looked thoughtful rather than bored.

Finally her timer went off.

Allie resumed, "Great, before we continue, I'd like you to consider these categories. They come from the Culture Map. We have to decide how we'll handle each category." She wrote each on the board, then explained each one.

Communicating

"This refers to low context and high context. Low context assumes everyone knows what you are talking about, high context states things explicitly."

Evaluating

"This is about feedback, but it's similar to the first. Do you like your negative feedback straight, no chaser, or do you prefer to have people break it to you gently?"

Persuading

"I know we all argue with facts here at SOS, but do we start with core principles, or lead with application and examples?"

Leading

"I know QuiltWorld has been hierarchical with George, but I don't want to assume anything. Do you prefer hierarchical leadership? Where the leader sets direction and finds the ideas? Or shall we pivot to a style where ideas can come from anywhere, and we set direction together?"

Deciding

"You can decide two ways: The team comes to a consensus, or everyone puts in their two cents, and then the leader makes the final call."

Trusting

"There are two ways to build trust. We can trust we have the right people in the room based on the fact they were hired, or we can build trust by spending time together and getting to know each other. I guess the real question is, do we want to make some time to get to know each other beyond our work roles?"

Disagreeing

"How confrontational do we want to be when we disagree?"

Scheduling

"When we say we're meeting at 10 a.m., does that mean 10:00, or does it mean 10:15?"

Arash, who came in last at 10:10, suddenly decided to examine his shoes. Allie smiled. "Okay, let's take another five minutes to add a few rules."

There was some furious scribbling. Allie thought adding a frame really helped people think of more potential issues. She had just finished the Culture Map on the plane back from Vegas, trying to figure out her crazy family of Mexico meets Chicago, and thought it might work. So far so good. Now for some Think/Pair/Share.

"Okay, time!" People looked up. "Please turn to a partner and share your ideas. Then combine them into the most important ones."

Another ten minutes passed, but the team was still talking animatedly. "Anyone need five more minutes?" Allie asked. Three-quarters of everyone's hands shot up. "Okay, keep going." She wasn't sure how long the Think/Pair/Share would take, and the "Do you want more time?" trick always worked well. Finally, she had to call the conversation to a close.

"Let's get some of the rules up on the board. Remember, we're working to listen, not interrupt, and advocate for each other."

There was silence for a second, and then Christie spoke. "Jheryn had a good idea, I think. He said he wanted to balance egalitarian and top-down decisions by having everyone discuss decisions, but if we can't come to an agreement, we'd like you to decide so we can move forward."

Jheryn then chimed in softly, blushing. "To save time so we don't argue too long."

Allie wrote it on the board. *Discuss, debate, decide. GM tiebreaks.* "Does anyone have a counterproposal?" she asked.

Kendra spoke up, "We wrote the same thing! Except we wrote, after thirty minutes of a stalemate, the discipline expert decides. That means I decide design stuff, Yosi decides engineering stuff, and you decide business stuff." Nadav, Kendra's discussion partner, nodded.

"I like that better, honestly," Christie said.

"Me, too." Noam chimed in.

Allie erased *GM* and replaced it with *Lead*. She added *after thirty minutes* to the end. It was awkwardly phrased, but made the point.

She paused. "I do need to hold the final decision. It's my job to care for the business, and everything we do here is for the business. But I do promise to listen to you as experts." The team digested that.

"What if we finish with, GM overrules only if dangerous for business?" Nadav floated the new idea. His team nodded.

"Works for me," Noam added.

"Are we good?" asked Allie. There were nods all around. "Okay, more rules?"

They continued to offer up rules and modifications, from tactical to inspirational. Allie wrote on the board:

- Trust good intent: Clarify before you criticize.
- Meetings start within five minutes of the agreed-on time no matter what.
- Make time to be people together—daily coffee klatch.
- Be respectful in delivering what you promised and when holding others accountable.
- Work is work: Disagreements and critique are not personal. Don't make it or take it so.
- Argue, decide, commit.

Then there was a knock on the conference room door.

Allie opened it, and was shocked to see Yosi holding a pile of pizza boxes. Seeing Allie's face he shrugged. "I was closest to the door when they came."

"You're back!" Allie said, overjoyed.

"It's okay. I'll tell you more later."

The team jumped up and had the boxes out of his hands before he could even put them on the table. Allie then walked Yosi though the recent decisions, leaving him reading the board as she joined her team chowing down. She thought that the team was talking more, laughing and joking more easily with each other. As she ate, Yosi sidled up to her.

"You know, I've been thinking," he said, after removing a bit of cheese from his scruffy beard with a paper napkin. "This has been really great. I don't want to set and forget though."

Allie gave him a puzzled look, her own mouth full of pizza.

"You know, with OKRs? You can't just set them, you have to check them every week. I'm thinking we should add a norm check to our weekly retros."

"Funny, I was thinking the same thing! We need a cadence of commitment to each other. And we can grade them, too, like we do OKRs, at the end of quarter."

Yosi nodded thoughtfully. "That should work."

CHRISTIE'S BIG IDEA

THE MEETING TO DISCUSS CHRISTIE'S VISION WAS AT TWO P.M. in Sonic. It had been two months since Christie's Advent Calendar had launched, and Allie was itching to launch the next big thing. But she trusted Christie too much to push her.

Christie had claimed the small conference room as her war room and covered the glass front with paper. The sign on the door said "Top Secret" and had a whimsical drawing of an angry hedgehog shaking a finger at the viewer. *Don't mess with Sonic.*

Allie walked in. Inside, every bit of wall was covered with drawings, writing, and photos. There were pictures of players, notes from playtesting, endless flowcharts, and diagrams. There were concept sketches, printed out and thus losing a bit of their vivid colors. The whiteboard was a mass of circles, boxes, arrows, and utterly incomprehensible handwriting. It certainly looked impressive.

But bad ideas could come in shiny packages. Allie stayed cautiously optimistic but skeptical. The perfect emotional state for a general manager, she felt. Ready to be dazzled or for everything to go to hell.

Christie came dashing in, her laptop open in her arms, cradled like a baby. Emma, one of the artists, followed her. Emma was a quiet Chinese woman, a recent graduate of the art school down the street. She rarely spoke, but if it was shyness about her English or just shyness, Allie didn't know. Then she thought about Carlton.

"Hey, did you invite Carlton?"

"I'm sure ..." Christie said, not sounding sure.

"I'll grab him. He should start getting caught up."

Allie walked over to the art team and tapped Carlton on the arm. He looked up from his laptop and blinked at her.

"If you are free, we're going to look at a new event Christie's been working on with Emma ..."

"Of course!" he said brightly.

When they returned to the room, Christie had her laptop connected to the projector and was ready for the pitch. They sat down and Emma dimmed the lights.

The door opened and Jheryn popped in. He was the tech advisor, there to make sure all concepts were buildable. "Sorry I'm late," he mumbled, and pulled up a chair.

Christie started. "After the Advent calendar bold beat, we realized there was an untapped desire for freeform creation." She showed slides of the some of the landscapes created on the Advent canvases. "It was our most successful bold beat so far, by an order of magnitude." She showed a chart; Advent had outperformed the strongest release half again. "And the bulk of that growth was driven by freeform creative play."

"Which led us to CountyFair. This is not an event. This will be an expansion."

Allie sat up. Events were important, but expansions ... were rare. It was almost like creating a new game. They took longer to make, and they had about the same chances of being successful as a new game. Though considering how successful QuiltWorld had been, it made sense. Like making a sequel to a hit movie. She became more excited and more anxious all at once.

"CountyFair has two parts. You have your property, where you have your house and workshop, and you have the fair itself." She showed an aerial view of a patchwork countryside, then clicked to show a small house and a big wooden barn. "We've got some ideas about events around the house later, but for now, it's all about the workshop." She went to the next slide. It showed the interior of the barn, filled with bookshelves, almost all empty, and bins. "You start with a limited amount of tiles and thread. We'll also provide some direction, probably in a play-tutorial." These were gamified tutorials, in which you tried to follow instructions as closely as possible to get maximum stars. "We'll use the play-tutorial to introduce another concept ... sending the work to the fair."

At this, Christie smiled broadly, full of glee to share this apparently brilliant creation. But she waited, savoring. "But before we move to that, I'll point out all this empty space.... Right now we think," she nodded to Emma, "it will act in two ways. Obviously players will want to shop for material. But also Emma was researching crafting stores, and ... you tell them, Emma!"

Emma cleared her throat and took a small sip of water. She spoke slowly and too softly. "I have researched people enjoy to buy materials because they like how pretty they are. Many people only use a small percentage of the materials. If we have many pretty things and much storage, we can appeal to collectors."

This was brilliant. Completionists can't resist getting all of a certain item. Empty shelves would drive them crazy. Some people preferred shopping anyway, the dream of making being more appealing than making. It was likePokémon; some collected and some battled. Because QuiltWorld always shipped just enough materials for whatever you were making in your kit, this was a world they hadn't explored.

"What's the model?" Allie asked. "Per item, or unlocked materials, more like Minecraft?"

"I'd like to test that. We've got a paper prototype test coming up next Friday. But please, can you hold questions? I'd like to show you the whole thing first."

"Oh, of course!" Allie reached for her notebook and pulled out a pen.

"So we've got collecting and making. We think you can also buy more instructions. Emma's research showed there is also a huge market for craft books that we theorize would translate to a market for instruction manuals, maybe crowdsourced. We could also use it to fuel community participation."

Emma smiled proudly.

"Okay, I mentioned sending it to the fair!" Christie continued. "When you are happy with your creation," she showed a slide of a hobbyhorse appearing to be made of calico scraps, "you click submit. For now, we think it'll just go to a tent," she showed an image of a tent full of toys made of fabric, "but we could do something more social, like voting. If people campaign, the virals could be incredible."

Allie could see it: a real reason to reach out to your social network. Better than begging for coins to buy the latest release, or lives so you could keep playing. She wrote herself a note to ask about energy management in the economy. She had never felt good about having to pay for more playtime or having to beg friends for it. It never felt integrated into the play.

"We already know one of the things that motivates play is pride in creation. So formally displaying work should be highly motivating. We're bouncing around ideas for blue ribbons as well. We think that could be a huge event, great for reacquisition."

She clicked back to another aerial view, this time of the fair. "We think some people may just like looking around, exploring the creations, like they do with YouTubes of Minecraft builds. We may be able to get longer session times. We're going to try out putting in a following mechanism, to encourage stranger play."

Stranger play was a holy grail. The longer players engaged in the game, the more likely they were to see their more dilettante friends drop out. To keep them engaged, they needed a safe way to play with people they didn't know. A following relationship might be the trick to build connections. Players could follow each other's work, ask for gifts, vote for each other. Over time it might create the kind of social bonds that kept players playing. World of Warcraft was notorious for having players who only logged on to socialize and never played anymore.

There were a lot of untested hypotheses in this expansion, but they were all built on hard-earned knowledge. Christie's design was packed with mechanics that would engage players over time. She'd pulled on both SOS knowledge and the best practices in the industry. This was a very calculated bet, but it was also a go big or go home bet. Allie was tingling with excitement now.

"How long do you think it will take? And what size team?"

Christie flicked on the lights, and Jheryn turned to Allie.

"Here's the thing. The whole thing will take at least nine, twelve months as scoped. That's with two pods of engineers, and probably most of the art team."

Allie shuddered.

"But I think we can break it up into releases, so we can start to get some numbers early."

Allie turned to Christie and she nodded. "I wanted you to see it as the final vision, of course. But if we release the workshop first, and the fair second … in fact, if we limit it to quilts in the first release, we might be able to have the first release out in under two months."

"Wait, people making quilts in QuiltWorld?" Allie laughed. "Imagine!"

Carlton cleared his throat. Everyone looked at him. He had a slight pinkness around his throat, like a flush. "I've got a few questions."

"Sure."

"Are you sure this is the right direction?"

"What do you mean?" asked Christie.

"Letting people make whatever they want?"

Christie bobbled her head, puzzled.

"If you let people combine things any way they want, make anything they want, do you know how ugly that will be? It'll be like a MySpace page!" His fair skin was becoming red and blotchy. Allie realized he was upset. "This project is a mess. QuiltWorld is where you make beautiful things! We design ways anyone can be an artist! Even when they have no talent, like most people. And now you're going to let people make ugly things?"

Christie clicked back to the first few slides, puzzled.

"We've covered the numbers … free-crafting looks to be a massive engagement driver. The numbers are telling."

"I don't care about numbers, this is an artistic decision."

Allie froze. What the … He was insane. He was against the very idea that would take QuiltWorld to the next level. And why? Because some players might make ugly things? Really? And then she imagined Yosi on her shoulder, whispering in her ear, "Give feedback right away …"

She looked straight into Carlton's too-blue eyes. "No, it's really not. We make decisions based on customer data in this studio, not based on individual opinion. We make our players happy, even if their taste isn't the same as ours." She swallowed, and licked her lips. "You're new here. Tell you what, let's grab lunch and I can fill you in on the background." Without waiting for a response, she turned back to Christie. "This is amazing work. All of you. After the first round of testing, if all goes well, let's prep for product council. We've got something here."

From the corner of her eye, she could tell Carlton was completely red now. She looked down at her notes, then turned back toward Christie. "So, tell me how energy works in the economy?"

* * *

Allie considered how to handle Carlton's weird outburst. She agreed with Yosi's model: fast, clear, and make sure the person understands there are consequences. It was hard. But doing the hard thing was the job description.

She walked up to Carlton's desk a little before noon. "Ready to grab some lunch?" she asked. She hoped he'd calmed down a bit. He was no longer pink, anyway.

"Sure." He pushed away from his desk aggressively.

She suggested Pazzo. They could get sandwiches and eat upstairs where it was quiet.

Allie got a chicken Caesar and Carlton got a meatball sub. This meant they had to sit downstairs, at least until his number was called. Hot food took a little longer.

They picked a table about halfway from the counter and sat down. Allie decided to wait to touch her salad until Carlton was served. She considered how to broach the meeting when Carlton exploded.

"You really disrespected me in that meeting! Emma works for me, and Christie is a peer. It's my domain, the look and feel of the game. I'm not sure

I can do my job if I can't make key calls that affect the final product. It goes on my portfolio, you know."

Jaw. Floor. Allie did not see *any* of that coming. "Carlton, let me ..."

"I mean, what is that? User-generated content? When has that worked well? Heard of MySpace?"

Now she stared at him, wondering what was going through his head. "Heard of Minecraft?"

"Oh, sure, a kids' game."

"Three hundred sixty-seven million last year. And some truly amazing projects. There is a city in Sweden that's using it for collaborative city planning."

Carlton paused and stared. Allie had finally shut him up. She decided to start with hard facts and wrap with inspiration. "Look, Carlton, I'm not sure what kind of relationship you had in the past with your GM, or what was expected of you. And I'm sorry we didn't get this out in the interview process. But it's important you understand where you work and our philosophy. SOS is a highly profitable, metrics-driven company that succeeds by making players happy. We hope to go IPO in the near future, and we want that to be a life-changing event for all employees. I don't know if you looked at your package closely, but if you vest fully, it will be for you also.

"While we respect the creative process, we also believe that constraints are part of great design. We do not express our individual vision in games. We use research and logic to make great games that touch our players' hearts and engage their minds. And in return, they pay us.

"We don't set out to make art. Art might happen, but our goal is to make our players happy. And if players are happy making ugly worlds with Tinkertoys, that's what we'll give them.

"I think they'd rather make beautiful things. The small percentage of players who do freecrafting do make wondrous creations. I'm happy to send you some. You need to have more faith in our players, and more faith in our game designers who make it possible. But most of all, as an executive at SOS, you need to know the end game. If you can't combine art and commerce, this may not be the place for you."

And as if to punctuate her comment, she stabbed her salad with a plastic fork and took a bite. As she chewed slowly, she stared at him and waited for him to absorb her speech. He was red again.

She swallowed her bite. "Oh, and your portfolio is not my problem. The game revenue is. But you are welcome to do great things with both."

Carlton's order number was called out. He rose stiffly and walked slowly to get his food.

Allie berated herself. That last bit was too much. This wasn't feedback anymore. She was just angry. She was trying to save a game she loved, and he just cared about looking good. Then she remembered what Yosi said about not knowing another person's intent. She should try to better understand what was motivating him. If only she'd done that in the interview. She pulled out her notebook and made a little note on her hiring page: "Find out interviewee motivation." She could ask Derek for question ideas for that later.

Carlton came back slowly as well, but he was back to a pale pink. "I think we might be talking past each other. Let's take a moment and try to figure out what our goals are here," he said.

Allie was surprised. Did he read her mind? "I'd like that. I'd love to hear more about what your goals are for taking this job in the QuiltWorld studio."

"I play the game," he said. "I love the game. I'd come home after a long day, and then I'd just pour myself a glass of wine and play. It was so relaxing, not too much thinking. I think that's part of what I was resisting in this change. But also the things I'd make were so lovely. And then, I started thinking of new things I could make, and thought how wonderful it would be to create them for others to assemble. It could be magical."

Allie frowned a bit. Did he not understand how game process worked? "Carlton, usually at SOS, the art director oversees the artwork for the game, but the actual modules are designed by the game designer, or sometimes if it's a smaller quest, a PM." And then she realized she was telling someone who really loved QuiltWorld, loved her game, she'd hired him to be an order taker.

"But the recruiter, she was telling me how collaborative you work, how ideas can come from anywhere."

Recruiters. They'll tell you anything, then when you arrive, you've got a signing bonus you don't want to give back and a bad surprise ahead of you. Then again, what he was describing was not unreasonable, just not how George had run things. She no longer needed to run things like George did.

Carlton was no longer pink. He just looked sad. And he hadn't touched his sandwich.

"Carlton, I'll be honest. I have only run this studio for a few months, even though I've been part of it for much longer. If you can familiarize yourself with how we develop and run games, and your ideas are expanding on the SOS framework, and not overturning it, I don't see why ideas should only come from a few people. In fact, that would be stupid of me. It's not like great ideas are so common I can just pick them up off the ground on my way in to work."

Carlton was still.

"Can we focus on getting you up to speed first? I'd like you to familiarize yourself with QuiltWorld, and we can look at revising the work flow to cast a wider net for new quests. But I want to make this clear: I do own final call on strategy for the game. That means all aspects of it, from design to architecture. I look to you for your expertise, but I'll always do what's best for the game. Are you going to be okay with this?"

Carlton put his head down, apparently staring at the meatballs covered with coagulating cheese. He looked back up. "I need to try it out. It's different, and it's not what I expected, but it's a different place." He paused, thoughtfully. "I think it's a special place."

That it is, Allie thought to herself. *Maybe together we can make it even more so.*

IT'S NOT COFFEE

ALLIE WAS DASHING DOWN THE STAIRS WHEN HER HEART started pounding. Then her chest tightened, and she found it hard to breathe. She sat down, suddenly dizzy. She could hear her heart in her ears, pounding fast. What was going on? She found herself gasping for air.

She felt a hand on her shoulder. "Hey, are you okay?" It was no one she knew.

"No. I don't know what's going on ..." Her chest was so tight. "It feels like a heart attack." But what did she know? She'd never had a heart attack. But she'd never felt like this, either. The person ran off, then was back a moment later. He handed her a glass of water.

"Try to take a sip."

She took a small sip, and the water tasted cool and sweet.

He took the glass from her hand. "Now can you breathe more slowly? I think you're panicking. See if you can slow your breath."

Allie had not done any yoga for years, but she tried to remember how to settle into her breath. It began to slow.

"Now drink some more water." He handed her a cup. She took another sip, the water opening up the tightness in her throat. "Help is on the way."

"What? I feel better already."

"No way. You're going to the hospital."

Derek picked her up three hours later. She was sitting on an uncomfortable plastic chair with her jacket in her lap. He dashed over to her as soon as he saw her, dodging nurses and gurneys. She stood to receive his embrace.

"What happened?"

"Look, we can go. I've already signed everything. I'm fine."

Derek glared at her.

"No, really. I'm fine. It's embarrassing."

He looked puzzled, but nodded. "Okay. The car is parked downstairs."

In the elevator he started to ask her what had occurred, but she silenced him with a look. When they got in the car, she felt private enough to admit what had gone down.

"It was a panic attack."

Derek took his hand off the key without starting the car and turned to her. "What? You're not afraid of anything! We snorkel with sharks! You've given talks in front of the entire company!"

"It's ... okay, well. I got heart palpitations, then that scared me, then I hyperventilated, and it sent everything haywire."

"But heart palpitations! That's serious, right?"

"The doctor asked me how much coffee I drink. I said, eight, ten cups a day. She said, 'Don't do that.'"

Derek stared at her. Then he started to laugh. Allie was briefly angry, then relieved, and she started laughing, too. "I did this to myself!"

Derek's laugh faded. "You have been running too hard. It could have been more serious. It still might. You need to cut out coffee."

"How about cut back?"

"How about cut back work? You sleep four hours a night. No wonder you are living on coffee. Soon it'll be an ulcer."

"You get ulcers from a bacteria."

"Which survives in the stomach because of stress!"

"Is that true?"

"Yes. You'd know it if you read more than industry news." He grimaced. "This is not sustainable. You have to find a better way."

"I was a little dehydrated also. I can drink more water."

"No, Allie, no. You have to find a way to take care of *you*, and take care of *us*. You can't sacrifice everything for SOS." He started the car.

"It's just for a little while."

"You know that's a lie. You know I know that's a lie. Killing yourself is the SOS lifestyle. You have to figure out how to do the job without putting yourself in the hospital. Literally." They pulled up to a red light. He turned to her. "Do you know how scared I was?" The light changed, and he pulled forward. "Also, I miss you," he said without looking at her. "I want my wife back."

Allie stared at the road. She didn't know what to do. She was so close to getting QuiltWorld where she wanted it. She just wasn't scaling well. She had to figure out what she could change.

Lying on the gurney had been horrible. They had oxygen on her and an IV, and she felt like she was on a crappy procedural cop show. She'd felt helpless and out of control. Then she started wondering if the ambulance could be made into a game. There was a time element and a mystery. Mysteries and secrets are always good for game engagement.

Then she'd had to wait forever for the doctor, and boredom had released all the tension in her body. She was sketching out a core loop for her ambulance game when the doctor finally came to talk to her. And then it was all her own dumb fault. Oh, God, what would she say when she was back in the office. Panic attack? Caffeine abuse? It all sounded so lame. And weak.

Derek was waiting for a reply, she thought. He seemed … extra alert. Or maybe he was just worrying. He was good at that. What would this trip to the emergency room cost? Would Patricia find out what it was? Would exhaustion sound good? Or weak? Maybe she could look up things on WebMD and lie. Would Patricia see the diagnosis via … HR stuff?

Where was she working that her diagnosis mattered? All that should matter was if she did her job. Which she didn't that day. But every other day, she did. Her head just kept spinning in circles. "Can I put on some music?"

Derek paused. "I think we should talk about this a bit more."

"Not while you're driving." She turned on the music. He acquiesced, visibly reluctantly.

Driving on the 101 was the most dangerous thing they did all day. There was an accident every day. But Derek was scared of flying. Every time he did it, he had to take a tranquilizer. Yet it was much safer than this drive. People didn't understand the odds. This panic attack—how she hated that term—was unusual, but not dangerous. It was certainly easily fixed, though she knew there would be ugly headaches along the way. But Derek wasn't going to see it. She didn't suppose having one every day until he got used to it was going to fix anything.

They walked in the apartment silently. It wasn't until the door was closed and she was on the couch that he jumped back in. "I want you to quit."

"What?"

"This is a wake-up call! This job is no good!"

"I've only been been GM for … not even six months!"

"You've been at SOS for two years. It's not being GM; it's this toxic company."

"Look, I know SOS is a problem, but QuiltWorld is a good game, and I've got some good people now...."

"Then they should leave, too. Get out of the house."

He'd hoped she'd laugh, she thought. *Nope.* "Look, I'm where I want to be. I don't have to stay forever, just long enough to have a track record."

"Is this Stockholm syndrome? What is wrong with you? Two years becomes three, then four? When are we going to start a family?"

"Oh, don't you dare. There is plenty of time for that. I'm not even thirty."

"I don't want to be an old man trying to keep up with my kids."

"Well, tough. If you make me choose between my career and having kids, you aren't going to like the answer."

"I ... I didn't mean it to be an ultimatum." He ran a hand through his shaggy hair. He needed a haircut. "I don't want to be an SOS widow. Widower."

"It really won't be like this forever. When the team is fully hired, it will quiet down."

"Until the next crisis." He paused. "When? When will you be home for dinner every night? When will we be able to go away for the weekend? When do I get to be married?"

"Soon. I swear soon."

Derek shook his head and stood. "I'll go make you some tea." He didn't believe her. Hell, she didn't believe her. Dinner *every* night?

NUMBERS CLIMBING, BUT...

ANOTHER MONDAY, ANOTHER NUMBERS MEETING. SO FAR, THEIR key health metrics—retention, revenue, acquisition—were slightly less than last year. Slightly was better than drop but not what she wanted to take to Rick. Allie cupped her hands around her mint tea, dreaming of coffee and miracles. Arash was going over the projected numbers for CountyFair and Advent calendar.

"I don't know why we are looking at CountyFair. It won't be close to shippable until February."

"January," Allie corrected. "It will go live in January."

Noam snorted. Jheryn looked thoughtful and scribbled on his notepad. Allie spotted it, and asked, "Do you have an idea?"

Jheryn hesitated, but he had everyone's attention. "If we put Nadav's team on the freecrafting on Advent calendar to make sure the code is modular, we can reuse it for CountyFair."

"It will make everything launch later," Noam replied flatly. Allie couldn't tell if he was hopeful or dismissive.

"How much later?" Arash spoke up.

"A week. Maybe two."

"That's cutting it kind of close." Allie sighed.

Christie raised her hand briefly, then put it down and spoke. "What if we cut scope? We were thinking a full month of Advent calendar, but it is traditionally the three weeks up to Christmas."

Carlton nodded. "We can adapt it for the other holidays. At least it's not Thanksgivukkah this year. If we made the holidays have the same functionality but different themes, that should reduce the work for engineering."

Arash looked at the numbers projected on the walls and sighed. "Are you sure we don't want to goose these? A daily slot machine, or … ?"

Kendra glared at Arash. "Do you?"

"Not really," he admitted. "But we have no historical data on this kind of bold beat. I don't have any sense if it's going to give us the numbers we need to hit our objectives."

Christie shook her head. "That would be like attaching a bobble head to the front of a Rolls Royce. Look, I've designed it to be viral but fun *and* make money. Please trust me."

"I've been playing it nonstop," Lawrence spoke up. "And it's magical. Even the bugs can't interfere with how fun it is. I say we don't ruin it for a couple more bucks."

Arash nodded. "I have a good feeling about it. I just wish I had more than a good feeling."

Noam spoke up. "I like it."

"And Noam hates everything!" Kendra teased.

Despite the mint tea, Allie felt her heart pounding. If Advent calendar went badly, she might not even be here to see CountyFair launch. She looked around the table. The team was talking happily about their favorite days in the calendar, about how fun the surprises were. She either trusted them, or she didn't.

"Okay, folks. Let's bet it all on red. Launch Advent calendar as designed, just pull back scope so we can double down on CountyFair. Let's show SOS what the future of QuiltWorld looks like."

"Yes!" yelled Jheryn, and the room erupted into laughter.

ROB IS BACK

ALLIE'S PHONE VIBRATED.
   "Rob: Emergency coffee"
   She picked it up and texted back.
   "Now?"
   "That's why I texted 'emergency.'"
   "Downstairs?"
   "Pazzo."

So it was a personal emergency rather than a caffeine emergency. She finished her database query and set it to run, then headed out.

   Rob was already in line at Pazzo. Allie joined him, cutting the quickly lengthening line for sandwiches. It was almost noon, so that was not surprising. He nodded as she stepped next to him, and they stood in a companionable silence for a few moments as the line inched forward. Rob ordered two decaf lattes and then moved to the other end of the counter.

   "So?" Allie prompted.
   "Not yet."
   They waited.
   "How is Christie working out?" Rob finally asked.
   "Pretty great, actually. I think we'll do a company-wide playtest next week of Advent calendar."
   "Can't wait to try it." His voice was monotone, automatic. They got their lattes. "Let's go upstairs."

Pazzo had a mezzanine that filled up last, after the first-floor tables filled up. Many people didn't even know it existed. It was a decent place to get privacy, until 12:30 or so when the lunch crowd arrived in force. And on a sunny day like today, people might choose the sidewalk seating instead. In San Francisco, a sunny November day could be positively balmy.

They grabbed seats in the far end of the mezzanine. There was only one other person up there, talking on the phone in Spanish.

Rob face-planted, narrowly missing his coffee. He tapped his forehead on the table, slowly and rhythmically.

"Cut that out. You'll spill the coffees."

Rob lifted his head and then threw it back with a long sigh.

"What is wrong with you?" Allie was alarmed. Rob was not prone to ridiculously dramatic gestures.

"I have to quit."

"What?"

"I have to quit! I have to. I just, I don't even know what to do."

"What is it?"

"Davis. I don't know why I thought I could work with him. I triaged the worst bugs, and it's not freezing and crashing anymore. Then I was working on seeing if we could move to Yosi's new platform. And he pulled me off to work on a brilliant idea he came up with that he's sure will double virals. And it's complete bull. He went to a growth hacker meetup the other night and heard about an exploit in the address book import for G+, and now he wants to drop everything and use it to spam our players' friend network before it's patched."

Allie leaned back. "That's old-school ugly."

Rob leaned on the table and ran his hand over his head. "It'll be patched before we get anything from it, other than bad will from players. And Google will be pissed off. They don't take violations of the TOS lightly. But Davis is just scrambling for something."

Allie leaned forward and cupped her hands around her latte. "So you'll tell him no, right?"

"He'll fire me."

"He can't. Not for that. Not for refusing to violate the contract."

"I've only been CTO for four months. I want it for my résumé. I don't want to take another dev role. I've been waiting for this chance. Sure, I like to code, but this is so much more fulfilling."

"Oh, you like firing, do you?" Allie teased.

"Actually, in a weird way, I kind of do. I don't like to fire someone, but when there is a bad fit, and everyone knows it's a bad fit, and you finally fire them, then everything gets better. When I fired Joe, the team started having fun again. He complained all the time and didn't get his cards done. Mike was always picking up his work. So when I fired him, it was like we'd all been holding our breath, and we could start breathing again."

"Especially Mike."

"Especially Mike." Rob now smiled, and took a sip of his coffee. "He's doing great now. More work, better work, and he's definitely more pleasant to be around. It's just when I code, I can make one thing better. But as CTO, I can architect a place where great things can happen. I like doing that. Of course, it's easier when my GM isn't a madman."

Rob sounded like Yosi just then. The work was the people, not the code. And here were the rewards. "I don't want to step backwards."

"Are you really going to tell me you're going to do something you find unethical because you want to keep your promotion? You? Rob, you can't even tip less than twenty percent. You stuff in extra money every time we split the check, in case someone shorted the bill."

"No. I can't do it." He put his hands flat on the table, as though seeking stability.

"Rob. There is another choice. I mean if you really are planning on quitting."

"What?"

"Come back. Yosi is not going to stay with us. Every candidate sucks. Be our CTO."

"I can't do that."

"That's just your pride. QuiltWorld is a higher priority than Bagboy."

"Will Rick really want two green execs on his cash cow?"

"Hey, we won't know unless we ask. Plus, Yosi is with us for at least another month to mentor you. He's a great mentor. Please. I need someone I can trust."

"I … don't know."

"Can you at least talk to Yosi about the idea? He's known Rick forever. He can help feel it out."

Rob nodded. They wandered over to the trash cans to recycle their cups and headed back. It wasn't until Allie entered the building she realized that now she didn't just have to succeed for her own dream, she would have to succeed for Rob's.

No pressure.

END OF QUARTER

THE END OF QUARTER NUMBERS REVIEW WAS ALMOST TWO weeks exactly before the end of the quarter. Allie would have loved to have been one of the last teams to be reviewed, but Rick was not going to go that way. He always hit the big earners first so he could figure out how to spin the story to investors and press.

She walked into the conference room fifteen minutes early, and Arash was already there. He looked up from his computer when she walked in. "Katelyn is reprinting the handouts."

"At this late stage?"

"She got really great numbers this morning. And we've got a backup in case we need to present the original deck." He waved at an innocuous gray cardboard box on the table against the wall.

"Okay." Allie hated last-minute prep, but today they needed every minute of good data.

Yosi and Christie walked in, chatting.

"You decided to come?" Allie smiled.

Christie replied, "You made your case. If Rick needs to be shown the big picture, I'm your woman."

George had always done these reviews with just Pete and her. Allie had followed his lead last quarter, but this time she decided to present ideas as more of a team. Or at least a republic, with representatives from the key groups.

Lawrence came in then, carrying a gray box full of printouts. "Katelyn asked me if I'd drop these by."

"Great," Allie smiled. "Take a seat." When she'd asked Lawrence to join, he'd demurred. He said surely there were better people to be at the meeting. But Katelyn had had Allie's back, and now community and customer service had a seat at the table.

Lawrence rolled his eyes at her, but took a seat. He flipped through the printout in front of him and smiled.

Rob then shyly popped his head in. "Rick suggested I sit in, since I'll be joining next quarter." Yosi waved him in vigorously, and Rob took a seat next to his new mentor.

Rick came in then, chatting with another GM whom he shooed off as he took a seat. The GM closed the door behind himself, and Rick turned to Allie expectantly. Arash dimmed the lights at the front of the room by the projector.

Allie spoke carefully and clearly, her voice low and resonant. After years of working with noisy gamers, she knew how to make herself heard. "Rick, we're here to share what we believe is the future of QuiltWorld. We've hit a vein of player happiness, and we're looking for permission to tap it. Arash will start with the numbers...."

Arash took Rick through the hockey-stick-shaped graph. The numbers rolled along, mostly flat, and then flew upwards in the last ten days like a flock of startled birds. Not long enough to be a real trend, but big enough to make a person imagine it could be.

Christie then walked Rick through the new strategy, illustrated with sketches and video. And Lawrence stepped up to explain the customer-service calls were tilting positive and message-board activity was up. They didn't have a lot of data, so they had to make what positive data they had sing. Yosi lent his gravitas with nods and the occasional "Exactly."

Rick asked many sharp questions and Allie answered them honestly. Finally, Rick glanced up at the clock. "Okay, keep going."

Allie felt her heart leap up. They'd done it!

"We'll talk again soon." He walked out the door. They'd done it ... for now. Time for the really important meeting.

After lunch, her direct reports were gathered together in Joust, the biggest conference room. Allie stood. "Okay, folks! We've graded our metrics. Now it's time to grade ourselves."

A couple of folks looked apprehensive.

"These aren't performance reviews. We're just going to take a little time to evaluate how we are doing as a team. Remember the norms we set beginning of quarter?"

"Nope," said Rob.

"Hush up, noob," Noam joked. Rob grinned back.

"Luckily for all of you, the new and the absent-minded, they are up on the wall."

"I made a poster," Kendra confided to Christie.

Sure enough, there they were:

- Trust good intent: Clarify before you criticize.
- Meetings start within five minutes of the agreed-on time no matter what.
- Make time to be people together—daily coffee klatch.
- Be respectful in delivering what you promised and when holding others accountable.
- Work is work: Disagreements and critique are not personal. Don't make it or take it so.
- Argue, decide, commit.

And more … The posters had been up in all the conference rooms for a month. Allie wondered if anyone noticed them. She hadn't.

"Now I'd like everyone to type in the URL I've written on the whiteboard, and rate each of our norms 1 to 5. 1 is 'We suck' and 5 is 'We live this norm' and the rest are 'Needs work,' 'Okay,' and 'Almost there.'" She wrote these on the board. Her team called up the survey, and the room grew silent as people filled in their responses. Allie had struggled about how to get this right. If they'd just put it all on the board, social pressure might have influenced opinions. If she had sent it out ahead of time, she knew half the folks wouldn't have bothered to fill it out.

Ten minutes later, she realized she couldn't tell who was done and who wasn't. "Anyone need more time?"

Two hands went up. The others were working or fiddling around, who knew. A couple of minutes later, Allie got everyone's attention by turning on the projector. There were the results. The room silently digested their own critique. "I like the sound of a daily coffee klatch." Rob broke the silence. The ratings on "Make time to be people together" were skewed from 1 to 5. "So what happened to that?"

"We tried to do it at three, but not everyone came," Kendra said.

"But Monday estaff is at three," Allie admitted.

"So is the biweekly cross-team design critique," added Carlton.

"I thought it was great," said Noam. "Do we really need every single person to be there every single day for it to work?"

"I'd like it to," Christie said. "Got me off my computer midafternoon."

"I want to keep it as is," Lawrence added. "It's nice to know it's there, and it's not enforced fun. And I wouldn't have ever learned Jheryn is a bowler, otherwise."

Jheryn looked at his feet. "I have my own shoes," he admitted.

Allie waited for the laughter to subside. "Okay, I motion we keep things as is for another quarter, and hold our next offsite at a bowling alley."

The motion carried unanimously.

Rob was smart to pick a fairly safe one to start with, Allie thought. Time to dive a little deeper. "Tell me more about why we aren't living up to 'Argue, decide, commit,'" she said.

The team spent a lively afternoon working through their issues. At the end of the meeting, Allie took them all out to the neighboring Thai restaurant for an impromptu celebration.

Rob leaned over to her, and said softly, "You're getting good at this boss business."

"Starting to," she said. *Starting to learn a great team bosses itself*, she thought.

EVERYTHING ALWAYS CHANGES

ALLIE SWUNG BY CHRISTIE'S DESK. SHE WAS SO EXCITED BY THE success of the CountyFair expansion, she felt like skipping. It was beautiful and fun and was growing acquisitions and converting beautifully. It was everything at once! There was a perfection when you put something good into the world, and people wanted to give you money for it. Something magical when you knew you didn't trick, cheat, or cut corners, and then an audience appeared. She wanted to hug herself. *She* had made this happen. She had been at the crux of making good work occur. This was what she had dreamed of.

"Ready for our one-on-one? I've got numbers to share," she sang out.

Christie gave her a tight smile. "Yes, let's talk."

"Conference room, or … ?"

"It's gorgeous out," Christie replied. "Let's take advantage of that."

"True. More rain forecasted later."

They stepped out, blinking in the sun.

"Mind if we walk?" Christie asked.

"Not at all," Allie replied. "How about the canal?"

"Oh, yes. I like to look for herons." They walked past Adobe toward the pathway the new condos had built along the canal. The canal was lined with houseboats. Christie wondered aloud if it was more affordable than San Francisco rent.

"So it's terrific!" Allie burst out. "New users are up! Finally! We're seeing virals like we haven't in six months! And NPS is pushing eight! We're going to blow past our OKRs! We did it!"

"That's wonderful," Christie replied.

"Hey, are you okay? You don't seem as excited as I thought you'd be."

"I have to tell you something. It's making me uncomfortable."

"So spit it?"

"I'm leaving QuiltWorld."

"What?"

"I didn't tell you when I joined that I was working on something else, and I feel bad about that. I just didn't know you yet. But when I came back, I had an agreement with Rick. I wanted to do this expansion, but I also agreed to kick-start a new game. So CountyFair is live. And it's time for me to go work on something new. It was the deal I made. I'm sorry."

Allie was gobsmacked. She had thought she had finally assembled a team that worked. But now she'd have to start over again with her game designer. "So what's the new thing?"

"It's actually a pitch I put in over year ago. It's called Twilight Carnival."

"Like the book?"

"Yes! Bizdev finally got the rights squared away, and we're doing it."

"I love that book," Allie replied.

"Me, too," Christie said. They walked along the sidewalk quietly.

"That's kind of amazing," Allie finally said.

"So you understand?"

"I think I have no choice. You came, you made something great, and now you're going to make something else that's probably even greater. I don't think I can argue with that."

Christie grabbed her and hugged her. Allie laughed. "I was really worried about telling you! I was afraid you'd hate me. I mean, everyone here ..."

"Yeah, hard to know who to trust. But I get it; I really do. This sounds like a once- in-a-lifetime chance to make a game that could be really amazing. If you were asking my advice, I'd tell you to do it."

"Thank you," Christie said. "I'll just be upstairs."

Allie paused and thought of something. "I'd like you to replace yourself, though." It was time for her to act like a GM and not a doormat. She couldn't let people swan in and out of her studio.

"That's fair. But we're supposed to start in a month."

"That's my deal. You make sure your successor kicks ass, or I hate you forever."

Christie grinned. "I'm sure we'll figure it out. I couldn't chance such a deadly fate."

Allie paused, and looked at her feet. "And I'd really like it if you'd coach me to interview game designers. I don't have a clue what makes a good game designer, I realize. I mean, it's like porn."

"Porn?"

"I know them when I see them!"

Christie shook her head in mock horror. "Okay, that we've got to sort out. Let's start with the basics."

And they walked for an hour.

GOSSIP

ALLIE WALKED INTO THE LOCAL THAI RESTAURANT WHERE she'd agreed to meet with Arash. The place was mostly empty at 5:30, but she noticed Brenda sitting at the end of the long chrome bar. She walked over to say hi.

The bartender spotted her as he came in from the kitchen, juggling a large container of fruit, a cutting board, and a knife. "The Sauvignon Blanc?"

"As always!" Allie replied.

Brenda looked up at her and waved. Allie pulled up the stool next to her.

"So, how is life in the big leagues?" Brenda asked.

"All kinda crazy. All of the crazies," Allie replied.

"No kidding. CookieWars just got funded up, but not sure how I'm going to grow the numbers to prove Rick was right. Hey, did you hear about George?"

The bartender placed a glass of white wine in front of her.

Allie took a sip and replied. "No. What's up?"

"I'm not sure exactly what's behind it, if Rick got impatient, or if he wants to double down …"

"You're killing me here, Brenda."

"Well, he hit pause on George's new thing. And he moved him onto SketchWorld."

SketchWorld was originally a joke. A stylus maker wanted a stylus-centric game and showed up with bags of money. Rick, being Rick, liked bags of money. So he quickly threw a team together and they made a game. The engineers on the game were a disaster, recently minted coders from everywhere from Stanford to the two-month coding boot camps San Francisco had on every other block. Patricia's team was always recruiting engineers, bodies to throw at problems. Allie knew it drove Rob crazy, but most CTOs didn't seem to care ... or they buckled to their GM's pressure. SketchWorld crashed perpetually during playtesting and launched with the worst bug count of any game at SOS. But the contract with the stylus people had a deadline, and contracts were contracts.

But the game itself ... They had just hired a mid-level game designer from an indie studio, Evan. He'd bounced from place to place, sometimes barely even lasting a year at a company. No one expected to keep him, so he was thrown on whatever project needed a brain. And apparently he had one, because SketchWorld was an elegant piece of game design. Rick had told the team to just reskin QuiltWorld. "Copy the mechanics and throw in something for a stylus to be used for. Do NOT waste time thinking!"

But Evan did think. He took the core idea of QuiltWorld, the world building. But instead of prefabricated fabric tiles, he gave players a mix of blank tiles and patterned tiles. He managed to tap into the Zentangle/adult coloring-book madness, and then on top of that, he built an elegant trading system, allowing players with high creativity to trade out tiles to those who just wanted to assemble premade tiles into worlds. Evan had been a history major in college and had studied ancient economies. He nailed his game economy in one.

The game was wonky and it was compelling, and it kept customer service busy with angry calls from passionate users. The worst bugs had been quashed, and now it was growing at a faster pace than QuiltWorld's first quarter.

"So George ..." Allie nudged.

"The whole team! Airlifted and dropped into SketchWorld." Brenda threw her hands up in the air

"Jeez." Allie shook her head.

"I know!"

"Do you know how George is taking it?" Allie asked.

"Who knows? He doesn't show his hand. But consider how much stock he has still vesting. Is he really going to fight for creative freedom just now?"

"Not George. Not now, with the IPO around the corner. But damn. He's been campaigning to do a game from scratch forever." Allie took a long sip of her wine. She was mad at George, but she couldn't help but empathize.

"He didn't have any viable concepts. He's been wandering in the wilderness too long, and Rick got bored."

"George can scale a game. So can Victor and Pete. Rick's decision makes sense for SOS." But not for George. He'd finally gotten untangled from

QuiltWorld, and now he was going to grow someone else's game. But he wouldn't be the most disappointed by this change. "What about Evan?"

"Pissed."

"No doubt." No doubt. He built a game that succeeded despite itself, and then it was taken away. Carlos was too senior to work for Evan; therefore, Evan would be pushed into a subordinate position, unless he was straight up moved to a different game.

Hmm, Allie thought. She pulled out her phone. "Sorry, just a sec. I forgot something."

Brenda shrugged, and took a sip of her scotch. The smoky smell drifted out toward Allie and she briefly longed for something stronger. But she was still working.

She quickly texted Christie, "Evan is unhappy. Check it out?"

Then Arash walked in. He waved franticly. "Sorry I'm late!"

Allie stood and turned to Brenda briefly. "Thanks for the intel, Brenda. Catch you later."

Brenda raised her glass. "Anytime, lady!"

Amazing she could down scotch and still be so coherent. But who knew? SOS was a hard-drinking company.

Allie and Arash moved to the other end of the bar, out of earshot. They ordered some food and settled into business.

Allie started. "I'm sorry I canceled our one-on-one earlier. And thanks for meeting me here. I missed lunch and I'm starving."

"I totally get it!" Arash replied. He'd ordered as much as she had.

From her pocket, Allie pulled out an index card covered with notes for their meeting. She had gone over the role canvas and his status email, and she knew what she wanted to talk to him about. But she started with GROW.

"So what do you want to get out of today's meeting?" What were his goals?

"I'm struggling with convincing market research to run a survey with male players. I don't know why they are digging their heels in."

"Okay, so what are they saying?" What was the reality of the situation? What did he know?

"The head of research says it's stupid to focus on men. But Jeff, the researcher who did last year's survey, he totally thinks it's interesting. He just doesn't think another survey is the right approach ..." Arash cheerfully ranted for a while.

"Do you have ideas of what to try next?" What were your options?

"Can you tell them to run this survey?"

"Really?" Allie countered, her face a clear *no*. "You can do better than that. A product manager uses their influence, not borrowed authority. You can't be using me like a baseball bat to hit people over the head with."

Arash sighed and came up with a couple new tactics. Allie critiqued them and eventually he settled on his game plan. *W* is what will you do next. And sometimes, though not in this case, *Who can help you*? "Because I said so" is not a sustainable strategy if you wanted allies in your professional goals.

Now it was her turn. She had picked the most important topic from her admittedly short list of concerns. "So Lawrence is worried you haven't met with customer service yet about next month's launch."

The food came, and they inhaled it while strategizing how to get their team prepped for the next big thing. Why had George skipped one-on-ones? It made such a difference to not have to solve every damn problem by yourself. And bless Derek and his GROW model. Finally, Allie was getting ahead of the game.

I DIDN'T ASK YOU TO QUIT

IT WAS TEN AT NIGHT WHEN ALLIE GOT HOME. SHE HAD GOT-
ten home even later than that all week, and was pleased that Derek would
still be awake when she got in. The lights were all on in the apartment, but
Derek wasn't in the living room. She walked through the hall to their bed-
room, where she heard movement.

Derek had the suitcase out on the bed and was carefully folding a T-shirt.
He rolled it and placed it in the suitcase before turning to her.

"Are you going somewhere?"

He turned to her. "I asked you to come home early yesterday. And the
day before that. Things have been happening at work." He looked at the floor
and rubbed his hands on his jeans and sighed. "Let's go in the living room."

"Okay." Allie didn't know what the hell was happening, but all her internal alarms were going off.

Derek sat down on the sectional, and she did too, only then noticing
there was an open bottle of red wine with one glass dirty and one clean.
Derek filled them both.

"Allie, I texted you I needed to go out to New York next week to help find
real estate for the new office. They moved the timeline up."

Allie nodded, but that didn't sound to her like a big thing she needed to
come home early for. "Go on."

"In that meeting, they also asked me to run the office."

Allie was reaching for the glass of wine, and froze for a second. Her
mind started running scenarios: *He's leaving me, he wants me to move, he
turned them down and now I get to feel guilty about working too much.* She

stopped herself then, and took a sip of the wine. Better to get facts. "Okay. Tell me more."

Derek smiled, but it didn't reach his eyes. "I know I changed jobs to spend more time with you, but you are never here. You're always at work."

"I didn't ask you to change jobs."

The muscle in Derek's jaw moved as he gritted his teeth. "We're married. I think it's okay to expect to spend time together."

"It's temporary. It's just things have been crazy."

"It's been temporarily crazy for over a year. More, even." He looked down at his hands, held his palm up, pleading. "Look, just stop. I don't want to have this argument again. I agreed to an interim position running HR for the New York office. I told them I'd give them six months, then decide."

Allie sat very still, waiting. She felt herself at the edge of the cliff in a strong wind, but maybe it was dying down. Maybe she wouldn't be blown off the end of the world. "What will you decide?"

"I can't know until then. But we have six months to decide if we want to be together. Actually *be* together. I won't be an SOS widower. I'm not telling you to quit, but you have to find a way to not let it take over your entire life. For your health as well as our marriage."

"That sounds like an ultimatum." Allie found herself swinging from fear to anger. She tried to keep it out of her voice, with mixed results.

"It's not, it really isn't. I'm just telling you what I need. I want love in my life every day. Right now there is no difference between being married to you in New York or married to you in Mountain View. I'm hoping this break will be a chance for us to both think about what we're willing to give to this marriage." He looked her in the eye. "Could be worse. We could have kids and be having this conversation."

There it was. He wanted kids. She wanted kids ... maybe? Someday? She wanted this job now, though. First. And he had to bring up some far-flung future. Again. Now her hot anger turned cold, and she felt her tight throat loosen enough to speak. "Okay. Go. That's fair. Go lose yourself in work a bit, and I'll see if I can sort out SOS. We'll touch base later."

Derek's Adam's apple bounced as he swallowed. "It's not the end. You can come visit. It could be fun; we could explore Manhattan. Maybe distance can help us, make our together time more special."

"Sounds nice." Allie drained her glass. "Why don't you finish packing? I have some spreadsheets to look at."

BRENDA DRINKS HEAVILY

ALLIE HEADED TO THE THAI PLACE TO MEET WITH HER POD TO toast the latest release. Brenda was there already, at one end of the bar, and a couple engineers were at the other. She walked up to her guys and clapped a hand on Tal's shoulder. "Hey guys! Order me a Sauvignon Blanc. I'll be right back."

She walked over to Brenda. "Hey, lady."

Brenda looked up at her, eyes slightly unfocused. "Hi, last gal standing."

"What?" She looked at Brenda's scotch glass. It was full. How many had preceded it?

"You haven't heard. Well, you will. They did it again."

"What did they do?"

"Busted to producer. In my own fucking studio."

Allie sat. The bartender took one look at her face, and placed the white wine in front of her. "What are you talking about?"

"They hired over me. Brought in a kid from Hurricane, latest hotness. He's twenty-three, for fuck's sake."

"What the? But Rick pulled Joe out of his GM spot last week. Hell, he ripped him a new one, told him every way he wasn't worthy of being a GM. But he's floating, coming up with a new game concept. He even has a dev and a designer with him."

"I know, I know. But Rick came in, and he told me, 'I've got this wunderkind,' and I need to stay on until he's got his feet under him. So, title change."

Allie couldn't figure out what had happened. It didn't make sense to her. Rick moved GMs around like chess pieces. But he didn't demote them. Or did he? She remembered Virginia. "Brenda, just stop. Please start over."

"Rick gave me that head count, and I hired, I hired. I got a couple keepers, too. I got one kid, he's working the PvP like no one's business. Our kfactor was above one last week."

Allie shook her head in wonderment. Viral growth was measured by kfactor. One person brought in X number of people. Usually it was a small percentage of a person. Sometimes a new game, if it got good press and was well tuned, could go over 1 for a week or maybe two. But an older game, like Brenda's? Never.

"But our revenue—I can't convert. I can't get any blood from that turnip!"

Allie stayed with Brenda, letting her rant, her wine untouched. Brenda took a long sip of her scotch, the heat of the alcohol no longer slowing her. "We do these things to our players. We make it fun, we give them something they need in their life, then we take their money, which is fair, I like money, don't say I don't like money, but we keep taking it, asking them for more money, more time, more connection, sell your friends to us, over and over."

Allie was completely in shock. She'd never heard anyone talk about SOS like this. It was a tough business, free-to-play. You were always on a treadmill, trying to make money, to convert engagement to cash, but …

Brenda stared at her. "I wanted to make games to connect people to each other. Like Christmas."

Allie gave a confused shrug.

"All the holidays, Thanksgiving too, right? You spend time with a bunch of relatives you don't give a rat's ass about, and you try to drink enough to keep from killing yourself from boredom, then someone takes out Apples to Apples or some idiotic game and you're laughing. Like you're at a bar with your pals, and it's almost okay. You feel like these relatives are not aliens. They might be related to you."

Allie nodded. Holidays were not anywhere that extreme for her, but games had allowed her to connect to the odder members of the family.

"And all Rick wants to do is win. He wins when he has all the money. And the games have to die for him."

"I hear you, Brenda," Allie replied. "Hey, we're going to order some food. Care to join us?"

"No. Don't want to be with people now."

No need to point out she was at a public place. "But perhaps order something to eat? You'll feel a bit better. And some water."

Brenda looked at Allie suspiciously, but apparently saw nothing to be worried about. She waved the bartender over.

"Jeff, get me that noodle thing. The one I like. And another scotch."

Allie looked into the bartender's eyes, and gave a tiny shake of her head. *Please not another scotch.*

"I'll put the order in," he said. "But we've just ended the bottle. Give me a minute, we've got another downstairs." Without asking, he refilled her water back. He looked at Allie and gave her a small nod.

"Hey, Brenda, I'm here with my guys, but we can chat more in a bit."

"Whatever. Go." Brenda waved at her.

Allie walked back to her pod. She sat on a stool, and Jeff—the bartender's name was Jeff?—returned the glass she'd forgotten at the other end of the bar. She grabbed his hand. "Do not let her leave unless you know she's not driving. Or it's on you." He looked frightened for a second. A bar could lose its license over a drunk driving incident.

Allie turned to the pod. "Guys, Brenda has had a few too many. Let's make sure we get her home okay, all right?"

Lawrence nodded. "I drove today. I can take her. I don't really drink anyhow."

Allie took a sip and tried to return the conversation to launch. But she was shaken. You didn't know. Who else has seen her like this? Did she talk trash about Rick to anyone else? That was career suicide. Why had he demoted her? She'd made a few base hits for SOS, small, solid revenue games.

No QuiltWorld, but good games, fun games. But Virginia had been pulled off GMing and was still a producer. She'd never been allowed another crack at running a studio. It was a small sample, sure. Allie couldn't think of a single male GM who'd been demoted. Everyone failed eventually. No one lived up to Rick's expectations forever. He was impatient, demanding, always expecting more and cold as ice when he didn't get it.

The thing was when things were unfair, you didn't know. When everything was crazy screaming and constantly changing, you had to wonder if you aren't good enough, or if there were loaded dice. You didn't know, and you didn't get to know.

THE PRIZE IS...

ALLIE FELT TRIUMPHANT. RICK WAS COMING TO ADDRESS THE studio. She'd done it. The CountyFair expansion was making money hand over fist, and players loved it. It had the highest NPS she'd ever seen for a game. This was her moment.

Yosi was back, his wife and baby at home with his in-laws. He hid at work. Christie was gone, but Evan had settled in. And Rob stood next to Yosi, soaking up his wisdom. Carlton was bouncing around on his toes, excited. He felt for sure he was going to get his first trip to Vegas.

Rick swept into the room. He had people with him—Patricia, Chuck, and a guy Allie didn't recognize. Well, this was special.

The room went quiet. Rick had all eyes on him once again in the panopticon.

"Hello, all! Congratulations! You have done some wonderful work this quarter!"

The room exploded into cheers.

"We are so proud of everyone, and I wanted to be the one to tell you, personally, you are going to Vegas!"

Louder cheers rang around the room.

"I want to be honest. I thought QuiltWorld had reached the end of its lifespan. You know there is a wisdom here that games do not have second acts. Well, you have proved them wrong!"

Cheers! Allie wished fervently that Christie were here. Her vision had been what truly saved them. Then Yosi leaned over her shoulder to whisper. "Good thing you made the Advent calendar quest. We might never have known that freecrafting was our direction."

And she realized that yes, Christie had designed the most profitable, and in her opinion, the most amazing expansion ever seen in SOS. But it had been built on the knowledge that was gotten by her leap of intuition. She had seen the potential in freecrafting. She had bet her career on it. And it had done her game and her career a world of good. Maybe she should stop doubting her vision. She knew what good game play was. She could do this.

"I have more exciting news!" Rick announced. "I wanted to introduce you to Stephen Parks. He was the VP of Your House games over at Digitl, and before that he was an Imagineer." Rick had the childish glee of a Disney fan. And he should be proud; it was quite a coup. Many people knew of the man who harnessed the unpredictable genius of Wilson Williams to build one of the biggest selling console games of all time. But why was he introducing Stephen here?

"Stephen is legendary, I think you'll agree. So I'm happy to announce he'll be QuiltWorld's new GM!"

A cheer began, but then faltered. The studio expected to celebrate, but the news was too confusing.

Allie was floored. It was like she'd been kneecapped. So she thought, anyhow, having never been kneecapped, but having been hit by a softball in the head once, it was like being hit by a softball in the head. It was so painful it didn't hurt. It was beyond. She nodded like she wasn't surprised. She nodded like she knew; it was all the plan, it was as expected.

Rick continued, "I can see you are worried about losing Allie, but don't be. She'll stay on as producer, to make sure QuiltWorld continues to thrive!" Here the team did cheer. And Allie nodded, nodded, nodded. Couldn't comprehend what she was hearing. It wasn't like a softball. It was like a very hard baseball the size of a basketball. She felt like there was a silent ringing in her ears. *Who does this? Who makes such an announcement without warning?*

Rick was talking but she couldn't hear. It was inconceivable.

Now Stephen was turning to talk to Yosi and Rob. She'd want to talk to him; he was a hero to her. But the softball was still embedded in her head. It was too big to let her think. Rick turned to slip out of the room. She followed him.

When they were out of the room, she grabbed his arm. He looked at her like she was insane for touching him. "What was that?" she spat out.

"What? You get to stay on the game you love and work for a great mentor."

"My ...? How could you announce that without talking to me?"

"It was an obvious choice. I'm surprised you are surprised."

"What are you ... oblivious? I don't even ..."

"Maybe you should take a walk, think about this."

"Look, if you are putting him in as GM ..." And honestly, she was surprised she had ever been GM at all. Now she thought of it, she realized she had always been a temporary, he had said interim, but had he ever meant to give it to her? Maybe he wanted her to work harder, maybe he thought teasing her with GM would do the trick. She felt tears in her eyes but refused them. She would not cry now, she would cry on her own terms in her own time. Patricia came up behind Rick, and started listening in, a vulture to document anything that was said.

"Look," she repeated, "why can't I float? I can move as GM, turn around another studio. Or better yet, I've proved I can bring new things into the world. Let me create a pitch." Now she got the tiniest ray of hope. "I can pitch a new game! Monetization baked in, made from ground zero to make money and delight users."

He stared at her coldly. Had he seen her tears? Did he see her as weak, unworthy to lead a new game? "Allie, we're going to IPO. Stephen is a big name, but I need the numbers to stay up. You are staying in QuiltWorld."

She saw herself through his eyes. A useful pawn. Property. Humans were just assets to be placed for highest return. Rage brought the tears she had dismissed back to her eyes.

"I quit." She turned her back and walked away.

She heard Rick say to Patricia, "She'll be back. She's being overemotional now, but she's a good kid. She'll come around."

IT'S TIME

ALLIE WALKED BACK TO THE STUDIO STRAIGHT TO HER DESK. She began packing it. She'd seen fired execs walked out with security, and she was damned if she'd take that perp walk. Better to get out while she still could stroll out in control of herself. She filled her backpack carefully with her things, leaving behind three staplers, two tape dispensers, and a large collection of gnawed pens. She wouldn't take a single thing of SOS's with her, damnit.

Then she felt eyes on her. She looked up. Rob was standing next to the desk, quietly. Kendra and Noam flanked him. Lawrence was there and Carlton, too. In fact, a good portion of the studio was there, and the rest were looking to her from their desks.

It was Carlton who spoke first. "Let me know where you end up. I'll send you my résumé."

Kendra spoke too. "Mine also."

"Whom will I argue with?" said Noam.

"I'm ready for a change," said Lawrence.

Allie felt her eyes tear up and she desperately swallowed, uncertain if her voice would work. Rob looked alarmed for her.

"Hey, folks, this is really great. But what if I take Allie for a little walk first? She looks like she needs … some air."

Thank goodness for Rob. He turned toward the door, and a path opened up. Allie walked out hurriedly, before she popped like a water balloon. She could hear Rob right behind her. She shot out the front door and she was halfway down the block before she could finally let go a little.

The tears ran fast and hot down her face. She didn't feel the fog as it materialized into a light drizzle, but Rob maneuvered quickly into Pazzo, and she took refuge in the ever-empty mezzanine. And then she cried for real. She couldn't have told Rob why she was crying, if he asked her. Relief? Anger? Joy?

He didn't ask her, but he did offer a shoulder, and she leaned against him and wetted his sweater. Finally she gasped, "Tissues."

Rob dug out a packet from his pocket. "I'll get you some water," he said.

She nodded, still not able to use her throat. It was closed tight with emotion.

He came back with water and tea. She drank half the water and then nursed the tea. Rob still said nothing. He could play silence like a violin. It was profoundly comforting.

"I'm done," she said.

"I know."

"I'm pretty much vested, anyhow."

Rob nodded. Whatever she needed from SOS, she had gotten. Actually, she'd gotten more. "They are willing to follow me?"

"Yes," Rob said.

She shook her head.

"Allie, it's time. You've just been shoved out of the nest. But hey, you've got wings. Time to fly."

"I don't know. Maybe I should take a job somewhere else, get a little more experience. I mean, I was GM of QuiltWorld for six months. I've got to be very employable."

"Allie, you are more than employable. Don't you get it? It's time to do your own thing. You've been talking about it forever. Or was it just all talk?"

Rob knew better. But he had to make her say it. "No. It wasn't talk. I want to build a studio that makes great games. In fact, I want to make games that make a difference. Christie always wanted to make educational games. Maybe she still does."

Rob nodded. "I sure want that."

Allie sighed. "You've got your CTO gig."

"Yosi is staying through the IPO. Need to make the studio look strong."

"Oh," said Allie.

"Yep," said Rob.

"So. We're starting a company."

"Well, I'd like a vacation first. And I don't cliff until February. But I hear New York is lovely in the winter."

"From whom? Are you really into black-and-yellow snow?" But she got the hint.

He continued, "New York bookstores can be very lovely in January. Cozy and romantic."

"Are there still bookstores in the world?"

"Restaurants then. Allie!"

"Subtle, you aren't."

They walked back quietly, talking about nothing important. It was like conversational hot tea. Soothing. When she got in the studio, her backpack was packed and waiting. Kendra stood by it. "I kinda hoped you'd change your mind, but I didn't think you would."

Allie picked up her backpack. "Thank you. You guessed right."

Kendra then swept her up in a hug, squeezing her just short of knocking the breath out of her. "You'll be fine, I know it."

"Thanks. Take care of QuiltWorld."

"Will do."

Allie walked around, saying good-bye to folks. Over and over, the team said, "I'll email you later. Let's talk."

At the door, Carlton shook her hand. "Remember. I'll send my résumé."

She walked out, wondering how the guy she once dressed down became her biggest booster.

ARE WE ON THE SAME PAGE?

WHEN SHE GOT HOME THAT NIGHT, SHE CALLED DEREK. THEY usually talked in the morning, since he was three hours ahead of her, but she hoped she might catch him since it was nine there: late enough he'd be home, but early enough to be awake.

He answered the phone on the second ring, which gave her a sense of comfort. He was there. His voice sounded normal, even pleased to hear hers. They began to exchange some pleasantries, but she couldn't stand it. "I quit today."

A long quiet pause. "Oh. What happened?" he asked.

She went over her day.

"Well, that was shitty," he replied. "I can't believe Patricia let it play out like that."

He would see the HR complications, wouldn't he? She hadn't considered that.

"It's Rick's show. It always has been, always will be. Patricia just sweeps up whatever mess he leaves."

"HR works for the company," he said.

She let that sit. He knew it, too. He just always tried to do the right thing anyhow. That was her Derek.

"Anyhow, it's got me thinking. A lot." She told him about Rob's advice, and the team's reaction. She felt her throat starting to close with tears again, and reached for a glass of wine. Derek was quiet, but she imagined she could hear him listening anyhow. "I would like to come out for a visit, if you'd like?"

"Yes, please."

"A long visit?"

"Yes."

"We've got a lot to talk about. I think we need to set our own team charter. I feel like we've just been talking past each other these last few months. I want to figure out what we both think is important, and make sure we're sharing goals."

"And roles and norms," he joked.

She replied quite seriously. "Yes. Actually. The other day I realized we never talked about kids before we got married. We both just kind of assumed the other one had the same ideas." *Oops, that came out suddenly.* Wine. Exhaustion. Emotions. "I mean, we've got a lot to discuss, really discuss. And I want to do it right, slowly, with my full attention. I love you too much to assume some relationship fairy will just make it work." Yeah, too much wine.

"I love you, too. You're right, you are so right. I thought everyone … Well, I assumed. You know what that does."

"Ass."

"Yup." The tone of his voice changed, signaling a change of topic. "So, when do you think you'll arrive? The corporate apartment is big enough for two. And not one more, honestly. New York. I bang my shins on the coffee table every day, I swear, and the efficiency kitchen is efficient if you are the world's tiniest chef." He'd told this to her before. He was nervous.

"I'll check flights. I could be there by this weekend … ?"

"I can't wait," he said.

And then they said little nothings until he had to beg off to sleep.

Allie laid back on the couch, and found herself there the next morning, rumpled but rested. She lay there for a moment, reveling in the lack of urgency. She didn't need to check email. She didn't need to look at her phone, which sat on the coffee table uncharged and unimportant. Soon enough, she'd be building a new company. Soon enough, she'd rebuild her marriage. But for right now? She looked at the sun streaming in the window, lighting up dust motes in the living room. Now she'd make some coffee. The slow way, the right way. Grind the beans, heat the water just so.… She staggered to her feet. Then breakfast, then … Everything else. The slow, right way.

NINE MONTHS LATER

ROB WAS IN THE TINY KITCHENETTE WHEN SHE GOT INTO THEIR office, brewing coffee.

"I think yesterday went well," Rob started.

She poured herself a cup of tea. "If you don't mind not making any of our key results."

"The numbers are good numbers. The team is overreaching in their goals! It's our first game."

"Our first game." Allie smiled. That felt good. And the numbers were fine, just not SOS-level numbers. But also, no SOS marketing team, no SOS PR group, no SOS cross-promotion. Sophia Games wasn't SOS, and Allie liked it that way. Yeah, the numbers were just fine, and they'd only get better with time.

"Fair. We still have a lot to learn about the education space."

"So fun!" Rob grinned. "And hey, we launched and are in the black in under a year. I think that's pretty good."

"That's because our costs are almost nothing. We're living on ramen and working out of my uncle's old garage." Her uncle had retired a few years ago from running a car upholstery repair shop, so though it was a garage, it was by no means small. Plenty of room to grow a team.

Rob's optimism was undaunted. "It's heated! And revenue means payroll."

"I like revenue," Allie admitted.

"Agreed!" said Christie, coming to join them for caffeine loading. "What are we talking about?"

"Still talking about our OKRs, and what it all means," Allie replied.

"Well, like I said yesterday, I don't think we'll really understand what the market thinks until after another quarter at least. I'm more proud of our sticking with our norms. 'Leave work by six.' That's a philosophy I can commit to!" She stirred her coffee. "So what are we doing today?"

Allie had blocked out a day and a half for "EOQ reviews." Yesterday they had spent the morning grading their performance against their goals. The afternoon had been the norm review. Today she was ready to try something new. She gave Christie a mysterious smile. "Come along and see."

Her little team was gathered in their only conference room. Sophia Games employees Jenny, Vihn, and Frank had joined former SOS employees Rob, Allie, Christie, Carlton, and Noam. That day they had one more person in the room, and the employees were eyeing her curiously.

Allie took her spot at the head of the room. "Hey folks, I want you to meet Rachel." Rachel was tall and brown, with strands of silver in her shiny black bob. She gave the team a small smile and nod.

"Rachel teaches at State and is an old friend. I've asked her to come help us rethink our performance reviews."

That certainly brought out some sour faces.

"We've been using a combination of the role canvas and OKRs pretty successfully to evaluate ourselves at the end of each quarter." Rob and Allie reviewed each other and kept each other honest. "But just as our OKRs and norms are accomplished as a team, I think we can commit to growing each other. I asked Rachel to facilitate because I want to participate. I want to grow and learn as much as I hope you all do. I'll let Rachel explain further."

Allie sat, and Rachel stepped forward. "Thank you, Allie. This method is one Allie and Rob came up with. I'm here to help the trains run on time, so to speak. We're going to do a visual 360 review, using the empathic feedback canvas. I've printed one for each of you and they are up on the wall.

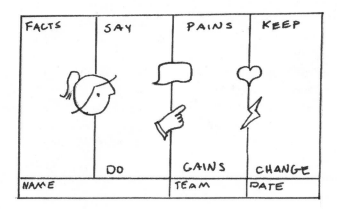

"Go ahead and stand in front of one of these. Oh, grab some Post-Its and pens first. There is a different color for each of you."

The team got up and stood in front of the blank posters. Allie was bemused at the lack of back talk. Oh, the power of a stranger! Or maybe it was Rachel's professor-voice that brooked no argument.

Rachel continued. "Let's take a second to customize these. Write your name and date, and make the person look like you."

There was some laughter as hair, glasses, and a couple hats were added to the images.

Rachel called a bit louder, "All right. Now step one poster to your right, to your neighbor's canvas." The posters were on all the walls, and it was easy enough to find their places.

"Everyone, we're going to write on Post-Its things we observe about our teammates. Not things we judge about them. Not 'he's a jerk' or 'she's nice,' but perhaps 'struggles to meet deadlines.' Observable facts. And we're going to move from left to right, spending two minutes in each column."

Noam raised his hand and spoke at the same time. "What's a pain and a gain?"

Rachel, unruffled, replied, "Let me go through the entire canvas. We want to build empathy for our teammates before giving feedback, so the canvas helps us reflect a little before we give our feedback. We start with some facts about the person, what they do, but maybe a bit about their personal life. Are they an only child? Married? Play basketball? Then we'll think about things over the last quarter we've seen them do and things we've heard them say, both good and bad. Did they accomplish a big project? Did they criticize someone's work unfairly?" She nodded at Noam. "Then consider how they experience their role. What do you see them struggle with in their role? That's a pain. What do they hope to accomplish? That's a gain. Finally, write down at least one behavior they might change next quarter and one behavior you want them to keep on doing. Does anyone have a question?"

The team looked slightly stunned. Rachel did not give them time to run away. "If anyone has a question while we're doing this, raise your hand and I'll come help." She set an alarm. "Start!"

Allie stared at Rob's chart. She knew so much about him. She slowly started to write down this and that, big family, ex-army, MIT, married to Marie, likes sugar and cream in his coffee. Then the alarm went off, and she was nudged to move to *say* and *do*. In the corner of her eye, she saw Rachel talking to Carlton, but she stopped herself from eavesdropping and refocused to Rob's canvas. She thought of all his optimism, and wrote, "We can do it!" and put it on *say*. *Do* was even easier, as not only did he code and hire, but he was always mentoring and helping out with dumb tasks like taking out the trash. And ... The alarm went off again. Bah. Too fast!

Pains and *gains*. Easy-peasy. He wanted to build a good team, and build good code with that good team. And if he didn't succeed? Ugh, back to the salt mines of big commercial games. Just like she would. She was staring at that horrible fate when the alarm shook her from her reverie.

Keeps and *changes*. Keep on being an optimist. Go home earlier. Keep on holding us to higher standards. Stop checking email on the weekends when it's not his turn on watch. Keep on being honest. Go ahead and be mad when it's worth getting mad about. He probably wouldn't take that advice, but hey, why not?

The alarm sounded again. Rachel spoke up. "Please move to the next person's canvas." Allie reluctantly moved from Rob's, certain there was more to say, but happily started in on Christie's. Then Noam's, Jenny's, Vihn's, Frank's, and finally Carlton's, already covered with Post-Its. Oh, Carlton. He had grown so much.

His work was magical, he and Christie were an incredible team, and he had even come up with the company's name ... Sophia, Greek for *wisdom*. She hardly had anything more to say than the others had written, but she did add, "Always willing to learn from critique." Allie marveled at how lucky she was to have such a wonderful team. Far from feeling painful, the exercise had filled her with joy. Even when she suggested Noam should "think a little before speaking," or Jenny might "understand the other person's POV before arguing," it was after celebrating how wonderful they were as a person.

When she returned to her own canvas, Rachel told them to take a few minutes to read through it all, then ask for clarification if needed from whomever had written the feedback. Allie stood glowing from pride in her team, but it slowly transformed into something else. There she was. The kid from East Palo Alto, older brother in New York, trying to be an actor of all things. Short, definitely. Feisty, apparently. Self-taught. That was true. Creative? She was hacker, not creative. But there it was, three times. Her team thought she was creative. Wow.

And in *say/do* she saw her team seeing her while she asked them what they thought and trusted them to figure out what the right thing to do was, brainstorming ways to teach with play. She felt their love as she saw how much she had to lose and gain with their first launch. And nervously, she read the *keeps* and *changes*. Keep trusting us. Go home earlier. Keep on experimenting. Trust your instincts. Turn off your phone on the weekends so we can all relax. Keep mentoring me.

If she cried now, it would be good tears. She decided to save them for later. She looked around the room at her team, talking passionately but not angrily, discussing and sometimes smiling. She got out her phone and took photos of the canvases. She'd use these with her other inputs. But really, no performance evaluation could make as big a difference in her team's lives as the feedback of their peers. Maybe it was time to go home earlier.

VEGAS, BABY

ALLIE REACHED ACROSS DEREK TO STEAL THE UMBRELLA FROM his ridiculous fruity drink. She stuck it in her hair and stuck out her tongue at him. He laughed. They'd been at the pool at the Bellagio all day.

"See, Vegas is not just a town full of sin and show girls!" Allie teased.

"Food is better than Disneyland. But not as many rides!" Derek complained, his big grin undermining his complaint. Allie was happy there was only one. She'd thrown up on their last anniversary trip after riding rides all day followed by an eight-course dinner. This year was going to be a lot gentler. On her turn to pick the vacation, she had decided to return to Vegas, and found it pleasantly unhaunted by memories of SOS.

"Wait until you see 'O'! It's the only Cirque du Soleil I haven't seen."

"What time is it? Do we need to get ready?" he asked.

"I don't know. I left my phone in my room."

Derek got up and came over to her bench. "Not worried?"

"They've got my back."

"Then I can have your front." He leaned over and kissed her. Leisurely.

~end~

The Model

HOW TO GET TO A TEAM THAT MANAGES ITSELF

ONE OF THE CRUELEST JOKES PLAYED IN COMPANIES IS WHEN you reward an individual practitioner by promoting them to manager. People management is a completely different job from any front-line job and requires completely different skills. It's not a step up, it's a step sideways. Some companies provide training, fewer provide mentorship, and a very few set up formal transition time so the recently promoted person can get her feet under her. Often people who have been succeeding their entire life suddenly are lost, uncertain how to get things done.

People management has three core components: hiring, firing, and feedback in between. Each one bears little resemblance to a front-line job, whether it's design, engineering, or product management. Being promoted is being reset to level one.

Even if you know what to do as a people manager, too often it's hard to let go of what made you successful in the past. There is a comfort in the familiar spreadsheet or code. But no matter how hard and long you work, there are only twenty-four hours in a day. This means you have to make active choices about where you spend your time. Delegation is a survival tactic.

You need to be able to lean on your team for another reason. Managers, like all humans, tend to do the work that has the most screaming associated with it. In a new team, or a dysfunctional one, the bulk of the screaming (and whining, and questioning, and requesting, and grousing) comes from the team. The next most frequent comes from the next level up—the general manager or the CEO. Thus when a manager chooses where to spend her time, it tends to be on team coordination and then business needs.

A manager working with a weak team spends all her time in reaction mode. After running around all day making sure everyone knows what they are doing, and has what they need, and WHY they are doing it, the manager stays up late, trying to fit in as much work on the business as she can handle.

But as teams mature, this gets better. You have less of a need for team coordination, because the teams know who is responsible for what. And you begin to see some institutional memory and shared values emerge just from working together over time. The team knows the product, and knows what its job is, and knows how to make it better.

In *The Discipline of Teams*, Katzenbach and Smith wrote, "Teams have four elements—common commitment and purpose, performance goals, complementary skills, and mutual accountability."

These first two properties can be addressed with OKRs, which I've written about in *Radical Focus*. (I also included a short primer in this book.)

The third—complementary skills—is a prerequisite for any sort of maker team. For example, in many game-design companies, a new game will start with a micro-team of a game designer, a business person (producer or product manager), an engineer, and an artist.

I remember back when I was first pitching my startup around, and an angel investor drew a triangle on his whiteboard. He said for a startup to succeed, it needed people with skills in product, business, and tech.

He said it didn't have to be three people each with one of the skills, but all three skills had to be there. It's good to remember that people are usually more skilled than their role requires, and there is more than one way to design a team.

But even in teams where the skills are very similar, such as a sales team or a customer-service team, people have complementary skills. Maybe someone is the best at cold calling, or someone is best with angry customers … All teams are made of people, and people vary. That's a feature, not a bug. You don't want a gang of robots all behaving the same, or a crew of "not my jobbers." You want a smart group of people all teaching each other their superpowers.

In a nascent team, the fourth requirement—mutual accountability—most often manifests as people demanding everyone pull their own weight. In a healthy team, the engineer will walk over to the designer and ask for a missing design component. In a dysfunctional team, he'll ask the product manager to deal with the designer. This wastes the PM's time and feeds resentment that hinders team performance.

Many people stop working on team health here, at the functional stage. But if you want the power of the high performing team, you have to take it farther. You want a team that is constantly getting smarter, learning from their mistakes and experiments, and building a competitive advantage. You want a learning team, because that's the only team that can keep up with our rapidly changing business climate.

In a learning team, not only is the team performing as a unit, but they are also working together to become better every day. They question each new status quo and make hypotheses about how they can be more effective.

A learning team shares a commitment to progress. Knowledge is shared as soon as it's acquired, and the team is continually developing new hypotheses to be tested.

A critical component to this team's success is a tolerance for creative conflict. Many teams are willing to put up with the storming that comes when you put people together who don't know each other. It's expected they'll fight, misunderstand each other, disagree on goals and outcomes. And it's a relief when it settles.

But it's a rare team that is willing to re-enter the land of conflict after it's figured out how to work well together. You've heard that you must break a leg again if it's set wrong. It's the same situation when a team has settled into bad (or even so-so) patterns. A great team must step back into conflict again and again to break the substandard status quo and find the best way to execute. The only way for a team to be willing to do this is if you, the team leader, have created psychological safety for the team.

Someday, you will want a team who can share decision-making and responsibility for meeting goals. You'll want all members to have a clear vision for what they want their results to be, so they both help each other and hold each other responsible. This is an autonomous team, and with this team, you'll suddenly find you have more time for strategy, for cooperation with other business groups, and possibly even for an afternoon nap.

Bruce Tuckman, a psychology professor at The Ohio State University, came up with the five stages of team development in 1965. He noted all phases were necessary and inevitable. The phases were Forming, Storming, Norming, Performing, and (a late addition) Adjourning. I will always be grateful to Mr. Tuckman for giving the phases memorable and descriptive names.

Because *Radical Focus* had made me so aware of the power of the cadence, I decided to adapt these phases from a story-like arc to a continuous improvement loop.

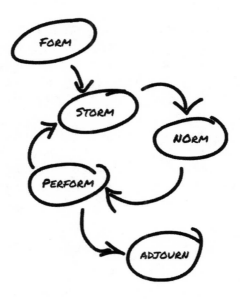

All teams are formed, and this is necessarily a onetime effort, like a hire. Storming comes from a clash of norms: workstyles, culture differences, etc. Norming is where those clashes are smoothed out through compromise and communication. Performing is when the team finds its rhythm and Adjourning might never happen.

Consider a favorite philosopher's puzzle: If it is supposed that the famous ship sailed by the hero Theseus in a great battle has been kept in a harbour as a museum piece, and as the years went by some of the wooden parts began to rot and were replaced by new ones then, after a century or so, all of the parts had been replaced. The question then is if the "restored" ship is still the same object as the original?Most teams are like this: People quit, are promoted or transfer, and new people come in. The team in name is still there, but as no person is the same as the one who replaced the last person, it has become a very different team. What if we acknowledge that change happens and leverage it for improvement?

Let's focus on three critical stages: Form, Storm-to-Norm, and Adjourn. We can map these to formal rituals (to steal the Agile term) held at the beginning of the quarter, weekly, and end of quarter.

Now, let's map that to the three critical elements of a functional team (borrowed from the great *Wisdom of Teams*): Goals, Roles, and Norms. We now have a road map for continuous improvement to become a high-performing team. These are the key rituals, what they do, and when they happen. I call this the 9x team process. By observing these nine quadrants you can have a team that's nine times better … or more.

The Cadence of a High Performing Team

	GOALS	ROLES	NORMS
SET (was Form)	Set objectives and key results	Hire formal roles (product manager, engineer, designer) Set information roles (facilitator, notetaker, agenda-maker)	Discover implicit norms Set shared norms via a team charter
CHECK (Was Storm-to-Perform)	Monday priority meeting to choose what tasks to do in hopes of achieving OKRs Friday bragging session to share successes and learnings. Weekly status email	Weekly 1:1, to coach and to give feedback	Retrospective, in which team quickly determines what's working and what needs to change
CORRECT (was Adjourn)	EOQ OKR grading	Quarterly individual performance review to determine promotions, commendations, or corrections.	Team Performance Review, in which the team collectively grades their group performance against their norms.

The goal for this cadence is to help a group of people become a team, but not to stop there. Once you have a team that performs, you want to examine weaknesses that have been left in place because you had bigger fish to fry. You want to examine wounds that might be festering, rotten apples that might be corrupting, metaphors that might be mixing. That last one doesn't bother me, actually.

Along the way to becoming a functional team, we'll make a lot of compromises just to get going. It's critical to not make any Band-Aids permanent. The Correct stage "closes" the quarter so we can reflect on where we are and where we want to be. It's also a good time for any new folks who have joined us to help shape the team's goals, roles, and norms.

It's not enough to become a functional team. We want to be a learning team, a growing team, an ever-getting-better team. That doesn't happen by accident.

It takes clear role setting, good hiring, regular feedback, and sometimes, corrective action. I'm going to go through each one, with its related cadence.

If you've read *Radical Focus*, feel free to skip this next section and move on to Roles.

SETTING GOALS WITH OKRS

WHAT MAKES A TEAM SUCCESSFUL IS A SHARED PURPOSE. Everyone must agree on the answers to some key questions: What are we going to accomplish, and why does it matter? How do we know we've done it?

We might assemble a team to build viral growth for the product we're all so proud of. How do we know we've succeeded? Would likes on Facebook be good enough, or do we measure conversion to users or paid sales? How much growth will it take to be considered a home run?

What, exactly, are we trying to do here?

Without a goal, however, team members tend to make assumptions about what they each think the goal is. The product manager might think conversion is the goal, but the designer wants to make users happy with a delightful experience. The engineer, meanwhile, is focused on writing beautiful code. The assumptions never line up; everyone gets mad that no one is working on what they assumed was the goal, and no one works together. It's a recipe for disaster.

The answer is to make the unstated stated. Setting OKRs, particularly setting a single OKR per quarter as I recommend in my book *Radical Focus,* forces the team to talk about what the goal should be. Once you've decided together on that one goal, everyone works together. Suddenly everyone has a sense of ownership. It increases velocity and decreases conflict—immediately. Every quarter, the team comes together to ask what the next quarter's goal should be. Then they work together week by week to make it happen.

Every Monday, the team has the tough conversations about what they'll do and what success will look like for each role. On Friday, everyone celebrates making progress toward something important. This renews the team's energy, determination, and focus every week. Everyone pulls together.

I've included a quick primer on OKRs in the next section, and you should read it as a reminder. That being said, I wrote an entire book on OKRs and I'm not going to repeat that information here at any length. OKRs are intensely focusing and productive for your teams, and you should use them. Go read *Radical Focus* for an in-depth look as to how.

OKR FUNDAMENTALS

THE OKR APPROACH TO SETTING GOALS HAS BEEN USED AT Google, Zynga, General Assembly, and beyond, and is spreading like wildfire across successful Silicon Valley companies. The companies that have adopted the approach are growing like weeds.

OKR stands for OBJECTIVES and KEY RESULTS. The form of the OKR has been more or less standardized. The Objective is qualitative and the KRs (most often three) are quantitative. They are used to focus a group or individual around a bold goal. The Objective establishes a goal for a set period of time, usually a quarter. The Key Results tell you if the Objective has been met by the end of the time.

Your Objective is a single sentence that is:

Qualitative and Inspirational

The Objective is designed to get people jumping out of bed in the morning with excitement. And while CEOs and VCs may jump out of bed in the morning with joy over a three percent gain in conversion, a sense of meaning and progress excites most mere mortals. Use the language of your team. If they want to use slang and say "pwn it" or "kill it," use that wording.

Time Bound

For example, doable in a month or a quarter. You want it to be a clear sprint toward a goal. If it takes a year, your Objective may be a strategy or maybe even a mission.

Actionable by the Team Independently

This is less of a problem for startups, but bigger companies often struggle because of interdependence. Your Objective has to be truly yours, and you can't have the excuse of "Marketing didn't market it."

An Objective is like a mission statement, only for a shorter period of time. A great Objective inspires the team, is hard (but not impossible) to do in a set time frame, and can be done by the person or people who have set it, independently.

Here are some good Objectives:

- Pwn the direct-to-business coffee retail market in the South Bay.
- Launch an awesome MVP.
- Transform Palo Alto's coupon-using habits.
- Close a round that lets us kill it next quarter.

and some poor Objectives:

- Sales numbers up 30 percent.
- Double users.
- Raise a Series B of $5M.

Why are those bad Objectives bad? Probably because they are actually Key Results.

Key Results

Key Results take all that inspirational language and quantify it. You create them by asking a simple question, "How would we know if we met our Objective?" This causes you to define what you mean by "awesome," "kill it," or "pwn." Typically you have three Key Results. Key Results can be based on anything you can measure, including:

- Growth
- Engagement
- Revenue
- Performance
- Quality

That last one can throw people. It seems hard to measure quality. But with tools like NPS, it can be done. (NPS = Net Promoter Score, a number based on customers' willingness to recommend a given product to friends and family. See "The Only Number You Need to Grow," *Harvard Business Review*, December 2003.)

If you select your KRs wisely, you can balance forces like growth and performance, or revenue and quality, by making sure you have the potentially opposing forces represented.

"Launch an Awesome MVP" might have KRs of:

- 40 percent of users come back 2× in one week
- Recommendation score of 8
- 15 percent conversion

Notice how hard those are?

OKRs Should Be Difficult, Not Impossible

OKRs are always stretch goals. A great way to do this is to set a confidence level of five out of ten on the OKR. By confidence level of five out of ten, I mean, "I have confidence I have only a fifty-fifty shot of making this goal." A confidence level of one means, "Never gonna happen, my friend." A confidence level of ten means, "Yeah, gonna nail this one." It also means you are setting your goals way too low, which is often called sandbagging. In companies where failure is punished, employees quickly learn not to try. If you want to achieve great things, you have to find a way to make it safe to reach further than anyone has before.

As you set the KR, you are looking for the sweet spot where you are pushing yourself and your team to do bigger things, yet not making it impossible. I think that sweet spot is when you have a fifty-fifty shot of failing.

Take a look at your KRs. If you are getting a funny little feeling in the pit of your stomach saying, "We are really going to have to all bring our A game to hit these…" then you are probably setting them correctly. If you look at them and think, "We're doomed," you've set them too hard. If you look them and think, "I can do that with some hard work," they are too easy.

WHAT MAKES OKRS WORK?

OKRS CASCADE.

The company should set an OKR, and then each department should determine how *their* OKR leads to the company's successful OKR. A team can focus their OKR on a single Key Result or try to support the entire set. For example, engineering might decide satisfaction is tightly connected with speed (and they'd be right).

So set an OKR like:

Performance Upon Launch Equivalent to an Established Company

- 99.8 percent uptime
- <1 second response time
- Instantaneous perceived load time (measure by survey, 90 percent of users say page loaded "immediately")

(I'm not an engineer, so please do not mock my KRs too hard.)

As you can imagine, some teams, like product management, can easily align their OKRs with the company OKRs, while others may have to dig a little more deeply to make sure they are supporting the company goal. Much of the value in OKRs comes from the conversations on what matters, how it will be measured, and what it means for the teams who are used to working from their own standards, apart from the business goals. Customer service, design, and engineering often have to work a little harder to find meaningful OKRs that will move the business goal forward. But it's worth doing. Can customer service upsell disgruntled customers to a better plan? Can design create an onboarding flow that improves retention? Can engineering increase satisfaction with a better recommendations algorithm? No department can be an island.

As well, each individual should set individual OKRs that both reflect personal growth and support the company's goals. If the company's OKRs are around acquisition, a product manager might decide she wants to "Get great at sales." She then might choose KRs of completing sales training with a high score, as well as improving the conversion rate of the product she runs.

Individual OKRs are about becoming better at your job, as well as helping your product get better. It's also a gift to managers struggling with a difficult employee. In the individual OKR-setting process, she can work with that person to set goals that correct those problems *before* they blossom into full disciplinary actions. By setting measurable KRs, she can avoid accusations of personal bias if things do not improve.

OKRs Are Part of Your Regular Rhythm

When people fail to achieve their Objectives, it's often because they set OKRs at the beginning of the quarter and then forget about them. In those three months, you are barraged by teammate requests, the CEO sends you articles you should read and incorporate, you get customer complaints ... There are always 101 interesting things to spend your time on that do not lead to success. I highly recommend baking your OKRs into your weekly team meetings (if you have them) and your weekly status emails. Adjust your confidence levels every single week. Have discussions about why they are going up or down. The cadence is what makes OKRs work.

OKRs Provide an Unmoving and Clear Goal

Do not change OKRs halfway through the quarter. If you see you've set them badly, suck it up, and either fail or nail them, and use that learning to set them better next time. No team gets OKRs perfect the first time. Changing them dilutes focus, and keeping teams focused is the entire point of the OKR. Changing them halfway through teaches your team not to take the OKRs seriously.

Get Ready to Fail ... BIG!

Let's be honest: we hate to fail. Everyone in the Silicon Valley gives lip service to failure, but really we still don't enjoy it. OKRs aren't about hitting targets, but about learning what you are really capable of. Failure is a positive indicator of stretching. OKRs are designed to push you to do more than you knew you were capable of and to learn from experience. If you shoot for the moon, you may not make it—but it's a hell of a view.

Objectives and Key Results are a tested and powerful way to accelerate your company's growth after you've found product market fit or to focus the search as you explore. I recommend them highly for anyone who seeks to accomplish extraordinary things. But they are just one part of three key areas you need to actively design, monitor and evaluate.

ROLES

MY STUDENTS HAVE THIS CRAZY IDEA THAT WHEN THEY GO OFF into the workplace, they're going to work with people they get to pick, that the team will be amazing off the bat, and everyone will get along all the time. That's not how it works.

Most of the time, if you're at a big corporation, you'll be given a team. Every team is the Bad News Bears. Every team you work with will have something wrong with it. You just have to figure out what is broken and what to do about it.

As you're looking at the brand new team you've been given, you have to figure a few things out. What is wrong with this team, specifically? Are the people in the roles people who are capable of doing the jobs? Is this person going to get good with a little coaching? Is this other person going to resist change? Do you have an egoist who wants to be the center of attention? You have to figure out if each person is going to be able to fulfill the role you need them to play on the team. And if not, what then? Do you fire this person? Do you change their role? Do you coach them?

This process doesn't happen only when you first meet your team. You'll do it over and over and over again. As a manager, you can be certain that the people on your team will be constantly changing. Some will get better, and that's great because that's what you want. Some are stuck at a level, which is sometimes okay and sometimes a problem. Some will get worse, and you have to understand why. And then they'll all change places. Just like with your goals, you will be constantly re-evaluating people's capabilities over and over again.

If you have a high performer, it will be tempting to ignore them while you focus on issues that are actively screaming at you. Be aware, however, that if you don't help a high performer grow into their next role, they will eventually get bored or feel neglected and leave. Successful people need coaching, advice, and a listening ear as much as those who struggle.

If you have someone who's been great and is suddenly not great, you need to understand what happened. Sometimes it's something personal, like a divorce or a life change. You support them through it, and push them to do the best they can. And sometimes it's just that someone is bored, and you help them find interest in the job or move to another job.

You cannot skip investing in your people. If you remember in the story, Allie's original manager George almost never made time for his one-on-ones. That means he didn't understand what was going on with his people. That means, in my opinion, he was failing as a manager, and one day, some problem he missed is going bite him where it's hard to repair.

You can never stop watching over and helping your people. There's a reason they call it people management. Not because you're bossing them around, but because you're helping them be the kind of person the company needs and the kind of person they want to be.

The Role Starts with Hiring

Hiring. Everyone says it's the most important thing you need to get right in your company. Yet it's the thing managers are mostly likely to do half-ass. Remember the last time you had to hire? You probably Googled around for some examples of job descriptions, found one that looked kinda close, edited it a little, and posted it wherever HR posts those things.

Then you got some résumés, and one or two had some company names you recognized, or maybe they just looked okay enough. And you called them for a phone screen. If they didn't sound like a psycho, you brought them in for an interview. If everyone liked them okay, well, you hired them, because you hate hiring and want to get back to the real work.

Oh, honey. Hiring *is* the real work. Companies are made of people. The wrong people make bad companies. Note I didn't say bad people ... there are rarely bad people, but there is often a bad fit. Your job—as a manager, recruiter, or member of a team who is vetting an interviewee—is to determine fit.

Interviewing is often done as haphazardly as writing a job description, thus bro-cos hire more bros, suits hire suits, and hipsters fill the room with hipsters. They seem okay to me, the interviewer says. *They seem just like me*, he thinks.

It's time to try something different.

Rethink the Process

Instead of thinking about hiring a person for a job description, think of hiring as the first step in defining and refining a role. We create a description of a role as we currently imagine it, including what goals, responsibilities, skills, and industry knowledge is needed to be successful. Then we evolve that description in partnership with the person inhabiting it via a weekly one-on-one. Finally, we have regular formal check-ins where we evaluate the person's fit with the role and determine what should be changed.

A BETTER WAY TO HIRE

Step 1: Define the Role

IN ORDER TO HIRE EFFECTIVELY (INTERNALLY OR EXTERNALLY) for a role, you need to understand the role first. Every role has four parts.

First, you describe the things the role does—goals and responsibilities—and the things the role knows—skills and market knowledge.

Responsibilities are the steady-state activities any job has; e.g., a people manager has to create and manage budgets, coach direct reports, and keep upper management apprised of progress.

A role also has goals it is asked to achieve, aligned to company OKRs. Since goals change as companies do, you won't know all the goals the role will be trying to achieve forever. But you should have a sense of what the goals are for the short term. Grow a new team? Build new efficiencies? Develop innovation strategy? Make sure that your goals—whether they use jargon or not—are concrete enough you'll know when your new employee has hit them. If you say, "Develop innovation strategy," ask yourself, what would that look like? What is the exit criteria? How will I know how successful it is? Vague goals are the enemy of progress.

In order to fulfill these responsibilities and achieve the desired goals, the employee must have market knowledge and the right skills for the role. *Market knowledge* is how well a prospect knows the space your company operates in: commerce, health care, education. *Skills* refers to the hard and soft skills it takes to accomplish the job, from Python to collaboration. Just like Kendra and Allie did in the story, I recommend free listing[1] the role's skills, stack-ranking them, and then drawing a line between must have and nice to have. Then put the top attributes in each category into the role canvas.

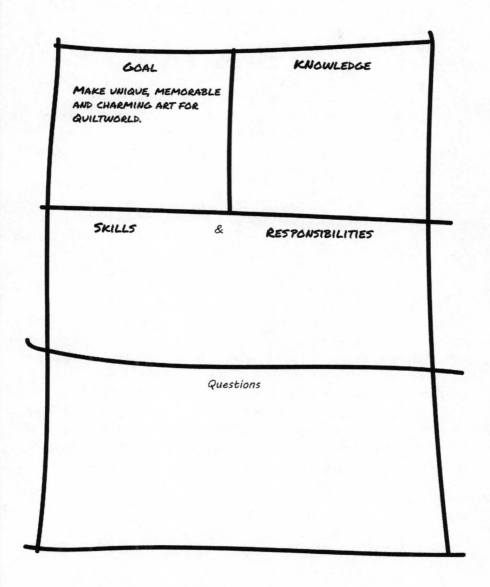

---

1   A design thinking technique in which you write down everything that comes into your head on the topic, one idea per Post-It.

Using the Role Canvas

A *canvas* is a visual worksheet that helps you think through an understood problem. I've designed the Role Canvas to be simple, so you can easily refer to it throughout the role lifecycle. I've included the four attributes mentioned above: goals, responsibilities, skills, and knowledge, plus an area for questions.

Filling in the role canvas is harder if you have a different background from the person you are trying to hire. If this is an existing role, you should ask the person who is already doing it to fill this out (assuming you are promoting them). If you are firing them, or if they quit, you can try getting a jump-start from another person who holds the same role in another team, an adviser, or—if desperate—you could do a content audit of other job descriptions and look for patterns. Make sure you understand what all those skills listed mean. You can't judge what you don't understand. Try to find a hiring adviser who can guide you.

In a big company, an adviser can be another manager who has held or managed the role. In a start-up, an adviser is that person collecting shares whom you never call.[2] Call them! If your adviser doesn't have the expertise, ask for an introduction to someone who does. Hiring a designer when you are an engineer is hard, hiring an engineer when you are a businessperson is hard … but sometimes you have to do it. The more you know before you do, the better.

Do the work. The right person makes the team stronger and the work easier for everyone. The wrong person does the reverse, and you'll be dealing with the fallout for months to years. Ask for help early or pay the consequences.

Next, take your giant wish list of qualities you'd like in the role that you carefully stack ranked. We're going to prioritize further.

In the goal, only put one to three goals. One big goal, clearly articulated, is best to give you focus on your hire. I know you have a hundred wishes for the magical unicorn you hope to hire, but it's more important to get someone who will accomplish the most important thing you need to get done.

Example goals:

- Build out an internal design team
- Transform engineering to Agile process
- Create a new product category for our portfolio

---

2   If you've been part of a startup, you just laughed ruefully. If you've never been, an adviser to a startup is an expert who is paid for their advice in shares. Sadly, those shares rarely turn into cash.

In responsibilities, try to get that down to five. There are only forty hours in a week, and most people like to sleep and see their families. Put in the most critical responsibilities, and let the job grow into more if it can. If it can't, at least the most important things get done.

Example responsibilities:

- Hiring, coaching, and firing direct reports
- Tracking and improving metrics
- Maintaining code base health

Knowledge refers to what area of the market should they be familiar with. Healthcare? E-commerce? Pick one to three areas of knowledge. Skills are like responsibilities, choose the three to five most critical. Skills can be taught.

Example knowledge:

- Familiar with best practices for e-commerce flows
- Understands social network dynamics
- Five years or more experience in online banking

Example skills:

- Photoshop
- Django
- Excel
- Usability practices
- Working with pattern libraries
- Multitasking

As you can see, skills are a bit of a catchall for everything from software to soft skills.

Now you have a description that covers the most critical elements of the role, but leaves space for surprising and interesting orthogonal skills to show up. You may get a marketer who knows how to edit video. You may get a programmer who has a great instinct for usability. Humans are complex and delightful. It's useful to make space for the unexpected candidate.

As well, you'll get more diverse candidates. Studies show[3] women will not apply for a job unless they are 100 percent qualified, while men will apply when they are 60 percent qualified. If you only list what you absolutely need in a candidate, you will get a bigger pool of prospects.

Once you have the canvas filled out, you can build the job description. This is the place where you stop thinking about "What do I want?" and start considering "What do they want?" The best people can work anywhere. Why should they work for you? Think about what makes working where you work so great. Ask others why they chose to work at your company. Even SOS, as toxic as it is, has its selling points. "A chance to work with top talent in the industry" or "Creating new categories of games." Maybe your company is "Reasonable hours" or "Provides mentorship and a chance to grow."

Next, reread your job description for gender coding. It turns out you will get fewer female candidates from a very masculine job description.[4] Some of this is obvious: Don't advertise for a salesman or a fireman. But it turns out more subtle language matters as well. Here are some examples from ERE[5], a Recruiting Professionals Community:

Engineer Company Description

AVERAGE DESCRIPTION: We are a dominant engineering firm that boasts many leading clients. We are determined to stand apart from the competition.

BETTER: We are a community of engineers who have effective relationships with many satisfied clients. We are committed to understanding the engineer sector intimately.

Engineer Qualifications

AVERAGE DESCRIPTION: Strong communication and influencing skills. Ability to perform individually in a competitive environment. Superior ability to satisfy customers and manage company's association with them.

---

3   Mohr, Tara Sophia. "Why Women Don't Apply for Jobs Unless They're 100% Qualified." *Harvard Business Review*. March 2, 2018. Accessed November 30, 2018. https://hbr.org/2014/08/why-women-dont-apply-for-jobs-unless-theyre-100-qualified.

4   Gaucher, D., Friesen, J., & Kay, A. C. (2011, March 7). "Evidence That Gendered Wording in Job Advertisements Exists and Sustains Gender Inequality." *Journal of Personality and Social Psychology*. Advance online publication. doi: 10.1037/a0022530

5   Shearman, Stephen. "You Don't Know It, But Women See Gender Bias in Your Job Postings." *ERE Media*, 22 July 2015, www.ere.net/you-dont-know-it-but-women-see-gender-bias-in-your-job-postings/.

BETTER: Proficient oral and written communications skills. Collaborates well in a team environment. Sensitive to clients' needs, can develop warm client relationships.

Engineer Responsibilities

AVERAGE DESCRIPTION: Direct project groups to manage project progress and ensure accurate task control. Determine compliance with client's objectives.

BETTER: Provide general support to project team in a manner complementary to the company. Help clients with construction activities.

In a study published in the American Psychological Association by the authors Gaucher, Friesen, and Kay called "Evidence That Gendered Wording in Job Advertisements Exists and Sustains Gender Inequality," six researchers studied gender wording in job advertisements and job descriptions and the effect of gender wording on job seekers. Among other findings, they discovered the language of competition was off-putting to women and the language of cooperation was appealing. If you are working toward the elusive high-performing team, you know diversity is a must.[6] A 2015 McKinsey report on 366 public companies found that those in the top quartile for ethnic and racial diversity in management were 35 percent more likely to have financial returns above their industry mean, and those in the top quartile for gender diversity were 15 percent more likely to have returns above the industry mean.

Wouldn't you like some fat financial returns? Focus on diversity from the very beginning.

Step 2. Interview

Before you interview, look over your role canvas and ask yourself, "How would I know?" How would you know if they had this skill? How would you know they could accomplish this goal? How do you know if they can fulfill this responsibility?

The answer is usually: Tell me a story ...

---

6   Grant, David RockHeidi. "Why Diverse Teams Are Smarter." *Harvard Business Review*, 4 Nov. 2016, hbr.org/2016/11/why-diverse-teams-are-smarter.

Sure, you could ask people, "Are you good at dealing with conflict?" They might say "No," if they are honest, but they are more likely to say "Yes," since it *is* a job interview.

Instead try asking, "Tell me about a time when you and your team were experiencing conflict." This avoids speculation and gives you something to reference check as well.

You can also ask, "Have you ever built a team? How did that go?" or "Have you done something similar? What were your greatest challenges?"

The important thing is to go over your role canvas and write up questions that will get you experience-based answers, not wish fulfillment.

Examples

1. Talk about a time when you had to work closely with someone whose personality was very different from yours.
2. Tell me about a time you needed to get information from someone who wasn't very responsive. What did you do?
3. Tell me about a time you were under a lot of pressure. What was going on, and how did you get through it?
4. Describe a time when your team or company was undergoing some change. How did that impact you, and how did you adapt?
5. Tell me about a time you failed. How did you deal with the situation?
6. Tell me about a time you had to be very strategic in order to meet all your top priorities.
7. Describe a long-term project that you managed. How did you keep everything moving along in a timely manner?
8. Give me an example of a time you managed numerous responsibilities. How did you handle them?
9. Give me an example of a time when you were able to successfully persuade someone to see things your way at work.
10. Describe a time when you were the resident technical expert. What did you do to make sure everyone was able to understand you?
11. Tell me about a time when you had to rely on written communication to get your ideas across to your team.
12. Tell me about your proudest professional accomplishment.
13. Tell me about a time when you worked under close supervision or extremely loose supervision. How did you handle that?

14. Give me an example of a time you were able to be creative with your work. What was exciting or difficult about it?
15. Tell me about a time you were dissatisfied in your work. What could have been done to make it better?

Optional Step 3: The Challenge

Determining if your candidate has the hard skills you need can be dealt with a number of ways, from tests to portfolios. Everyone has their own tricks, and I'm not going to get into the weeds with whether the design challenge is ethical or writing code on a whiteboard is moronic or not. Find someone who knows their business (a senior designer, engineer, what have you) and have them vet the individual. Again: Ask for help. Your job is to determine if the person can do the job or not. You don't have to do it alone.

Be sure to share the questions across the members of the interviewing team. Asking the same questions over and over bores the interviewee and reduces your information.

Consider rating each person 1 to 5 on the key attributes you've outlined in Goals, Responsibilities, Knowledge, and Skills. Compare the ratings across the interviewing team to look for biases or for anything you might have missed.

The Beginning, Not the End

Once you've checked in with other interviewers and made the best selection for the job, congratulations. You've done something hard. But the journey isn't over yet. Hang onto the role canvas, because you'll be using it for your one-on-one meetings with this person as well as regular team cadence reflections.

As such, be sure to update the role canvas as you go along. You may find some aspects are less important than you thought, and some were originally missing that you'll need to add. You'll want the document for feedback and for when you hire again.

Yes, you'll hire again for that same role. Life happens, and even the best workers don't stay forever.

UNSPOKEN TEAM ROLES

WITHIN TEAMS, THERE ARE THE SPOKEN ROLES, AS IN DESIGNER, marketer, engineer, etc. There's also a host of additional unspoken roles. There will be a facilitator, a person who takes notes at the meeting, a person who organizes the office party or the retreat, and a hundred other small tasks and roles that won't be on anyone's official job description. And yet you can't do without them.

I like to call these tasks the office housework. Nobody wants to do these things—they take up time and energy and are usually thankless. Over and over again, unless there's a plan otherwise, studies show that women end up with most of the office housework. If there's a woman on the team, even if she's an engineer, she is still asked to organize the Christmas party, and she still takes notes at meetings. Why is that?

So when we set up our team norms, we also need to list all the office housework and set up a schedule to rotate the housework logically. There's this saying about domestic housework that applies here: "Everybody hates housework. Mommy hates housework. Daddy hates housework. I hate housework, too. But it's just better if everybody does it together and gets it out of the way." If you let the housework sit with one group out of knee-jerk bias, hidden resentments build. The anger builds to the point it fractures teams and destroys any progress you're making toward diversity as well as most progress you're making on your goals.

People avoid dealing with the issue because they believe it's easier to make assumptions and move on rather than deal with conflict. But hidden resentment compounds over time until it costs you exponentially more. It's like buying a refrigerator in cash versus a small monthly payment. An $800 refrigerator kills your budget and you eat ramen for a month or two. Then you're done. Paying a little bit each month doesn't hurt as much, but in the end you've paid $1,700 for a refrigerator that should cost $800. It's far better to take the initial hit than to let the resentment collect interest.

Bring up the team roles and office housework as part of your norms. The tall guy shouldn't always make the decisions. The women shouldn't always take the notes. Instead, decide first how to decide, and then decide who does what and how. If the leader decides, who's the leader? If we say we come to consensus, how do we make sure everyone's voice is heard? What does that mean? If there are elements to the roles beyond what you were hired for, how do we portion those up fairly? What's the office housework and how do we deal with it fairly? When you make the unspoken spoken, everyone will ultimately be happier.

Or you could bicker and snipe at each other and hobble your progress for months, I suppose.

WHY DO WE MAKE NORMS?

I APOLOGIZE FOR STATING THE OBVIOUS, BUT TEAMS ARE MADE of people. People differ. People have different personalities. People come from different cultures. Yet everyone expects everyone else to behave the same as they would in a given situation.

There is an old saying: When you assume you make an ass out of you and me. With teams, if you assume shared understanding, you invite conflict and underperformance. Instead of spending time innovating and executing, you'll spend it arguing and undermining.

Companies often spend a lot of time applying Myers-Briggs tests or the actually-based-on-science Big Five tests[7]. It doesn't matter if you use these or horoscopes—what does matter is that you become aware that people think differently from you. When you realize that you love a good argument but your coworker would rather eat office chairs than disagree in public, you begin to develop the empathy needed to collaborate.

Culture also plays a big role in creating assumptions that lead to conflict. In her book *The Culture Code*, Erin Meyer explains how eight elements of cultural differences can cause friction. Her book is an excellent read, so I won't go into the details here, but she points out that in some cultures ten minutes late is polite, in others on time is the only right choice. In some cultures the boss decides, in others you have to build consensus.

---

7   Gladwell, Malcolm. "Personality Plus." *The New Yorker.* June 20, 2017. Accessed December 02, 2018. https://www.newyorker.com/magazine/2004/09/20/personality-plus.

When I was reading the book, I quickly saw that it isn't just countries that have cultures, companies do. When I worked at Yahoo, everyone was so very, very nice and you had to get consensus to get things done. At Zynga, it was dog-eat-dog and the boss always had the final call.

Now imagine starting to work with a group of people who all have a different idea of how to operate. Of course we're going to have stormy weather. But just like with OKRs and the Role Canvas, there is a cadence of rituals that can smooth the waters so we can navigate to success.

- Take a chunk of time up front to design who you want to be together. Create team norms.
- Set aside a tiny bit of time each week to tune how your progress is reaching toward those goals. Hold a retrospective.
- Quarterly, grade your performance against your stated vision of what kind of team you want to be.

This "extra work" will end up saving time in miscommunication and arguments as well as making happier and more productive workplaces. Slow down to go faster.

Design the team you want to be part of. Design the team you need to succeed. Design the life you want to live every day. Or choose to accept whatever dysfunction (and inaction) shows up.

SET THE NORMS

"WHAT ARE NORMS?" YOU ASK ME. THEY ARE THE RULES OF CON-
duct in a group. Often they are emergent and unspoken. But what if different
people have different ideas of what the norms are? They will behave in a
way that they think is appropriate, but their behavior will be perceived as
inappropriate. Then the judging begins: That person is a jerk, a bully, pushy,
pushover, etc. Americans deal with a huge number of messages about what
is normal. We get them from the many cultures that make up this country,
from national to regional to familial to corporate. We navigate high context/
low context values (blunt vs. subtle communication) to cooperative/competi-
tive to conflict averse/conflict accepting and more.

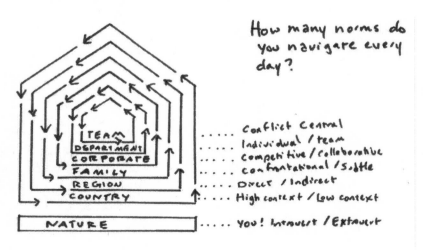

How many norms do
you navigate every
day?

TEAM
DEPARTMENT
CORPORATE
FAMILY
REGION
COUNTRY

..... Conflict Central
..... Individual / team
..... Competitive / collaborative
..... Confrontational / subtle
..... Direct / Indirect
.... High context / Low context

NATURE

...... You! Introvert / Extrovert

For example, let's look at the behavior of interrupting. Let's say one team member, Margot, came from a big family in Chicago where talking over each other was normal. Only way you could get a word in edgewise! She also works in sales, where fast talking is valued. Now she's on a team with Jim, who is from Maine, a Quaker, and Japanese-English. Jim thinks Margot is the rudest person he's ever met, and can't stand to be in a meeting with her. Margot thinks Jim is a doormat.

I suspect most initial storming (conflict) is teams trying to normalize varying norms. You could avoid the worst of inter-team conflict by collectively designing the team norms. Instead of letting norms be unspoken and emergent, speak about them and choose what the team will accept and what it won't. A lot of headaches can be solved if you're willing to have conversations to make the norms explicit.

Educator Andre Plaut taught me an exercise to help classrooms determine their norms. Andre specializes in adult education, and found when classes decide how they want to learn—as opposed to accepting the benevolent dictatorship of the professor—they learn more quickly and completely. I still use that exercise with my classes, and I adapted that norm setting exercise for teams. It's easy to run this exercise with new teams, as creating a team charter and/or "rules for our team" is a pretty typical part of team forming. But even if the team has been around a while, you can use the start of a quarter as a "do over" moment, and run this exercise.

EXERCISE FOR TEAM NORMING

THIS EXERCISE CAN BE RUN QUICKLY, IN ABOUT THIRTY TO FOR-
ty-five minutes, or you can let it run long and people will go for two hours.
Talking about what makes teams work or fail is often therapeutic.

If you want to run this, set aside at least an hour. No one complains when
meetings end early. Timebox (i.e., put a time limit) on each exercise, unless
you suspect it's a critical conversation. You can lose the trust of the team if
you force them into the next exercise when they clearly need to talk through
an issue. If you can bring in a facilitator so you can be a participant, do so. A
trained facilitator can spot when a team needs to go long, and it allows you
to join into the fray.

There are two ways to run this exercise. One is as a single group talking
to each other, similar to the traditional brainstorm. This works well when
the group is small and comfortable with each other.

The other is silent listing of norms, then share to breakout groups, then
share with the larger group. This is effective if the group is larger, or made up
of introverts and extroverts, or strangers. There is less social cost to writing
something down and sharing with a small group than having to yell out your
thoughts in front of everyone.

Step One: the Good

Picture the best team you've ever been on. The one where you felt you were part of something special. Can you recall its characteristics? What made it so awesome?

Share them with the facilitator *or* write them down on Post-Its.

Give folks about five to ten minutes for this.

If writing down on Post-Its, take a moment (five minutes) to share with your smaller group (three to five people.)

Step Two: the Bad

Now picture the worst team you've ever been part of. You know, you wake up each morning dreading that you'll be facing *those people*. What made it so dreadful?

Share *or* write them down.

If writing them, take a moment to share with the small group.

If working in small groups, take a moment to stack rank your issues. Then share your top three goods and top three bads with the larger group. The facilitator should write them on the wall so they can be remembered as you create your norms.

Step Three: Rules of Engagement

Finally, make a list of rules for your team. It should be easy to think up rules after a moment of reflection on your experiences. Call them out to the facilitator, and have them listed on a flipchart—something that invites editing and updates. Fancy posters will make team members reluctant to update the norms.

If you are working in breakout groups, the small groups can generate them, then share with the big group. Duplication is fine … it just means the issue is really important.

When I run this exercise, I question the "rules." If someone says, "Speak your mind," I'll ask:

- What does it look like when someone "speaks their mind"?
- Why does that rule matter?
- How can we tell if people aren't following the rule?
- How do you plan to call each other out if someone violates this rule?

The rules need to have the same meaning for all team members. I often have to get clarity around a phrase that everyone knows what it means, like "Speak your mind." What does it look like when everyone speaks his or her mind? Is everyone yelling? Does it mean we'll tell people when their sweater is ugly? Or are people honest but still appreciative of each other's feelings?

Many teams in the Silicon Valley are composed of people from both high context and low context cultures[8]. A rule like "Speak your mind" has a very different meaning for a person from China, a person from Holland, and a person from Texas. By describing what it looks like to speak your mind, it's recognizable by people whose culture doesn't favor direct confrontation. Some people need formal permission to speak up.

Let's say Jim suggests the rule, "No interrupting."

Margot is confused. "What do you mean?"

Jim says, "It's rude."

Margot says, "I don't think it's rude. It's important to get your ideas out while they are fresh."

Jim says, "But when you interrupt me, I forget what I'm saying. It's upsetting. I feel like my opinion isn't valued."

The facilitator can then ask others what they think (if they don't jump in). The group will decide if interrupting is okay, at which point the facilitator can ask the group how to help Jim make sure he can participate. Or the group may decide interrupting is not okay, which means they need to figure out how to help Margot adjust.

Two things need to happen:

- Pick what is acceptable behavior in your group
- Decide how to help everyone live with that choice

After you've got about ten rules people believe they can live by, ask if anyone has any other burning issue they wish to address. If not, set aside the rules until the weekly retrospective, where you'll review and revise.

---

8   *"High-context cultures are those in which the rules of communication are primarily transmitted through the use of contextual elements (i.e., body language, a person's status, and tone of voice) and are not explicitly stated. This is in direct contrast to low-context cultures, in which information is communicated primarily through language and rules are explicitly spelled out."* Study.com. Accessed December 2, 2018. https://study.com/academy/lesson/high-context-culture-definition-examples-quiz.html.

CONTINUOUS FEEDBACK, CONTINUOUS IMPROVEMENT

CONGRATULATIONS! YOU'VE HIRED WELL, SET EXCELLENT GOALS, and created team norms! Now we just have to wait for the success fairy to come along and put good metrics under our pillows![9]

When I put it that way it sounds ridiculous, but many people act as if that were the case. They spend a ton of time finding that perfect hire, but no time coaching them. They set goals, but don't check them weekly. They set norms, then forget them as the team slides into old habits (and arguments). You need check-ins, so the team can live their intentions.

The cadence here is weekly: the weekly one-on-one, weekly status email, Monday commitment meetings and Friday brag sessions, weekly retrospectives. These rituals are where the team starts to learn how to hold each other accountable, how to question each other's decisions, and how to work together toward a shared goal.

---

9   Apologies to everyone who doesn't have a tooth fairy in their cultural mythos. You'll have to search it up. Yes, American children really do believe this. It might explain a lot.

The chart below is from Amy Edmondson[10]. As you can see, the team leader takes on two critical functions: setting the goal and creating psychological safety for the team. I've described setting the goal sufficiently.

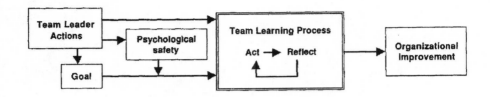

10   *International Handbook of Organizational Teamwork and Cooperative Working.* Michael A. West, Dean Tjosvold, Ken G. Smith, eds.,John Wiley & Sons, 2003, pp. 255-275

LET'S TALK PSYCHOLOGICAL SAFETY

WHEN I WAS AT LINKEDIN SO MANY YEARS AGO, WE WERE LOOK-ing into creating a product where people would ask questions and other professionals would answer them.

When we conducted user research, we discovered that the target audience was uncomfortable posting publicly. Their boss and coworkers were on Linkedin, and they wondered what would happen when they posted. "Will my coworkers think I'm an idiot?" "Will my boss think I'm not capable?" In fact, they were even afraid to share an article. "What if everyone has already seen it? Will I look stupid?" Eventually we came up with a solution by creating LinkedIn Groups, where you knew whom your audience was. But it taught me how rare psychological safety is.

Psychological safety is when you know you won't be ripped a new one for asking a question. It's when your boss thanks you when you point out she made a mistake. Psychological safety is when your coworker gives you advice and you know they want to help you, and not put you down. It seems like it should be the norm, but sadly it is not.

The team leader is responsible for setting the tone of the team. Simply setting norms together has already done part of the work. It sends the message, "We are all responsible for our team." But how you respond day-to-day is even more critical. This is where you prove you truly trust the team.

In *The Fearless Organization*[11], Amy Edmondson lists critical behaviors a team leader must show to encourage psychological safety:

- Reframe failure. As Astro Teller of Google X says, "I'm not pro-failure. I'm pro-learning."
- Show situational humility. Don't be the one with all the answers. Be willing to say, "I don't know." Admit when you are wrong.
- Listen completely and ask good questions. Nothing says "I care" more than listening.
- Compliment, offer help, brainstorm solutions. Be the person who makes answers happen, not the person who has answers.
- Sanction clear violations. If someone has broken the norms the team agreed upon, model effective feedback. Let them know what they've done is inappropriate quickly and clearly.

The difference between guilt and shame is you feel guilt when you do a bad thing, and shame when you are convinced you are a bad person. A team member who is acting inappropriately is (hopefully) not a bad person, just a person with bad habits. Treat norm violations like spelling errors. Everyone makes them sometimes, but you don't want to make it a regular thing—it's unprofessional. A person who violates the team's norms may feel a bit guilty, but they should never feel ashamed.

By showing you're human, seeking answers from the team, showing humility, and gently guiding them toward the behavior they have stated they want, you can be an effective leader of a high-performing team.

---

11   Edmondson, Amy C. *Fearless Organization: Creating Psychological Safety in the Workplace for Learning, Innovation, and Growth.* Wiley & Sons Canada, Limited, John, 2018.

THE AUTONOMOUS TEAM

NOW THAT YOU'VE COMMITTED TO BEING A NEW KIND OF MAN-ager, let's build (or remodel) a new kind of team.

All teams are made up of individuals with a variety of skills that complement and support one another. A team is united by a shared purpose, offers mutual accountability, and sets goals for performance. That's the fundamental nature of a team. But what makes the truly good teams good?

An autonomous team goes many steps further. This team collectively sets goals. It can debate, in a healthy manner, why that OKR set is the right one to focus on for this quarter. The manager doesn't have to dictate; instead, he or she brings information about what other teams are working on and what upper management is particularly interested in. He or she becomes the ambassador for the team, while the team largely sets their own direction.

The team can help each other get better at doing their jobs through open and honest feedback. Over time, the psychological safety of the team increases. They start to trust each other to look out for one another, and the feedback cycles become smaller. As they become more comfortable with one another, they are able to call each other out when bad behavior happens. Issues don't fester.

Imagine a world where a teammate is talking and another interrupts because she suddenly got a great idea. The first teammate might get angry, thinking that she doesn't care about him, that she's disrespecting him and talking over him. If he speaks up rudely to stop her, both people might leave seething with anger.

Imagine instead a team where both have already been working together. She might interrupt him in the same way, excited about that new idea, but now he says, "Hey, Pam, hold on a second … Can I finish my idea? And then I'm totally excited to hear your idea." It takes a while to build trust on both sides, to call someone out on bad behavior but to trust their motives, and to take that call-out in good grace.

Healthy teams have done the work of building norms. They've decided who they want to be, and how they will call each other out when they don't meet those standards. They've decided on goals that they believe in that they're going to set together. They've decided on both the spoken and unspoken roles they've agreed to fill. They've agreed to rotate who brings coffee to the meetings. That's a team that's comfortable and committed to each other, and that's a team that can work on getting better and better over time.

As Daniel Pink talks about in his book *Drive*, humans are motivated by and find fulfillment in autonomy, mastery, and purpose. These three conditions are the largest predictors of happiness, and the self-regulating team has all three. They have autonomy because the boss isn't telling them what to do—they decide how to reach the goals set before them. They have purpose because they've jointly decided on a shared goal to strive for, pulling together in the pursuit of something meaningful. They've got mastery, because they constantly evolve to get better at their jobs through the process of safe feedback. It's a formula for truly amazing, fulfilling work.

Once you begin to evolve a team to this level, everyone wants to be a part of the success. You get to go from Bad News Bears to the World Series winner. The team coaches itself. The people manager eventually becomes a member of the team who happens to have some deep insight into the business and the rest of the company. It's a good place for the team to be.

Evolving a Team for High Performance

As a reminder, once again here are the different stages of a team in its various aspects.

	GOALS	ROLES	NORMS
SET (was Form)	Set objectives and key results	Hire formal roles (product manager, engineer, designer) Set information roles (facilitator, note taker, agenda maker)	Discover implicit norms Set shared norms via a team charter
CHECK (Was Storm-to-Perform)	Monday priority meeting to choose what tasks to do in hopes of achieving OKRs Friday bragging session to share successes and learnings. Weekly status email	Weekly 1:1 to coach and give feedback	Retrospective, in which team quickly determines what's working and what needs to change
CORRECT (was Adjourn)	EOQ OKR grading	Quarterly individual performance review to determine promotions, commendations, or corrections.	Team performance review, in which the team collectively grades their group performance against their norms.

In the last section, we talked about forming the team, with its norms, roles, and goals. When a team forms, the group actively designs how they'll work together. It's the first step toward making a high performing team. In this section, we'll be talking about performing as a team, Stage 2. Here, the team realizes its potential through continuous feedback and iteration.

It's not enough to become a functional team. We want to be a learning team, a growing team, an ever-getting-better team. That doesn't happen by accident.

It takes clear role setting, good hiring, regular feedback, and sometimes corrective action. I'm going to go through each one, with its related cadence.

If you've read *Radical Focus*, feel free to skip this next section and move on to Roles.

THE WEEKLY OKR CADENCE

From *Radical Focus*

MANY COMPANIES WHO TRY OKRS FAIL, AND THEY BLAME THE system. But no system works if you don't actually keep to it. Setting a goal at the beginning of a quarter and expecting it to magically be achieved by the end is naïve. It's important to have a cadence of commitment and celebration to ensure you stay on the right track.

Scrum is a technique used by engineers to commit to progress, to hold each other accountable, and to support each other. Each week an engineer shares what happened last week, what they commit to doing next week, and any blockers that keep them from their goals. In larger orgs, they hold a "scrum of scrums" to assure teams are also holding each other accountable for meeting goals. There is no reason multidisciplinary groups can't do the same.

Monday Commitments and the Four Square

Each Monday, the team should meet to check in on progress against OKRs and commit to the tasks that will help the company meet its Objective. I recommend a format with four key quadrants:

INTENTION FOR THE WEEK: What are the three or four most important things you must get done this week toward the Objective? Discuss if these priorities will get you closer to the OKRs.

FORECAST FOR THE MONTH: What should your team know is coming up that they can help with or prepare for?

STATUS TOWARD OKRS: If you set a confidence of five out of ten, has that moved up or down? Have a discussion about why.

HEALTH METRICS: Pick two things you want to protect as you strive toward greatness. What can you not afford to eff-up? Key relationships with customers? Code stability? Team well-being? Now mark when things start to go sideways, and discuss it.

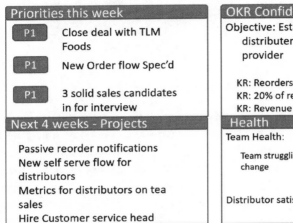
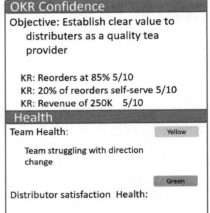

This document is first and last a conversation tool. You want to talk about issues like:

- Do the priorities lead to our hitting our OKRs?
- Why is confidence dropping in our ability to make our OKRs? Can anyone help?
- Are we prepared for major new efforts? Does marketing know what product is up to?
- Are we burning out our people or letting hacks become part of the code bases?

When you meet, you could discuss only the four-square, or you can use it to provide a status overview, then supplement with other detailed documents covering metrics, a pipeline of projects, or related updates. Each company has a higher or lower tolerance for status meetings.

Try to keep things as simple as possible. Too many status meetings are about team members trying to justify their existence by listing every little thing they've done. Trust your team makes good choices in their everyday lives. Set the tone of the meeting to be about team members helping each other to meet the shared goals they all have committed to.

Have fewer priorities and shorter updates.

Make time for the conversations. If only one-fourth of the time allotted for the Monday meeting is presentations and the rest is discussing next steps, you are doing it right. If you end early, it's a good sign. Just because you've set aside an hour doesn't mean you have to use it.

A Note about the Health (Maintenance Metric) Box

OKRs are stretch goals. They are shoot-for-the-moon goals. But not everything needs to be pushed. Some things need to be maintained. That's why I recommend the bottom right box of the four square. While you're focusing on one big objective, there are probably some metrics you want to monitor to keep an eye on the company as a whole. Revenue, for example. Customer satisfaction. You need to make sure teams are healthy, key hires are made, and the code base is not turning into septic waste. So pick a handful of key metrics you want to keep in the green while you are making heroic efforts toward the OKRs.

I typically mark the health metrics simply as green/yellow/red. Green means all fine, yellow means keep a watch out. But red means something critical to the health of our company is in free fall.

At this point you call a "Code Red" and prioritize a fix (or finding a path to a fix) over OKR efforts.

Keep your health metrics to a minimum. Three to five is enough. If you are a data-driven company, you can hold a biweekly or monthly full metrics review to get deep into the data. But you still want a very short list of numbers you can truly live by.

Health metrics and OKRs are different things. Don't put maintenance efforts in your OKRs. Don't put OKRs in your health measures.

Fridays Are for Winners

When teams are aiming high, they fail a lot. While it's good to aim high, missing your goals without also seeing how far you've come is often depressing. That's why committing to the Friday wins session is so critical.

In the Friday wins session, teams all demo whatever they can. Engineers show bits of code they've got working and designers show mockups and maps. But beyond that, every team should share something. Sales can talk about whom they've closed, customer service can talk about customers they've rescued, business development shares deals. This has several benefits. One, you start to feel like you are part of a pretty special winning team. Two, the team starts looking forward to having something to share. They seek wins. And last, the company starts to appreciate what each discipline is going through and understand what everyone does all day.

Providing beer, wine, cake, or whatever is appropriate to your team on a Friday is also important to making the team feel cared for. If the team is really small and can't afford anything, you can have a "Friday Wins Jar" that all contribute to. But as the team gets bigger, the company should pay for the celebration nibbles as a signal of support. Consider this: The humans who work on the project are the biggest asset. Shouldn't you invest in them?

OKRs are great for setting goals, but without a system to achieve them, they are as likely to fail as any other process that is in fashion. Commit to your team, commit to each other, and commit to your shared future. Renew those vows every week.

WORKING THE WEEKLY ONE-ON-ONE
A Primer on Coaching

THERE ARE A LOT OF WORK "RITUALS" THAT SUCK SO BADLY YOU want to hunt down and interrogate whoever invented them. The dreaded weekly status email is one of them. The weekly one-on-one between a boss and a direct report can be another. What should be a chance to get on the same page with the person critical to your success is often awkward, overly chummy, or even skipped.

In my life, I've been a manager, a coach, and a teacher. You could argue they are all variations of management. All three share a common misconception, which is that the job is to tell people things—what to do, what to think, or what to know. But it's not. If you want to be good at any of these, you have to become a facilitator in another human's journey to self-management.

The job of a manager is to make yourself as unnecessary as possible.

A teacher who only lectures is no more valuable than a YouTube video. A teacher who asks great questions makes life-long learners.

A coach who tells you how to solve your problems is giving you a one-size-fits-all answer, creating dependency if the advice works, and blowing up in your face when it's wrong. But a coach who pushes you to closely examine your situation and develop your own solutions is a great coach.

A boss who tells you what to do is a micromanager. As well as annoying the subordinate, a boss like that doesn't scale. No CEO has the time to tell their direct reports what to do in every situation, much less all their employees. Although I know plenty of startup founders who try …

A manager has to learn to create a workplace where all employees feel comfortable both making decisions alone and asking for advice when it's needed. The one-on-one is where that habit is built.

I recommend using an approach based on John Whitmore's GROW model[12] (based on the Inner Game[13] approach). I could gush about the Inner Game approach to coaching for days. The big idea is that everyone can be their own coach, because everyone is an expert on themselves. Instead of an advisor, we need a thinking partner to help pull those insights out.

Here's how that model works for one-on-ones:

Step Zero: Start with at Least a Little Prep

Before the one-on-one, scan the person's status report. Is there anything there that you should address? A worry, a missed goal, a drop in confidence?

Or you might have something you need to discuss with your direct report, such as a concern about a behavior issue.

I told you you'd use your role canvas again—this is where. Before the one-on-one, review the Role Canvas. Are they making progress toward the goal? Are they fulfilling their responsibilities? Do they have the needed knowledge and skills to do their job?

Now pick the most important topic to discuss. That very well might be feedback you've heard about them from another team member or a skill you believe they need to learn.

Make a note to yourself on what the topic is and any salient details. Don't trust memory. Emotion can disrupt it.

Try not to have more than one to three things on your list. Just one is best. Remember, you meet every week. Discuss fewer things better.

Consider going for a walk rather than sitting in a conference room. It will be easier to talk, more relaxing, and it will get you out of the building. Start the conversation by asking an easy personal question about an interest you and the person share, such as sports or entertainment. If you don't know

12   Whitmore, John. *Coaching for Performance: GROWing Human Potential and Purpose*. Boston: Nicholas Brealey, 2009.

13   Gallwey, W. Timothy. *The Inner Game of Tennis*. New York: Random House, 1975.

what they care about, ask! The best work is done when we all know each other as human beings.

Step One: Now You're Ready to Coach

G is for Goals. Ask your report, "What would you like to get out of today's meeting?" Let their topic lead the discussion. You can make space for your issues after.

R is for Reality (or Reflection). Ask questions about the topic they are struggling with: What facts do they have? What insights? What hunches? What is their reality?

Some questions to try out from *Coaching Mastery*[14]:

- What's your gut tell you?
- How's that make you feel?
- What's exciting?
- What's scary?
- What's making you [sad, angry, happy]?
- How does your culture or history affect this?
- What *do* you know? (Can be used when someone says, I don't know.")
- What surprises you about this?

O is for Options. Have the report come up with their own solutions to the situation.

This can be tough if you are a "fixer," like I am. As soon as I hear someone say they have a problem, I start thinking of solutions. But this keeps you as the holder of all answers. Sit on your hands, resist the urge, and ask, "Do you have any ideas for what to do about this?"

More possible questions to ask:

- How can you make your dream happen?
- What's possible?
- What if you had a magic wand, and what you wanted just happened?
- What's a new way?

---

14   Smith, David W. *David Smith's Coaching Mastery: The Ultimate Blueprint for Tennis Coaches, Tennis Parents, Tennis Teaching Professionals*. St. George, UT: David Smith, 2008.

- What if there were no barriers?
- What's the ideal?

W is for Wrap-Up. If you have gotten through the issues you need to, you can discuss next steps, e.g., "Let me know how it goes," "Email me that report," or "Looking forward to learning more next week!" Ask, "How can I help?" Then you can restart the cycle or finish the conversation.

Wrap-Up questions:

- How can I help?
- What resources are available?
- What's next?

Step Two: Giving Feedback, Positive and Negative

Feedback is a word that strikes terror into many people's hearts. Feedback is often used to mean, "I'm going to tell you what's wrong with you." I used to be terrified of feedback, because all I heard was, "You are a bad person."

Over the years, I've studied feedback: How to give it, how to take it, and how to use it to live in a state of constant growth. It still scares me a little, but I value it because it makes me more effective. Feedback helps you see yourself as others see you.

When people engage in a behavior that upsets us, we often attribute intention: "They don't care," "They're selfish," "What a privileged asshole!" But intention is unknowable. Only through feedback and conversation can we create a common understanding that leads to better cooperation.

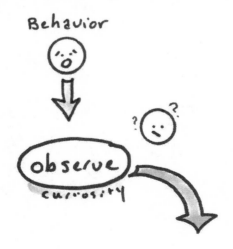

The prompt to give feedback is usually emotion. It can be anger, frustration, or resentment. People feeling strong feelings often vent or repress. You cannot do either, for the sake of your team.

This is the hard part. You have to transform your negative emotion into curiosity.

I feel angry. Why? What triggered the anger? What are the stories I'm telling myself about my anger? What other stories explain this trigger? Is the behavior appropriate in another context? Could it be personal? Have I seen this before, or is it atypical? Is this the individual, or is this how our culture asks us to behave?

The next step is to try to put the behavior into context via compassion.

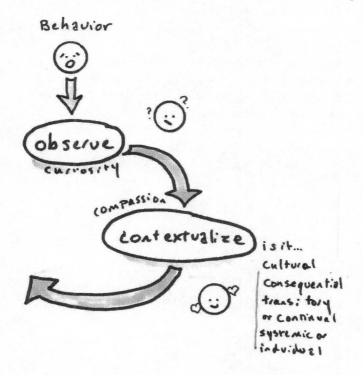

Watch for High Context-Low Context Culture Clashes

Everybody has an internalized idea of appropriate behavior. It comes from multiple factors, from geography to family to corporate culture. When people grew up in one place, got jobs, and worked for one company for most of their life, there was very little cultural tension. In other words, your family played by the same rules as your country and your company.

As we become more global, we run into issues when people have to work together but are playing by different rules. When we see a behavior we think is inappropriate, it must be examined for context.

At Yahoo, we had a culture of passive-aggressiveness. At Zynga, we had a culture of aggressive-aggressiveness. I grew up in Iowa, which is a mix of high context and low (because of its Dutch-English mix). My family, however, were very non-confrontational. You can imagine which company I found easier to navigate.

Mind Your Motivations

From curiosity, change your emotional state to sympathy, then empathy, and finally compassion. Sympathy allows you to see they have a different experience; empathy allows you to feel their struggle as well as your own. Compassion is empathy with an action item. Compassion gives you the right posture to communicate feedback. When you move from wanting to give feedback because you're hurt to wanting to give feedback to help them be more successful, then you are ready to shape your message.

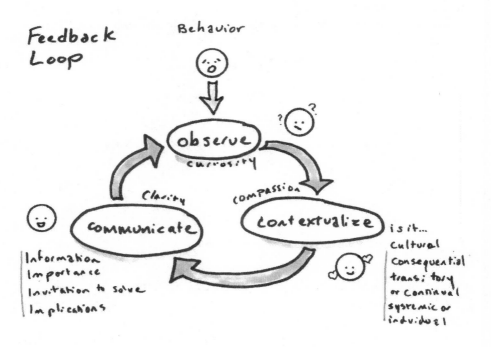

Structuring Effective Feedback

Matt Abraham, lecturer at Stanford Business School, uses the four I's as a model for structuring feedback. His steps are:

- Information—what is the behavior I observed that is not working for me?
- Importance—why is it problematic?
- Invitation to change—a nice way to say, "I'd like you to cut that out."
- Implications—if you don't, these are the results I expect will happen, from not being able to work together to firing.

I shorten this to simple sentences like, "You've turned in your designs late three times now, and this means I don't have time to code properly, or I have to stay up all night working, and my husband gets mad at me. How can we change this? Otherwise, I'm not sure I can continue to collaborate with you."

The touchy-feely approach works, but you may wish to modify messaging to match your company and team culture. But no matter how you say it, keep feedback *about the behavior* and *not* the person or the intentions. For example, delivering promised work late can be called out as bullshit nonsense, but *never* call the person a jerk or assert, "You don't care about my life." People get upset if you judge them as a person or ascribe intent. They know you are making stuff up about them (even if you are right).

INTENT   BEHAVIOR   REACTION

I know, You can't know (unless you ask)   WE can see   You know, I can't know (unless I ask)

The only thing you can both be sure about is behavior. Talk about that, share your reactions, inquire about intention.

David Bradford, professor at Stanford University, calls this moving from your area of expertise (your feelings) and moving to your area of ignorance (their motivations). In *Power Laws*, he describes it thusly:

"Crossing the line between objective remarks about performance and judgments about the person is common in workplace feedback:

- "You have a poor attitude."
- "All you want to do is build an empire."
- "You are a controlling person."

"Each of these statements contains assumptions about another person's motives and intentions. None address observable behavior or its consequences. The person on the receiving end of this inept feedback will naturally become defensive."

Stay with what you both know: This happened.

There are four strong ways you can stay with what you know, but still offer clear feedback:

1. Tell them how the behavior affected you. This we've discussed.
2. Tell them the behavior is not meeting their apparent goals. In the fable portion of this book, Mick wants Kendra to work faster. Allie has to point out this has the opposite effect.
3. Your behavior may meet your goals, but it is costly to you. For example, being so persistent in pushing your agenda that another person might dig in out of sheer annoyance. The pushy individual may get a poor reputation and find it hard to accomplish goals that take cooperation.
4. Ask, "In what ways am I part of the problem?" Perhaps Kendra could say, "Mick, I know I deliver late a lot, and I really want to fix this. But when you hover over my cube, I can't focus, and it takes me longer to do my work. Can we find a way to make you more comfortable so I can settle down and focus?" Hopefully Mick and Kendra could find a way to find a balance, perhaps via short daily check-ins.

What if You Aren't the Boss?

It can be tough when your boss isn't the best coach. But you can still coach upward. Ask your manager what she wants to cover or suggest a topic, then ask her what she knows about the reality of the matter, share what you know, bounce options off her and so on. Help her help you.

As well, look for peer-to-peer coaching. You can read a book like *Inner Game of Stress* with a small group of coworkers and discuss it after. Then coach each other, using the GROW model. Question-based coaching with GROW allows you to coach anyone, even if you don't have expertise in that area. That means a designer can coach an engineer or a QA person can coach a marketer. You might even get greater team cohesion along the way.

Managers, Avoid the Seduction of Bossing

Advice is thrust upon us so often in our everyday life. It's kinder to ask first, even when you are the boss. Maybe especially when you are the boss.

If you do have advice, ask for consent first. Try saying something like, "I have an idea I think might help. May I share?" That little gesture of respect prevents you from appearing bossy and makes space for your report to hear what you have to say.

The combination of deep listening, directed questioning, and respectful and restrained advice changes the power dynamic in the employer-employee relationship. It becomes a partnership in which each person has a distinct role to play and in which both are responsible for each other's success. Which they are.

This model is so effective I've been using it in my office hours with my Stanford students. When a student comes by, I ask them what's on their mind. I ask them what they know about the situation, and if they had thought of any solutions already. I offer advice when I have it and when the student wants it. But often they figure it out just by talking it through.

My students are bright and passionate humans, and I won't be teaching them for long. I'm better off teaching them to teach themselves.

RETROSPECTIVES AND POST-MORTEMS

A HIGH-PERFORMING TEAM HAS TO BE A LEARNING TEAM. IN A learning team, not only is the team performing as a unit, but they are also working together to become better every day. They question each new status quo and make hypotheses about how they can be more effective. I believe in this type of team the stages look more like this.

A learning team (or maybe I should call it a Lean team, as it closely resembles the continuous improvement of Lean Manufacturing and the learning cycle of Lean Startup) shares a commitment to progress. Knowledge is shared out as soon as it's acquired, and the team is continually developing new hypotheses to be tested.

There are two key rituals I'd like to call out, both from Agile[15], that support learning. One is the Post-Mortem and the other is the Retrospective. There is a LOT written on the internets about both, so I'll keep this section short.

---

15   Agile is a time boxed, iterative approach to software delivery that builds software incrementally from the start of the project, instead of trying to deliver it all at once near the end. It has a number of best practices (rituals) for delivering software iteratively, and both my OKR and team methodologies borrow from the practices I've seen succeed.

The Retrospective happens every week. The team quickly notes what worked last week and what sort of things they'd like to try next week. Different teams use a lot of formats. I'm a fan of two columns: keeps and changes.

The keeps + and changes Δ columns used on retrospective.

It's good to go with an approach that matches your team culture. Personally, I prefer the very simple one, because I think it's more important to do regular, small, fast check-ins than make a production out of it. If every week you just improve one to three things, that adds up very quickly to a great team. A lightweight ritual is less likely to be skipped because you are low on time. It can take just ten minutes, tacked on the end of another meeting.

The team's leader can make a big difference in how willing the team is to admit mistakes and learn from them. From Edmondson, *The Fearless Organization*

> "To create psychological safety, team leaders also can demonstrate tolerance of failure, such as by acknowledging one's own fallibility, taking interpersonal risks, and religiously avoiding punishing others for well-intentioned risks that backfire. Self-disclosure by team leaders is one way to do this (Gabarro, 1987).

> For example, one surgeon team leader repeatedly told his team: "I need to hear from you because I'm likely to miss things."

"The repetition of this phrase was as important as its meaning: People tend not to hear or not to believe a message that contradicts old norms when they hear it only once. Soliciting feedback suggests to others that their opinion is respected; it may also contribute to establishing a norm of active participation."

In early retrospectives, expect to go first, admitting a mistake of your own. You can also "seed" the retrospective by keeping an ear to the ground for good items for reflection, and say things like, "You folks really figured it out. I hope you'll mention it Friday at retro so others can learn from it." Or "You really struggled with that. Would you mind bringing it up Friday so we can figure out how it doesn't happen again?" But nothing beats being willing to go first.

Your reception to mistakes will make a huge difference to the team's psychological safety. Treat them as failed experiments that reveal new potential solutions. You don't have to condone incompetence, but a well-intentioned, well-researched, well-executed failure that did nothing wrong but be unable to predict the future? If you punish good people doing their best for not succeeding, you'll soon have a group that doesn't want to take any risks.

The motto of product-design firm IDEO is, "Fail often, so you'll succeed sooner." Innovation is hard, and if you really want it you'll have to make a safe place for risk taking.

Post-mortems are more formal retrospectives held at the end of a project. They don't fit the set-check-correct model as closely, as they can be held anywhere in the quarterly cycle.

A learning team creates a rhythm of introspection and evaluation. Some do it at the end of each project, some will make a simple "keeps" and "changes" tally each week. What matters is the learning cycle. (I recommend both, by the way.)

QUARTERLY REFLECTION RHYTHM

IN THE LAST SECTION, WE TALKED ABOUT USING A WEEKLY reflection practice to constantly learn and improve. The weekly reflection cycle allows you to note progress, course correct, and celebrate small wins as a team in order to stay on track for your big-picture goals. This allows for evolution. For revolution, you need to formally step back and move from examining the trees to taking a look at the forest. A deep and thorough retrospective allows you to address thorny problems that resist change. I recommend quarterly, as many business functions mark progress by quarters.

Quarters are useful temporal landmarks. A temporal landmark is an artificial moment in time that a group shares, like New Year's or a special birthday (30, 50, 75) or an anniversary. A temporal landmark is a place where people pause, reflect, and commit to change. Monday is a tiny one, quarters are midsize ones, annual is a big one … perhaps too big? If we wait until the end of the year to examine our performance, first, we probably can't remember back to last January and second, it's way too long to wait to fix a recalcitrant problem.

Spotify Labs notes, "Quarterly seems to be a good starting point. Every month seems too often (people get fed up with it, and the data doesn't change fast enough to warrant it). Bi-annually seems too seldom (too much happens within that period). But, again, it varies."

Quarterly has three key advantages:

1. If you know you are going to be discussing what's going right and what needs improving again in three months, you can keep it short. Less information is more likely to be taken to heart. I've found when I give three pieces of feedback, all are acted upon. When I gave twenty, none were. It's just too overwhelming. Save little things for the one-on-ones, and cover the big issues in the quarterly.

2. It's hard to remember what happened last February, but the last three months are pretty memorable. Over time, we tell ourselves stories about what happened, often making ourselves the hero, and the other person the villain. Doing a check-in every three months means you will hopefully remember things the same way as the employee. (But always document anyhow. Paper doesn't forget.)

3. Reviewing reduces the stakes. If you only get a shot at a promotion or a bonus once a year, it can be devastating when employee expectations and hopes aren't met. But in a three-month cycle, there is always next time.

If your company is stuck in the annual review cycle, you can still do a formal sit down with your direct reports every three months. Document the conversation, and you might actually have a shot at remembering what happened in February. And you'll be providing invaluable feedback regularly.

What to Cover

During this adjourn-and-reflect quarterly review, I recommend spending time reflecting on the following three areas:

	GOALS	ROLES	NORMS
Adjourn	Grade	Promote / Fire	Question Evolve codify

1. GOALS. How did we do on the goals we set ourselves at the beginning of the quarter? If you use OKRs, this is when they get graded. Then, using what you've learned, you'll set OKRs for the next quarter.

2. ROLES. Performance reviews are based on three things: How well is the individual living up to their goals, role expectation, and team norms? The quarterly assessment is an excellent time to grade the individual's performance, give feedback, and decide whether to promote or fire.

3. NORMS. Bring out your rules and ask folks if they are living up to their own standards. Discuss changes. Make updates.

This may sound like a lot of time, but really it's just two meetings with some prep. Moreover, it's an investment in moving your team from a workgroup to a learning team to eventually an autonomous team. Wouldn't you like to leave your phone in the room someday, rather than be tied down with the emergency du jour? Invest in your people, and they'll invest in you.

QUARTERLY GOAL EVALUATION: GRADINGS

TWO WEEKS BEFORE THE END OF THE QUARTER, IT'S TIME TO grade your OKRs and plan for the next cycle. After all, you want to hit the ground running on day one of Q2, right?

There are two common systems for managing OKRs: confidence ratings and grading. Each has its benefits and downsides.

We'll start with confidence ratings, the system I've outlined in my book *Radical Focus*. Confidence ratings are a simple system best used by startups and smaller teams, or teams at the beginning of OKR adoption. When you decide on your objective and three KRs, you set a difficult number you have fifty percent confidence in achieving. This is typically noted by a 5/10 rating on the status four square.

In your Monday commitment meeting, everyone reports on if and how their confidence levels have changed. This is not a science, it's an art. You do not want your folks wasting time trying to track down every bit of data to give a perfect answer, you just want to make sure efforts are directionally correct. The first few weeks of OKRs, it's pretty hard to know if you are making progress or not on achieving your key results. But somewhere in week three or four, it becomes very clear if you are getting closer or slipping. Each team leader (or team member, if a very small company) will start to adjust the confidence rating as they begin to feel confident.

Then the confidence rating will start to swing wildly up and down as progress or setback shows up. Eventually around two months, the confidence levels settle into the likely outcome. By two weeks from the end of the quarter, you can usually call the OKRs. If they were truly hard goals, the kind you only have a fifty-fifty chance of making, there is no miracle that can occur in the last two weeks to change the results. The sooner you can call the results, the sooner you can make plans for the next quarter and start your next cycle.

The advantage of this approach is twofold. First, the team doesn't forget about OKRs because they have to be constantly updating the confidence level. Because the confidence level is a gut check, it's quick and painless, and the key for getting a young company in the habit of tracking success. The second advantage is this approach prompts key conversations. If confidence drops, other leads can question why it is happening and brainstorm ways to correct the drop. OKRs are set and shared by the team, and any team member's struggle is a danger to the entire company. A leader should feel comfortable bringing a loss of confidence to the leadership team and know that he'll have help.

At two weeks before the end of the quarter, you mark your confidence as 10 or 0. Success is making two of the three key results. This style of grading leads to doubling down on the possible goals and abandoning effort on goals that are clearly out of range. The benefit is to stop people spinning their wheels on the impossible and focus on what can be done. However, the downside is some people will sandbag by setting one impossible goal, one hard goal, and one easy goal. It's the job of the manager to keep an eye out for this.

The second approach to OKRs ratings is the grading approach. Google is the most famous for using the grading approach. At the end of the quarter, the team and individual grade their results with data collected. 0.0 means the result was a failure, and 1.0 means the result was a complete success. Most results should land in 0.6-0.7. From the Google official site on using OKRs, *ReWork*:

> "The sweet spot for OKRs is somewhere in the 60-70% range. Scoring lower may mean the organization is not achieving enough of what it could be. Scoring higher may mean the aspirational goals are not being set high enough. With Google's 0.0—1.0 scale, the expectation is to get an average of 0.6 to 0.7 across all OKRs. For organizations who are new to OKRs, this tolerance for "failure" to hit the uncomfortable goals is itself uncomfortable."

Google sets high value on transparency. As well as all OKRs, individual and team, being posted on the intranet, team progress is shared throughout. Again, from *ReWork*:

> Publicly grade organizational OKRs. At Google, organizational OKRs are typically shared and graded annually and quarterly. At the start of the year, there is a company-wide meeting where the grades for the prior OKRs are shared and the new OKRs are shared both for the year and for the upcoming quarter. Then the company meets quarterly to review grades and set new OKRs. At these company meetings, the owner for each OKR (usually the leader from the relevant team) explains the grade and any adjustments for the upcoming quarter.

And *ReWork* warns against the danger of set and forget:

> Check in throughout the quarter. Prior to assigning a final grade, it can be helpful to have a mid-quarter check-in for all levels of OKRs to give both individuals and teams a sense of where they are. An end of quarter check-in can be used to prepare ahead of the final grading.

This is also done differently across teams. Some do a midpoint check, like a midterm grade. Others check in monthly. Google has always had an approach of hire smart people, give them a goal, and leave them alone to accomplish it. As they've grown OKRs are implemented unevenly, but OKRs continue to allow that philosophy to live on.

Ben Lamorte is a coach who helps large organizations get started and sustain their OKR projects. He shares a simple technique to keep OKR progress visible: progress posters. Several of his clients have set up posters in the hallway that are updated regularly with progress. Not only does this make OKRs more transparent and visible across teams, it can be effective for communicating scores on key results and really creating more accountability.

It doesn't look good when your team hasn't updated any scores and when you're already a month into the quarter. Most of these posters include a placeholder to update scores at four to eight planned check-ins throughout the quarter. Certainly OKR posters are not for all organizations, but they can be quite effective in some cases.

No matter if you use confidence check-ins or formal grading (or a combination of both), there is one last piece of advice from *ReWork* that is important to keep in mind:

OKRs are not synonymous with performance evaluation. This means OKRs are not a comprehensive means to evaluate an individual (or an organization). Rather, they can be used as a summary of what an individual has worked on in the last period of time and can show contributions and impact to the larger organizational OKRs.

Use the accomplishments of each person to determine bonuses and raises. If you use the status report system described in Radical Focus, it should be easy for each person to review their work and write up a short summary of their accomplishments. This report can guide your performance review conversations. Some things shouldn't be automated, and the most important part of being a manager is having real conversations about what employees have contributed. And what they haven't.

If you rely on OKR results to guide your decisions, you will encourage sandbagging and punish your biggest dreamers. Reward what people do, not how good they are at working the system.

QUARTERLY NORMS EVALUATION

TEAM FEEDBACK HAS TWO PARTS: THE GROUP LEVEL AND THE member level. A team has to look at each member and their contributions AND how the individuals come together and work as a unit. If you only give individual feedback and never examine group dynamics, you've only got half the puzzle.

It's easier to begin with team feedback because we all share responsibility for the team's performance, and thus all share responsibility for fixing problems. So I recommend starting with feedback about how we are together, rather than starting with the more difficult "This is how I see you."

Team Evaluation

The norms you set at the beginning of the quarter and evolve throughout are the base of the team evaluation. Each norm should be rated on a simple three-point scale. You can use red-yellow-green as Spotify Labs does, or Happy-Meh-Sad, as long as it's clear. Have the team rate the norms before the meeting. Then have them put it up on the wall.

Next, the teammates compare their answers to the prework and discuss their findings.

Look at where you felt they could grow, where you are succeeding, and where people disagree in their assessments. The places you disagree are the best places to learn.

Why does one person think communication is going poorly and another person think it's awesome? Do people have different needs? Are different people being supported in different ways? A group is complex, and you have to cautiously navigate expectations and outcomes.

"Are we talking about the same product when we sit in that conference room? Do we know what our roles are? Are we getting closer or further away from our goals and a clear understanding of what we came here to do?"—Noam Zomerfeld

The team then revises norms and moves forward. As the team grows in maturity, this process should get faster. The first time you hold this meeting it could be an hour or more, but you'll find it becomes a short fifteen minutes you can tack on the end of an OKR review.

Quarterly Role Evaluation

Members of a learning team need fast and regular feedback. You achieve this with the quarterly performance review, covered in the next section. As psychological safety in the team increases, you can consider introducing peer performance reviews, covered in the second section. You can even combine them, doing quarterly one-on-one reviews, and an annual peer review. As the team becomes autonomous, the team will be able to decide what works and discard or evolve what doesn't.

Performance Reviews for Maximizing Learning

To this day, the words "performance review" make me feel a bit ill. When I was at Yahoo, I had to add extra time to any project that occurred around the performance review time, because the team would be so depressed after the evaluations that work would grind to a standstill. I also recall other workplaces where managers would spring all my faults on me once a year and I'd be left shaken and contemplating job hunting. You can rename it the quarterly "conversation" or the quarterly "reflection" but the name isn't the problem: The problem is you if you are delivering performance reviews in the traditional way. If you manage people, you have got to learn how to give feedback well. I recommend the marvelous *Thanks for the Feedback* by Sheila Heen and Douglas Stone.

Rather than reproduce their book here, I'll give a short outline of a good evaluation session done in accordance with the goals-roles-norms model.

Be sure to give feedback quarterly, even if you still do annual performance reviews. This gives both you and your direct reports an opportunity to grow throughout the year by addressing issues and reinforcing positive behaviors swiftly. Do not use the company's schedule as an excuse not to have difficult but necessary conversations.

The quarterly performance review has two parts: prep and delivery. You absolutely cannot skip prep. Memory is untrustworthy. You have to do your homework in order to give fair feedback.

Review the weekly status reports and your notes from the weekly one-on-one meetings. Note how many times positive and negative behaviors come up. Look for patterns. Determine what is important and what is trivial.

Imagine a design agency. There is a team that likes to play music in the afternoon while they work. One member has a tendency to start it, so he can play his music. This annoys some of the more introverted folks, who aren't willing to confront him. This same designer has a bad habit of interrupting clients in presentation meetings. One problem is critical to address formally in the evaluation. The other is important to the health of the team, but can probably be addressed some other way, like rotating music choices on a chart.

Each problem should be addressed, but not all rate being discussed in the evaluation. If you give someone a lot of feedback, they'll become overwhelmed and tune out. Select the top two or three issues you wish to address. Or one. Then decide how you want to address the rest of the issues (if there are any). Some things can be discussed in a one-on-one. Some things can be addressed as a team. And some things just aren't worth addressing. None of us are perfect, and it's not a manager's job to try to make us so. As a manager, you are seeking problems that interfere with the team health and ability to perform.

As well, make sure you find opportunities to praise. While the famous "sh*t sandwich" of two compliments and one criticism has been proven not to work (look it up), you want to make sure people know they are appreciated. They may not be able to hear you in the meeting, especially if they are affected emotionally by your feedback, so make sure you write down your key points and give it to them.

Some quarters there will be nothing to critique. That's a good thing. Don't look for something. However, if there is nothing to praise, that is a bad thing. Consider if you really want to keep adequate people around. They tend to set the bar low. Use the quarterly evaluation to ask them to step up.

Day of Review

Schedule at least fifteen minutes beforehand to go through your notes and get yourself in the right frame of mind.

What is the right frame of mind? You are here to help. You work for the team. In service to the team, you are going to help this person be the best teammate they can be. You're going to celebrate their strengths! You're going to coach their weaknesses. You're going to be there for them.

You are not punishing them. You are not giving them bad news. You are just like a golf or tennis coach. Bad form is something to be corrected. Bad behavior doesn't mean someone is a bad person. They just need help to see it and correct it.

But most of all, you are there to listen. Don't get so caught up in what you have to say that you don't listen to the other person.

In his new book, *If I Understood You, Would I Have This Look on My Face? My Adventures in the Art and Science of Relating and Communicating*, Alan Alda promotes active listening—it's required for acting and doing improvisational theater.

"I don't say my next line in a play because it's written in the script and I've memorized it," Alda says. "I say it because you do something—you the other actor—do something or say something that makes me say this next line, and makes me say it in a certain way."

Actors listen deeply to each other in order to understand what the other character is saying, so that they can make sure their character responds authentically to the other. You need to listen so you can react authentically *and* appropriately to the other person. Your goal is not to tell them what's wrong or right, but to point out problems in their contributions to the team, understand how they see the situation, and invite them to come up with solutions to fix the issue. Understanding takes listening.

The first time you hold a coaching-style performance review, you may need to say that you are there to help explicitly. I know every time I've walked into a review, I've been afraid. So many managers see this as a time they need to get tough, even if that is not their natural style. By explicitly saying you are there to help a report reach their potential, you can begin to build trust. And with time, that trust will go both ways.

At the end of the conversation, ask your report if they have any advice for you, either about your feedback style or leadership. The first evaluation, they probably won't have anything to say. Ask them to think about it and let you know in your one-on-one. Over time, it will become a habit to exchange coaching. You'll get better at your job and help build psychological safety as well.

Finally, document everything. Memory is fallible.

PEER-TO-PEER FEEDBACK

THIS IS AN EXERCISE I ORIGINALLY DEVELOPED WITH STUDENTS, and then used with clients. It's proven to be powerful and transformative. Only you know the current climate of your team, and if this is too touchy-feely for your team, wait until you've built up the psychological safety and mutual trust to allow for it.

I recommend, as Allie did, that you hire an outside facilitator. This allows the leader to participate, further creating a sense of mutual accountability and interdependence. A trained facilitator will have the distance to not be caught up in any interpersonal conflicts, they have skills to mediate any emotionally difficult moments, and they free you up to participate.

This is how a typical peer-to-peer feedback session goes when I run it:

Begin with Empathy

First, I like to warm up with a Nonviolent Communication exercise called "Sometimes I ..."

In this exercise, you place two chairs next to each other, facing the opposite way. It's like sitting in a car together, except one person is facing backward. We all know the best conversations happen on road trips, right?

In the exercise, you take turns finishing a sentence that starts with "Sometimes I..." One person talks for three minutes, only finishing that sentence, and the other listens *silently*.

You can be silly—"Sometimes I pretend to be Supergirl" or serious—"Sometimes I pretend I know what I'm doing."

Then you switch, but with a new sentence.

Sometimes I pretend ...
Sometimes I wish ...
Sometimes I'm afraid ...

This is a powerful empathy building exercise.

It's hard to describe how magical it is. Because you are not looking at each other's eyes, you are free to confess. Because you are being listened to, you feel cared for. And hearing someone be silly, be brave, be vulnerable, be released from the pressure of having to respond, is intimate and precious.

Each person speaks to each member of their team, and listens to each. Elissa's blog post[16] from my class captures the experience:

"We had sentence starters such as "I wish people ..." "Sometimes I pretend ..." "I worry about ..." "I hope ..." which got personal pretty quickly after we all ran out of general hopes and wishes. I felt uncomfortable and vulnerable talking about these things with people who aren't my mom or best friend. I did feel closer after listening to my group's responses, it made me know them deeper and feel more personally connected to them. I felt happy to be closer to the people that I work with so closely. We see each other for 6–9 hours a week or more, yet I realized I barely know anything about them.

It's difficult to share who you are, yet it also connects you in a way ordinary communication, such as ..."

"Hi, Bob."
"Hi, Joe! How's things?"
"Fine. How's things with you?"
"Fine!"

... can never do.

---

16   Welsh, Elissa. "Teamwork, What Does That Mean?—The Creative Founder : NightCap Edition—Medium." Medium.com. October 31, 2016. Accessed December 21, 2018. https://medium.com/the-creative-founder/teamwork-what-does-that-mean-42abab5554b8.

Team Member Feedback

Next, we work on team member feedback. I have Allie in the story use this exercise with the team at her new company, and you can see how powerful the results are once you've got a healthy team, what I call an autonomous team.

When I first developed this exercise, I was working with Dave Gray's Empathy Map[17]. He had designed it to help designers understand their customers. But I found it useful to have my students use it to think deeply about each other. Over time, I evolved it to better support creating empathy and turning that into constructive feedback. Finally, I was able to use it with clients as well as students.

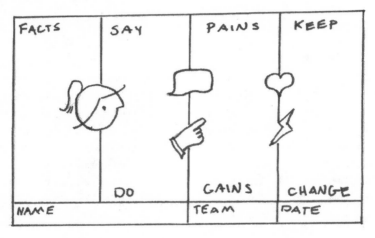

Every person on the team has this chart in poster form on the wall, and you stand in front of it, and decorate your face and fill in the bottom. Then each person steps to the right, in front of a teammate's poster. They answer the following questions on sticky notes for two minutes for each section, and place them on the poster.

- What's everything you know about the person? Family? Friends? Hobbies? Interests?
- What are things they say and do in meetings that you notice, whether good, bad, or indifferent?
- What do you think they struggle with? What could they gain if they overcame that struggle?

17   Gray, David, Sunni Brown, and James Macanufo. *Gamestorming: A Playbook for Innovators, Rulebreakers, and Changemakers.* Beijing: OReilly, 2010.

- Finally, what is at least one thing they should keep doing and one thing they should change?

Since there are four questions, each poster should take eight minutes, though I often let the first round go longer as people are warming up and the page is blank.

Next, you move to the next teammate's posters and do the same. If you have a large team (more than four or five) you may want to do this in break-out groups of three, to avoid being at this all day.

Eventually you return to your own poster, which is now filled with reflections of how your team sees you.

This exercise is a pure act of empathy. Everyone feels seen, even if they are sometimes surprised by what is seen.

My student Jherin Miller's sketchnote of his experience. https://medium.com/ the-creative-founder/sketchblog-midterm-feedback-537ce05ff413

Filling out the compassionate feedback canvas can bring up deep emotions and lead to important conversations. One year, my student Analisa wrote a poignant post on what it felt like to realize everyone on her team was conscious that she was the only woman.[18] "I've never really thought about this but I've now started re-analyzing everything that has happened

---

18   Chaosanalicia. "A Woman Amongst Men." *Voxum Design: Analicia.* October 18, 2015. Accessed December 21, 2018. https://chaosanalicia.tumblr.com/ post/131374320964/a-woman-amongst-men.

from the start of this team to where we have come to. I'm beginning to identify these smaller moments where there were differences in how I was being acknowledged, treated, and spoken to in comparison to others on the team. Even as I meet with my group now, or talk to other males in general my senses have enhanced to be aware of every detail of differences I am receiving."

That's the real value of the canvas. It's bringing up difficult subjects and then spending time discussing them. Unspoken tensions fester. You have to make time for the conversations after, as things are unveiled.

What I like about the compassionate feedback map is that it's observation based: It keeps people in the realm of behavior and out of the world of speculation. "I see you not showing up on time," rather than "You don't care about the team."

At the end of a session, everyone is exhausted. It's about a two-hour meeting, but it feels longer. Some people will fall into deep conversations, unpacking a Post-It note comment. Others may slink out quietly, their emotional reserve empty. Others may joke boisterously. Let people recover in their own way.

As Danielle Forward wrote in her wonderful essay on getting feedback,[19] "There's a big difference between who we want to be—who we imagine we are—and what we actually are."

She goes on to say:

It's easy to tell yourself a narrative of who you are. We probably do it all the time. "I'm a good person, a good leader, and a good teammate," but am I? Are you? How would you know? It's this same skepticism, this same curiosity, that I think makes me a designer. That last week in class, I was the "product"—and I got to view the data about myself.

This is the true "gift" of feedback. To see yourself how others see you, and decide what to do with that information.

That's all feedback is: information about how someone sees you.

19   Forward, Danielle. "Week 8 of Creative Founder: Midterm Feedback—The Creative Founder : NightCap Edition—Medium." Medium.com. November 07, 2016. Accessed December 21, 2018. https://medium.com/the-creative-founder/week-8-of-creative-founder-midterm-feedback-7f32058f6705.

"I'm really glad I know that I've been coming across differently than I intend in group discussions."—Allesandro Battisti[20]

That is the secret of feedback. Before it, you know what you meant and what you said, but you don't know how it's received. Learning how you are perceived allows you to change what you choose.

It wasn't all kumbaya. One person was wounded by the feedback he got, and I shared Chapter 10 from Thanks for the Feedback (marvelous book!) with the team. I now suggest assigning this chapter BEFORE the feedback sessions (perhaps even before your quarterly reviews) because it is so powerful in helping create psychological safety.

It's vital to decide which feedback to accept and which to discard. Learning that NOT ALL FEEDBACK HAS TO BE ACTED ON may be the most valuable information I have ever gotten, and I was happy to share it out. Here are two quotes, as Thanks for the Feedback quotes Anne Lamott:

> In fact, being able to establish limits on the feedback you get is crucial to your well-being and the health of your relationships. Being able to say no is not a skill that runs parallel to the skill of receiving feedback well; it's right at the heart of it. If you can't say no, then your yeses are not freely chosen. Your decision may affect others and it will often have consequences for you, but the choice belongs to you. You need to make your own mistakes and find your own learning curve. Sometimes that means you need to shut out the critics for a while so you can discover who you are and how you are going to grow. Writer Anne Lamott puts it this way:

> '... Every single one of us at birth is given an emotional acre all our own. You get one, your awful Uncle Phil gets one, I get one. And as long as you don't hurt anyone, you really get to do with your acre as you please. You can plant fruit trees or flowers or alphabetized rows of vegetables, or nothing at all. If you want your acre to look like a giant garage sale, or an auto-wrecking yard, that's what you get to do with it. There's a fence around your acre, though, with a gate, and if people keep coming onto your land and sliming it or trying to do what

---

20   Battisti, Alessandro. "Team Feedback—The Creative Founder : NightCap Edition—Medium." Medium.com. October 31, 2016. Accessed December 21, 2018. https://medium.com/the-creative-founder/team-feedback-f7d1457b6e73.

they think is right, you get to ask them to leave. And they have to go, because this is your acre.'[21]

Feedback is anecdata. Sometimes it tells you something about you, sometimes it tells you something about the other person, and sometimes it tells you something about the interpersonal dynamic. Listen thoughtfully and choose strategically what you do with that information.

---

21   Anne Lamott, *Bird by Bird: Some Instructions on Writing and Life* (Pantheon, 1994), 44. Buy it, read it, give to someone you love, buy a new copy and reread it.

WHEN FEEDBACK ISN'T WORKING, FIRING MAY BE THE ONLY CHOICE

THE BIGGEST PROBLEM WITH FIRING IS WE'RE AFRAID TO DO IT. If you've watched *Up In the Air*[22], you probably have a picture in your head of what a bad firing can look like: people cursing at you, crying, throwing things.

What we don't make a movie of, though, is letting a bad person continue to work with good people, demotivating them, depressing them. Good people will quit and leave for other companies. Maybe they only switch to another part of the company in order to avoid the person you should have fired. Eventually, you have a team of people no one else wants. It's a boring slog into mediocrity. This story ends with you, bad manager, getting fired yourself.

Now that I've (hopefully) convinced you firing is necessary, let's move to thinking of it as potentially positive. First we must reframe the PIP. PIP is an acronym for Performance Improvement Plan. When we use acronyms all the time, we often forget what the original words were. (OKRs anyone?) PIP

---

22   *Up in the Air*. Performed by George Clooney. Paramount, 2009. Film.

has come to mean "firing someone very slowly with lots of documentation so we don't get our asses sued." We have to take back the original meaning—performance improvement plan.

The long walk toward change starts with anger. Or frustration. You ask yourself, "Why does that person keep doing that thing?"

Next you have to interrogate yourself about your role in the problem. "Have I given clear feedback that this behavior needs to change or there will be consequences?"

"Well, I did say I was really upset when he delivered the report late."

"But were there consequences?"

"I had to reschedule with my boss, and that made our team look disorganized. We ended up being taken off the list for the launch."

"Did he know that was a problem?"

"No. I didn't want to be confrontational. In fact, I gave him a bonus at the performance review because I didn't want him to be upset."

STOP.

You are the one who needs to improve your performance.

STEP ONE: When an undesired behavior occurs, you must tell the person about it *as soon as possible*, and show consequences for the action.

Examples: A late delivery from a designer means a front-end engineer has to stay up all night to try to make the deadline. Interrupting the marketing person in meetings all the time means she won't help your team anymore. Calling everyone on the team *guys* or *dude* is making the female team members uncomfortable, and we don't want them to leave because they are talented. Refusing to compromise your vision means the list of people who will work with you is shrinking.

If you have a company lawyer and/or HR, this is a good time to get advice about what is and is not a firing offense at your company. As well, there are some offenses so egregious you don't put someone on a PIP, you simply fire them. This can include theft, sexual harassment, and more, but I am not a lawyer, so go find one and make sure you are doing the right thing.

STEP TWO: If the undesired behavior doesn't disappear overnight (and sometimes it does!), up the stakes. Make sure that the person you're coaching understands that if they don't change, they may have to leave the company. Start documenting incidents, if you have not already.

A short word about documenting: Document behaviors only. You cannot fire someone for having a bad attitude. You can fire someone for repeatedly bad-mouthing the company, skipping meetings, being chronically late, and more (again, talk to HR/your lawyer). You need to give the problem employee clear behavior to change, because it's unfair to ask someone to change something whose criteria is "I'll know it when I see it."

Vague complaints also leave you open to litigation. "You have a bad attitude" can be interpreted as "I am sexist/racist/ableist and I just don't like you." In the state of California, you cannot fire someone for having a mental illness, and a bad attitude and depression can sometimes look alike. Stick with clear, unambiguous evidence of undesirable behavior. Again, I am not a lawyer. Get one.

STEP THREE: Okay, the individual is still refusing to change. Putting a person on a PIP is often a wake-up call. It sends a message that you were serious when you said that change was required, not advised. Many motivated employees will respond well to a PIP. They may initially be upset, but having an opportunity to change bad habits is a career maker.

There are three kinds of problem employees:

1. Those who don't know their behavior is a problem. Feedback fixes this.
2. Those who do not want to change. Being put on a PIP will either change their mind or encourage them to take their talents elsewhere.
3. Those who can't change. If they don't see the axe coming at the end of the ninety- day PIP and find another job, you'll have to wield it. Honestly, I can't tell the difference between those who cannot change (perhaps because of deeply held beliefs or lack of a key talent, like empathy), and those who don't want to. It doesn't matter. At the end of a PIP, the person either has changed, or they have not. And if they have not changed or chosen to leave of their own free will, you have to escort them to the door. It's for the good of the team.

If someone does move to another part of the company, be sure to pass on what you know to the new manager. I passed off a problem employee early in my career because I was a wimp, and I paid for it later, when my peer held a grudge for not giving him the heads up. It's immoral to pass on your problems, and if that isn't enough to motivate you, it will bite you on the bum later. What goes around comes around, often with interest.

HR or legal should walk you through the company's firing process. No matter what they say, don't do it alone. It's best to have someone sit in the room with you as you deliver the bad news, both as a witness and in case something unexpected happens.

Be brief, be compassionate, be clear. Reference the PIP results and offer any package (severance pay) that is appropriate. All companies do this differently, so you'll want to consult your boss and HR. If you are a startup CEO without these capabilities, find a lawyer. (I know, I keep repeating myself. But four paragraphs in, I continue to not be a lawyer.)

Only you know if the person needs to be walked to the door or can be allowed to gather up their things unsupervised. When in doubt (and without company policy) stay with them while they pack up. A moment of anger or resentment can lead to unexpected retribution. Or at least some epic office supply thievery. Be pleasant and social, but professional. The urge to hide is strong, but put on your big-girl pants and see the firing to its end.

A very long time ago, I worked with a manager who put a problem employee on a PIP three times. It made her crazy that she couldn't fire him, but he kept shaping up long enough to get out of the PIP and then would slide back into old habits. Finally, during the third PIP, he quit and went to work for another company. There, he built a transformative product that made his company do very, very well. Then he started his own software company that got bought by a different very wealthy company. Sometimes the person is the problem, but sometimes the problem is fit. Sometimes being kicked out of a place where you struggle is a gift. Not always. But sometimes.

George Clooney's corporate hatchet man character in *Up in the Air* points out to people that a firing is a moment to acknowledge that where they are has been proven to be a bad fit. He challenges them to reexamine their life choices and make new ones.

It's important to remember you didn't ruin someone's life. You were clear about what the team needed from the team member, and they were unwilling to give it. Now it's time for you to find someone who will help the team excel, and for the other person to find a way forward past their bad habits and toward a better fit.

What isn't fair is to suddenly fire someone without ever letting them know what they did wrong. This is cruel and easy and I want you to promise me it'll never be you. Everyone deserves a chance to be their best self.

SCALING FROM TEAM TO LEARNING TEAM TO AUTONOMOUS TEAM

"I have not failed, not once. I've discovered ten thousand ways that don't work." —Thomas Edison

I KNOW THIS BOOK COVERS A LOT OF GROUND. I LIKE TO WRITE short books, but this book refused to be summed up in a few pithy bits of advice. Interpersonal and group dynamics are really hard and really important. Go slowly. Do not try to transform your organization overnight.

Start with you. Are you creating psychological safety, or are you making things worse? Attend a T-Group, get coaching, find a local Nonviolent Communication group ... or try a combination! Just do what it takes to become the kind of leader your team needs.

Next, transform your group into a learning team. Learning teams constantly learn from each other so they can constantly evolve. You don't have to be everywhere, you don't have to micromanage, you can trust the team to start helping each other reach the team potential.

Don't hop straight into all the touchy-feely stuff right away. OKRs are hard, but they can be the easiest place to start your revolution. They are now widely accepted, and have proven value.

Your role as leader in this phase is to:

- Co-create the OKR set with the team.
- Make smart failures acceptable.
- Value calculated experiments over safety and mediocrity.
- Listen *hard* to your team, and ask smart questions (the kind you don't know the answer to and that don't have a yes/no response).
- Remind your team what you are all trying to accomplish.
- Hold people accountable for their efforts. If they don't achieve a goal or accomplish a task, make sure they learn why.
- Show you are fallible. Have situational humility.[23]

So now you have led the team to higher performance in setting and achieving their goals. Can the team move toward self-regulating? Can the team manage itself? I think so.

Autonomous Teams

When you want to give power to people who have been traditionally power-less, norm setting is a great first step in returning them control. Norm setting says, "This is your team. How do you want to run it? How do you want to be in it?" It also says, "I the leader don't have to be in charge of everything."

The beginning of every quarter is a magical moment for a do-over. It's never too late to try something new. Create a team charter or "rules of engagement" or whatever you want to name it. Run weekly retrospectives.

Your role as a leader here:

- Keep asking for input and live with long uncomfortable silences until you get it. Repeat phrases like, "You have to share what doesn't work, so we can get better." When you are tired of saying it, they are starting to hear it.

---

23   Learn more: Edmondson, Amy C. *Fearless Organization: Creating Psychological Safety in the Workplace for Learning, Innovation, and Growth.* Wiley & Sons Canada, Limited, John, 2018.

- Listen and respond with "Yes and …" rather than "No, but …" when people have suggestions for change. Never shut down an idea, only unpack it.
- Trust the team.

Get serious about your weekly one-on-ones. If the schedule is difficult, make them biweekly but not less often. But don't treat them as something you can cancel and not reschedule. They aren't disposable. Even when nothing critical is discussed, you have still connected with your report as a human being, increasing psychological safety.

Your role as a manager:

- Let your reports lead the conversation as much as possible.
- Listen to and coach reports to solve their own problems.
- Offer advice only when asked, or ask for consent to give advice. Just saying "Do you mind if I give you a few of my thoughts?" shows you really do value the other person's experience and builds psychological safety.

Change how you run performance reviews, unless you are running them quarterly and compassionately already. Your ability to coach people is the difference between team members who keep getting better and team members who get a new job.

Your role as a manager:

- Hold regular evaluations, even if the company is on an annual review cycle. Quarterly is usually a good rhythm, but you know your team's needs.
- Ask for feedback on your performance. Ask how you can help your reports do their job better.
- Listen. Listen. Listen.

If you'd like to change your entire organization to the 9x team process, try starting with one team first. Let them be the pilot. I've seen so many companies fail epically with OKRs when they try to "roll it out company-wide." Go slow. Evaluate. Adjust. This is not a religion, this is just a set of best practices. They will work best if you try them as is with a small group, let that group make adjustments, and then roll them out slowly.

CONCLUSION

I KNOW THIS APPEARS HARD, BUT ONLY BECAUSE IT'S DIFFERENT. Once you've worked with a team that manages itself, you'll wonder why you did it any other way. Having a team be capable of running itself is easier than doing it all yourself. You can go to sleep at night and not get woken up by a freaked out person wondering what to do. You can promote ideas far crazier and much better than any you can come up with by yourself. You can have time to focus on strategy and impress the CEO with your brilliance. You can even be a better CEO.

My last bit of advice is simple: Don't do this alone. Get a coach or find an accountability buddy. It's easier if you have others to work with. They are support, they keep you honest, they give you advice. Hard things take help. But it's worth it to have the team you've always dreamed of.

You've got this.

BOOKS, THANKS, AND NEXT STEPS

IF THERE IS ONLY ONE OTHER BOOK YOU READ NEXT, IT SHOULD be *Fearless Organization: Creating Psychological Safety in the Workplace for Learning, Innovation, and Growth* by Amy C. Edmondson. You cannot succeed in reaching your goals without psychological safety, and she is the master of explaining how it works in groups. If you are in a hurry, skip to section three—though the entire book is fascinating. It came out as I was finishing this book, and I wish it had been available earlier.

There are additional valuable works in the bibliography below, especially *Thanks for the Feedback* and *The Tao of Coaching*. Finally, if you can take a T-Group at Stanford or elsewhere, do so. It will change how you perceive yourself and others.

I want to say thanks to all the people who read a draft, chatted ideas, or just reminded me to eat and sleep. Amelie Sarrazin, my daughter, is first in my heart and her support and belief make me who I am. I want to also thank Andrea Corney, Ed Battista, Erin Malone, Michael Bernstein, Andre Plaut … and you, person I managed to forget. You were the best.

References

Battisti, Alessandro. "Team Feedback—The Creative Founder : NightCap Edition—Medium." Medium.com. October 31, 2016. Accessed December 21, 2018. https://medium.com/the-creative-founder/team-feedback-f7d1457b6e73.

Chaosanalicia. "A Woman Amongst Men." Voxum Design: Analicia. October 18, 2015. Accessed December 21, 2018. https://chaosanalicia. tumblr.com/post/131374320964/a-woman-amongst-men.

Edmondson, Amy C. *Fearless Organization: Creating Psychological Safety in the Workplace for Learning, Innovation, and Growth*. Wiley & Sons Canada, Limited, John, 2018.

Forward, Danielle. "Week 8 of Creative Founder: Midterm Feedback—The Creative Founder—Medium." Medium.com. November 7, 2016. Accessed December 21, 2018. https://medium.com/the-creative-founder/week-8-of-creative-founder-midterm-feedback-7f32058f6705.

Gray, David, Sunni Brown, and James Macanufo. *Gamestorming: A Playbook for Innovators, Rulebreakers, and Changemakers*. Beijing: OReilly, 2010.

"Introductory T-Groups." Stanford Graduate School of Business. Accessed December 21, 2018. https://www.gsb.stanford.edu/experience/learning/leadership/interpersonal-dynamics/facilitation-training-program/intro-tgroup.

Landsberg, Max. *The Tao of Coaching: Boost Your Effectiveness at Work by Inspiring and Developing Those around You*. London: Profile Books, 2015.

Stone, Douglas, and Sheila Heen. *Thanks for the Feedback: The Science and Art of Receiving Feedback Well (even when it is off base, unfair, poorly delivered, and frankly, you're not in the mood)*. NY, NY: Penguin Books, 2015.

Up in the Air. Performed by George Clooney. Paramount, 2009. Film.

Welsh, Elissa. "Teamwork, What Does That Mean?—The Creative Founder—Medium." Medium.com. October 31, 2016. Accessed December 21, 2018. https://medium.com/the-creative-founder/teamwork-what-does-that-mean-42abab5554b8.